RT HON HENRY MCLEISH began his political car
local government in 1974 and was leader of Fi
years. In 1987 he was elected as a member of tl
as Minister for Devolution and Home Affairs Government
from 1997 to 1999. In the first Scottish Parliament he was Minister for Enterprise and Lifelong Learning from 1999, and in 2000 he became First Minister of Scotland until 2001. Retiring from politics in 2003, he is now an adviser, consultant, writer, author and broadcaster and lectures in the USA and elsewhere on the European Union and politics. He chaired the Scottish Prisons Commission, which produced a report into sentencing and the criminal justice system entitled 'Scotland's Choice'. In 2010 he conducted a major report on the state of football in Scotland, which had been commissioned by the Scottish Football Association, and chaired a commission into sport requested by the Scottish Government. He is now an honorary professor at Edinburgh University.

JAMES MITCHELL is Professor of Public Policy, University of Edinburgh having previously been Professor of Politics, Strathclyde University and Professor of Public Policy, Sheffield University. His research has included studies of political parties and public opinion in Scotland. His most recent work has included studies of the SNP, Scottish elections and the independence referendum. All of his work is informed by an appreciation of the importance of the past in its impact on current concerns.

Previous books by Henry McLeish:

People, Politics, Parliament: The Settled Will of the Scottish People, (Luath Press, 2022)
Scottish Football: Requiem or Renaissance?, (Luath Press, 2018)
Citizen's United: Taking Back Control in Turbulent Times, (Luath Press, 2017)
Rethinking Our Politics: The political and constitutional future of Scotland and the UK, (Luath Press, 2014)
With Tom Brown, *Scotland: The Growing Divide*, (Luath Press, 2012)
With Tom Brown, *Scotland: A Suitable Case for Treatment*, (Luath Press, 2009)
With Tom Brown, *Scotland: The Road Divides*, (Luath Press, 2007)
With Kenny MacAskill, *Wherever the Saltire Flies*, (Luath Press, 2006)
With Kenny MacAskill, *Global Scots: Voices from Afar*, (Luath Press, 2005)
Scotland First: Truth and Consequences, (Mainstream Publishing, 2004)

Previous books by James Mitchell:

With Lynn Bennie & Rob Johns, *Surges in party membership*, (Routledge, 2024)
With Jim Johnston (eds), *The Scottish Parliament at 20*, (Luath Press, 2019)
Hamilton 1967, (Luath Press, 2017)
With Gerry Hassan (eds), *Scottish National Party Leaders*, (Biteback Publishing, 2016) [part of Biteback's The British Leaders series]
With Rob Johns, *Takeover: explaining the extraordinary rise of the SNP*, (Biteback Publishing, 2016)
The Scottish Question, (Oxford University Press, 2014)
With C Carman & R Johns, *More Scottish than British: The 2011 Scottish Parliament Election*, (Palgrave Macmillan, 2014)
With Gerry Hassan (eds), *After Independence*, (Luath Press, 2013)
With R Johns & L Bennie, *The Scottish National Party*, (Oxford University Press, 2011)
With R Johns, D Denver & C Pattie, *Voting for a Scottish Government: The Scottish Parliament Elections of 2007*, (Manchester University Press, 2010)
Devolution in the United Kingdom, (Manchester University Press, 2009)
Governing Scotland: The Invention of Administrative Devolution, (MacMillan, 2003)
With C Jeffrey (eds), *The Scottish Parliament 1999–2009: The First Decade*, (Luath Press/Hansard Society, 2009)
With D Denver, C Pattie & H Bochel, *Scotland Decides: The Devolution Issue and the 1997 Referendum*, (Frank Cass, 2000)
With L Bennie & J Brand, *How Scotland Votes: Scottish Parties and Elections*, (Manchester University Press, 1997)
Strategies for Self-Government, (Polygon, 1996)
With A Midwinter & M Keating, *Politics and Public Policy in Scotland*, (Macmillan, 1991)
Conservatives and the Union, (Edinburgh University Press, 1990)

Unfinished Business

The Evolution of Devolution

HENRY McLEISH and JAMES MITCHELL

Luath Press Limited

EDINBURGH

www.luath.co.uk

First published 2025

ISBN: 978-1-80425-205-5

The paper used in this book is recyclable. It is made from
low-chlorine pulps produced in a low-energy,
low-emission manner from renewable forests.

FSC
www.fsc.org
FSC® C023367
The mark of
responsible forestry

Printed and bound by
Robertson Printers, Forfar

Typeset in 11.5 point Sabon by
Main Point Books, Edinburgh

Contents

SECTION TWO – THE NEXT TWENTY-FIVE YEARS

Preface

WE APPROACHED WRITING this book with different backgrounds and experiences but each of us had long been committed to the establishment of a Scottish Parliament, and today we are open-minded about future reforms and keen to see the Parliament contribute to making Scotland a better place. We hope the combination of a former politician – who has served as a councillor, council leader, MP, UK Government Minister, MSP, Scottish Government Minister and First Minister – and an academic who has spent over 40 years studying government and public policy with a particular focus on Scotland would be able to stimulate discussion and debate. This is not a manifesto, though we make some policy proposals and institutional reform proposals, insomuch as they are reflections and a contribution to a debate on Scotland's future. This book grew out of many conversations over a number of years. Through these conversations, we found much common ground, learned from each other, rethought and honed views and positions. We firmly believe that respectful dialogue is important. We do not claim comprehensive coverage of all challenges and issues – that could not be possible in one book – but have focused on areas with which at least one of us has engaged at length over time.

We do not expect anyone will agree with everything but that is not the primary purpose of the book. We hope it contributes to and stimulates further debate on matters discussed.

Introduction

THE FIRST ELECTIONS to the Scottish Parliament were held more than a quarter of a century ago. Anniversaries are appropriate, even if somewhat arbitrary, moments for reflection. Enough time has passed for the Parliament to have become embedded in the life of Scotland. Sixteen-year-olds who will vote in the next Holyrood elections were born over a decade after the first elections. Much has changed economically, socially and politically over the intervening period, including dramatic and rapid technological innovations. Brexit, the rise of populism and increased geopolitical uncertainty had not been anticipated.

Every constitution and institution needs to be revisited periodically even if there may be disagreement on how this should be done, how often and how radical the revision. One of the great exchanges on this took place in 1789 between Thomas Jefferson and James Madison. Jefferson, who became America's third President, argued that the US Constitution should expire every generation, by which he meant every 19 years. He had used mortality tables to reach this figure. The 'earth belongs to the living, not to the dead' he insisted and 'one generation, is to another as one independent nation to another'. Madison, who succeeded Jefferson as American President in 1809, was unconvinced and concerned that a completely new constitution was impractical, fearing that it would 'engender pernicious factions that might not otherwise come into existence'. He also argued that a generation was not a fixed period.

We hear echoes of these debates in Scotland today. What is the appropriate time between holding referendums on Scotland's constitutional future? Who decides what should be on the ballot paper? What is a 'generation'? Is a referendum essential before major changes are implemented? And what is a 'major' change? How 'major'? One view is that the issue should be reopened when there is evidence of a demand for change, but that leaves many questions unanswered. How should we measure demand for change? Former Scottish Secretary Alister Jack suggested the 'duck test'. 'If it looks like a duck and sounds like a duck and waddles like a duck, it's probably a duck'. The trouble is we can't agree on what a constitutional duck looks or sounds like. And should independence be the only option for change on any future ballot paper? The view adopted in this book is that devolution is in need of review, regardless of whether a second referendum is needed. By devolution we mean both the Scottish Parliament but also the Scottish Government and attendant institutions. Indeed, we go further. It is not only devolution that needs to be reviewed but Scottish governance more broadly, including Non-Departmental Public Bodies and local institutions.

We want to move beyond politics in which each party seeks to outmanoeuvre others and score a decisive victory. This leads to political stalemate. We want to reflect on the successes and failures of devolution and offer a series of proposals for reform that could be embraced by a broad swathe of opinion. This is not to dismiss debates on independence and more powers for Holyrood, only that other issues require our attention. In the first section of the book, we begin with reflections on the hopes and expectations of devolution before turning to early experience and then to consider more recent times. The second section offers ideas on how reform might take place.

The early years of the Scottish Parliament coincided with a period of relative political calm and economic 'good times'. It was not without controversy however, especially related to the Holyrood building. It was a formative period for the new devolved institutions. There was little prospect that the new Scottish Parliament could live up to the exceptionally high ideals of its founders, though this is not to dismiss these ideals as naïve or mistaken. Expectations of change and idealism play an important part in any political movement, providing momentum to mobilise support. They also provide important reminders of the institution's aims, a yardstick against which progress can be measured, though often enough used as a stick to beat the institution or its supporters when it has fallen short. It is easy in retrospect to identify weaknesses and problems that might have been foreseen but this book is more concerned with learning lessons, recognising that much in political life falls under the category of 'known unknowns' or even 'unknown unknowns'. The test of any institution is not only how it lives up to its ideals but how it deals with unanticipated developments and crises and, crucially, whether and how it learns and reforms itself.

We should also take heed of words spoken by the late Queen when she addressed the Parliament three years into its existence. Speaking in its temporary setting in Aberdeen University, when the Kirk reclaimed its building for its annual General Assembly, the monarch noted that the process of creating a new Parliamentary culture would take time.

'After what might be considered a parliamentary adjournment of almost 300 years, that process will inevitably take time.' Notwithstanding that perspective, the best time to create a new culture is at the outset. Habits and practices tend to become rooted and more difficult to change as time passes.

This creates challenges. Standing still or resting on our laurels is not an option in our view. The growth of populism, feeding on disillusionment and distrust, cannot be ignored. There is much speculation on the possibility of a major breakthrough for Reform UK. UKIP, its antecedent, wanted to replace MSPs with Westminster MPs, which would amount to a return to the pre-devolution arrangement of having a Scottish Grand Committee, though UKIP never developed or explained the idea clearly. Nothing should be taken for granted.

Tim Harford, in a column in the Financial Times in November 2024, noted that in countries 'gripped by anger and frozen by polarisation, there is not much room for the curious, humble, practical problem solving of the experimenting society. Yet somehow the vicious circle must be broken'. Scotland is far from alone in being caught in such a vicious cycle and will need to find its own way of breaking out. This book is a contribution to a debate on how this might be done.

SECTION ONE
The Last Twenty-Five Years

CHAPTER 1

Hopes and Expectations

Give us our Parliament in Scotland. We will start with no traditions. We will start with ideals. We will start with purpose, with courage.
Jimmy Maxton before being elected MP for Glasgow Bridgeton in 1922

What is devolution?

LANGUAGE IS IMPORTANT in politics and various terms have been used for what is now commonly called devolution. The Irish Nationalist TP O'Connor joked that devolution was 'Latin for home rule'. 'Home rule' was the much more common term used in debates on the Irish Question in the late 19th and early 20th centuries. It was not until the 1970s that 'devolution' was commonly used. Michael Foot, a strong supporter, preferred home rule over devolution but his was a minority voice in the Labour Government in the late 1970s. Whether devolution is, as some maintain, a dry and uninspiring term, it is the term that has come to be associated with Scotland's constitutional status today.

Not all those who campaigned for devolution in the September 1997 referendum were strictly speaking supporters of devolution. They included people who saw it as a stepping stone to federalism, independence or some variant thereof. Devolution became the favoured term, as commonly happens with political language, as a means of distinguishing what was proposed from other options – usually the status quo ante and independence. Home rule might have been an appropriate term and, as we will see, had been used by earlier generations who supported what we now call Scottish devolution, but was associated in some minds with nationalism. Ironically, many nationalists were equally suspicious of 'home rule' for its association in their minds with unionism.

A phrase commonly associated with devolution was 'Scottish control of Scottish affairs'. This was used to refer to a Scottish Parliament but had previously been used for almost any special institutional arrangements for governing Scotland. The term 'administrative devolution' had been proposed by a civil servant in the interwar years to refer to the Scottish Office, the department of UK government with responsibility for Scottish affairs. The Scottish Office incorporated a growing range of responsibilities from its establishment in 1885 but also, crucially, its Ministers and officials were expected to 'stand up for Scotland' on all manner of issues. It was, in essence, Scotland's voice at the centre of government.

The Scottish Office is central to any understanding of devolution today. Created in a pre-democratic age to acknowledge Scottish distinctiveness within the United Kingdom and ensure that Scotland was not swallowed up into a Greater England, the Scottish Office had one major flaw that gave rise to the demand for legislative devolution. The Scottish Office was accountable to Westminster, with the Scottish Secretary appointed by the Prime Minister. So long as the largest party was the same in Scotland as in the UK as a whole then this was not seen as a major problem. But it was difficult to see how Scottish Office Ministers could claim to 'speak for Scotland' when the UK governing party lacked support in Scotland.

The complaint that Scotland was neglected in London had led to the establishment of the Scottish Office in 1885. As Prime Minister Lord Salisbury explained to the first holder of the office, the Scottish Office was established to 'redress the wounded dignities of the Scotch people – or a section of them – who think that enough is not made of Scotland'. There was 'so much sentiment about it' but he warned that 'measured by the expectations of the people of Scotland it is approaching the Archangelic'. More than half a century later, Churchill appointed Lord Home to a new post as Minister of State at the Scottish Office, telling him to 'Go and quell those turbulent Scots, and don't come back until you've done it'. The turbulent Scots Churchill was referring to were those arguing for Scottish home rule. But it was less the activities of Lord Home than James Stuart, Churchill's Secretary of State for Scotland, who had a close relationship with the Prime Minister, that ensured there was a Scottish voice at the heart of government. Stuart won concessions in Cabinet. He made the case for a bridge over the Forth and argued for greater resources for Scotland. The problem was that while Stuart had access to the centre of power, Tory Secretaries of State were not representative of Scotland as a whole. This point was driven home frequently by Willie Ross, as Labour's Shadow Scottish Secretary. Even when Ross became Scottish Secretary (1964–70; 1974–76), and arguably the most effective holder of that office in winning concessions for Scotland, the Scottish voice was once again one chosen by the Prime Minister.

Scottish Office Ministers and officials became adept in making the case for treating Scotland as exceptional, requiring greater resources – often successfully, even when a stronger case for extra resources might be more deserving in other parts of the UK. Peter Hennessy, one of the keenest observers of Whitehall, has remarked that the Scottish Office was one of the few institutions, along with the military, to most successfully and persistently gain extra spending from the Treasury. While it was successful as an institutional lobby within the system, it also allowed for distinct policy development that ensured Scotland continued to be different from other parts of the UK. But such policy divergence invariably had to be agreed in Cabinet and Whitehall, and that meant within the ideological framework of the governing party. The Scottish Office could not have pursued a left-wing policy agenda under the Tories even if that was what Scots wanted and no Tory Prime Minister would appoint Scottish Secretaries with such views. But there was always some scope for variation.

Administrative devolution provided the basis of what would become the Scottish Parliament's competences. Matters devolved to the new Scottish Parliament were, more or less, competences previously under the Scottish Office. At the time, the Scottish Office had accumulated a wide range of responsibilities piecemeal over more than a century. Initially, the Scottish Office's responsibilities were limited to education and aspects of local administration, but law and order were soon added. Its responsibilities increased broadly in tandem with the increasing role of the state. Though not all new state intervention came under the Scottish Office and much was organised on a British or UK-wide basis, there were significant additions to its responsibilities over time. Agriculture was added before the First World War; housing and health were added after the war and grew in importance. More were added after 1945 including aspects of planning and economic responsibilities. The Scottish Office won major concessions and extra resources, sometimes based on additional needs, but also due to effective lobbying made possible by having a voice at the core of government. Its responsibilities included a general oversight of Scottish affairs, even where there was no formal responsibility. The Scottish Office was expected to 'speak for Scotland', to ensure that the Scottish voice was heard on matters that had an impact in Scotland. There were inevitably many grey areas. European Union matters, for example, were formally not within the Scottish Office's purview but it did have responsibilities regarding European policy areas, including regional development and aspects of social policy.

The principal case for legislative devolution focused on the unrepresentative nature of the Scottish Office's political leadership. Hence, much of the best debate and ideas favouring a Scottish Parliament focused on this. Less attention was paid to competences, not least as it was assumed these would be inherited from the Scottish Office. The translation of administrative devolution into legislative devolution involved a very different understanding of 'Scottish control of Scottish affairs'. 'Scottish control' meant control by Scottish elected representatives accountable to Scottish voters. 'Scottish affairs' may have initially been taken to refer to Scottish Office responsibilities but would become subject to debate involving other policy areas.

Parliamentary reforms paralleled the development of the Scottish Office. A Scottish Grand Committee was established initially on an experimental basis at the end of the 19th century and then continuously from early in the 20th. The Scottish Grand consisted of all Scottish MPs plus added Members to ensure it conformed with the party balance in the Commons as a whole. It considered Bills after second reading initially but its remit was extended in 1948 when it was able to consider Scottish Estimates – ie public spending under the Scottish Office – and it would consider the principle of any proposed Scottish legislation before second reading. In 1958, a Scottish Standing Committee was established which would consider Scottish Bills at Committee State. As the Committee stages of Scottish legislation in the Commons had been handed to Scottish Standing Committees in 1958, reflecting the composition of the Commons as a whole, there was little reason to continue with the practice of including (invariably) English Conservative MPs on the Scottish Grand Committee in the 1980s. In his 1966 book, *Parliament and Mumbo-Jumbo*, Emrys Hughes, Labour MP for South Ayrshire and son-in-law of Keir Hardie, had described how Iain MacLeod, London Tory MP whose family came from Lewis, had been 'quick to remind us the English would demand an English majority on committees dealing with purely English bills and in these the Labour Government would always be in a minority'. The West Lothian Question had its precursors.

Scottish Standing Committees dealt with Scottish legislation and a Scottish Select Committee was created in 1979, though one had briefly existed a decade before. Scottish Questions were taken in the Commons, though fairly rarely despite the growing scope of Scottish Office responsibilities.

Scotland was given generous representation in the Commons from 1922 until devolution but Scottish MPs were still inevitably a minority in the Commons simply because Scotland was much smaller than England. Nonetheless, Scotland was over-represented on a strictly population basis.

Anti-devolutionists

It is worth considering devolution's opponents before considering the devolutionists. It should not need to be said that opponents of devolution were not anti-Scottish or anti-democratic, though that is how supporters of a Scottish Parliament often described them. There were those, predominantly on the right of politics, who saw devolution as incompatible with the sovereignty of the Westminster Parliament and the UK as a unitary state. The notion of another Parliament that might challenge the authority of Westminster was anathema to such people. These opponents did not disappear with the creation of the Scottish Parliament. Some became constructive critics, some even embraced devolution and subsequently argued that the Scottish Parliament needed more powers to make it more fiscally responsible. Others remained staunch critics, insisting they would still vote against devolution. David McLetchie, the first leader of the Scottish Conservatives in the Scottish Parliament, maintained this position, though this did not prevent him from making constructive contributions, including making Ministers accountable for decisions as a powerful interrogator during Parliamentary Questions. But it would be a long stretch to describe McLetchie as a devolutionist.

Scottish nationalists would not necessarily describe themselves as devolutionists, though many campaigned for devolution in the 1979 and 1997 referendums. Scottish nationalism's objective was never as clear-cut as some would have us believe today. There were those who adopted a Scottish version of sovereign statehood, who opposed sharing power with others and were the mirror image of defenders of Parliamentary sovereignty at Westminster. For the most part, Scottish nationalist objectives have been contingent on circumstances. Go back 90-odd years and we find Scottish nationalists supporting a vague form of home rule within the Empire. Go back 70 years and senior figures in the SNP were arguing for what amounted to a confederal UK. Support amongst Scottish nationalists could range from something similar to legislative devolution through federalism and confederalism, to 'sovereign' statehood. Some of these positions might simply reflect a pragmatic view that full statehood was unlikely at the time. The lack of precision was understandable. For most of the 20th century Scottish nationalism was nowhere near the point of needing a clear, detailed outline of objectives. Its first objective was getting the broad principle of a directly elected Parliament firmly on the agenda. It is far from clear how many of the early Scottish nationalists would have supported the objective that was outlined in the SNP Government's 2013 White Paper on independence. Indeed, that very question is meaningless as we should not try to lift people from an earlier era and try to fit them into today's politics. Context is all-important. Anyone who doubts that a variety of forms of independence is possible need only look at the differences on elements of that 2013 white paper that have since emerged to realise that independence is a contested idea even amongst nationalists.

There have also been many opponents of devolution in the Labour Party. Many saw devolution as an irrelevance, associated with nationalism. It was a distraction from pursuing social justice and socialism. Others went further and opposed devolution as they believed a strong central government was needed to deliver equality and feared that the central demand management of the economy would be undermined by devolving power. This did not mean that Labour opponents of devolution believed in uniformity. Few could doubt Willie Ross's commitment to Scotland. Ross stands out amongst post-1945 Scottish Secretaries in his pursuit of Scottish interests. His close and loyal relationship with Wilson helped him win concessions. Richard Crossman, his Cabinet colleague, noted in his diary that there was already 'deep separation' between Scotland and England in policy terms and that while Ross accused the SNP of separatism, 'what Willie Ross himself actually likes is to keep Scottish business entirely privy from English business'. Ironically, Ross was then hostile to devolution, though he was converted by the rising electoral threat from the SNP, and Crossman was a keen advocate of legislative devolution.

There is an apocryphal tale that encapsulates a strain of Labour thinking pre-devolution. When Frank McElhone was appointed as a junior Scottish Office Minister, he is supposed to have asked Secretary of State Ross what he should do. Ross replied, 'You'll do as yer tellt'. It spoke of paternalism, enlightened as it may often have been, and very much framed in Scottish terms. Though Ross was vehemently opposed to Scottish devolution for most of his career, he was no less Scottish than anyone. Ross jealously guarded how Scottish interests should be defined. In their study of Labour and Scottish Nationalism, Michael Keating and David Bleiman noted that, in opposition, Ross made great play of the Tories' alleged neglect of Scotland, turning Scottish grievances to Labour's advantage without making any concession to home rule. Ross doubted that a Scottish Parliament could articulate the interests of Scotland as well as he could, at least until electoral pressure forced his change of mind.

Labour had been a keen advocate of home rule in its first 50 years, as discussed below, but abandoned that commitment after 1945. The abandonment was explained by John Taylor, Scottish Labour's secretary and organiser, in straightforward terms to delegates at the party's Scottish conference in 1947. In the past, he told delegates, there was strong support 'based on the fact that under Tory rule Scotland never had a fair deal'. But now, Scotland was in a 'much more favourable position than ever before in her economic history' after two years of the Attlee Government. There was also a view that achieving equality required centralised policy making that provided the same levels of support to citizens regardless of where they lived. Decentralisation was suspected of undermining social citizenship rights and equality. These views held sway amongst a large contingent of Labour members and supporters up to the 1980s. It was a view built on the assumption that Labour would remain in government much more often than would be the case.

In 1958, a special report from the Scottish Labour executive was presented to a party conference in Glasgow. It concluded that Scotland was not a separate economic unit and to treat it as such would be 'against the best interests of both sides of industry in Scotland and the United Kingdom'. It called for more Parliamentary time to be devoted to 'special problems requiring special provision in respect of Scottish domestic affairs' in light of the extension of Scottish Office responsibilities. While rejecting home rule, the report declared 'our belief in the principle of the maximum possible self-government for Scotland, consistent with the right to remain in United Kingdom Parliament and continue full Scottish representation there'. Labour was then staunchly opposed to a Scottish Parliament but equally committed to maintaining distinct Scottish institutions with a type of devolution that allowed for

> a) the need for direct contact and the personal touch;
> b) the need to adjust centralised services to the special needs of particular localities;

c) the need to avoid delay;
d) the convenience of the public;
e) the complexity which has accentuated the desire to devolve as far as possible;
f) the advantage derived from regional devolution in time of war.

In the late 1960s, Labour once more rejected home rule and re-committed itself to the 'greatest possible devolution consistent with our absolute determination to retain the maximum possible influence on the economic and political polices of the United Kingdom'. This was, Donald Dewar insisted in 1970, very little different from that adopted back in 1958. It is acceptable sentiment which could offend no one. The difficulty is that ten years later the party is 'not one bit the nearer knowing what it means'.

Dewar was then in a minority within the Labour Party on devolution. His view was that Scotland's government should be looked at holistically, including reforming local government alongside devolution. This should not be 'reduced to a narrow exercise in political tactics when what is required is anxious debate about the case for change'.

The SNP threat to Labour in the late 1960s had led to the establishment of the Royal Commission on the Constitution, initially chaired by Lord Crowther, former editor of the *Economist* and later by Lord Kilbrandon, a Scottish judge, following Crowther's death. The Royal Commission was charged with examining the functions of Parliament and Government in relation to the several countries, nations and regions of the United Kingdom. Crowther was not sympathetic to devolution as was clear when he volunteered that the Royal Commission should be wound up after the 1970 general election which was widely, though mistakenly, interpreted as evidence that the Scottish nationalist threat had gone. Lord Kilbrandon was much more favourably disposed to devolution. In October 1973, Kilbrandon reported recommending, inter alia, a devolved Assembly for Scotland. At this point the term 'Assembly' was used to distinguish what was being proposed for Scotland and Wales from Parliament at Westminster.

Scottish Labour's initial reaction to the rise of the SNP was, in the words of Gordon Brown and Henry Drucker, 'one of horror and contempt'. Scottish Labour's submission to the Royal Commission opposed devolution. Chair of the Labour Party in Scotland, John Pollock, whose view would change dramatically over time, said his party would prefer the 'obnoxious possibility' of a Conservative Government to separatism or federalism.

Scotland needed administrative not legislative devolution, with scrutiny provided by Parliamentary committees in the Commons. Devolution, Pollock then insisted, would take Scotland on a 'slippery slope', a phrase that would be repeated time and again by those hostile to devolution. A crucial argument, frequently articulated, was that devolution undermined working-class solidarity across Britain. Class was then much more important than national identity. Working-class families in Glasgow, it was argued, had more in common with working-class families in Liverpool than they had with Highland lairds. An example of this thinking was provided in 1977 in a debate on devolution when Bob Hughes, Aberdeen North's Labour MP, spoke against devolution,

> I believe in the unity of the working class in this country, and, far from devolution benefiting those people, I believe that, in the longer term, it will damage the advance of Socialism and the control of the commanding heights of the economy.

A strong view amongst Labour councillors in the 1970s was that a Scottish Assembly would undermine local government, especially that the proposed Assembly's powers would be used to cut grants to local government to provide the devolved government with more resources for its own areas of responsibility. The fear amongst many, and not just Labour councillors, in the new regional and district councils created in the 1970s was that power would be sucked up by a Scottish Parliament.

Labour was forced to rethink its position on devolution when the SNP won seven seats with 22 per cent of the vote in February 1974. This U-turn was motivated less from principle, though there were always genuine supporters of home rule in Labour's ranks, and more from fear of the SNP electoral threat, a threat that had been fuelled by the opportunities the discovery of North Sea oil offered. In October 1974, the SNP won 30 per cent of the vote and 11 of Scotland's 71 MPs and was in second place in 35 of Labour's 41 seats. It was these 35 second places that concentrated Labour minds. Ironically, had the decision been left to its Scottish MPs or to Scottish party activists, Labour would have remained hostile to devolution. The decision to support a Scottish Assembly was taken, largely due to the trade union block vote, at a special conference held between the two general elections in 1974.

As ever in politics, our preference for neat boxes makes complexity more manageable but also exaggerates differences. Not only is it more accurate to view preferences on Scotland's constitutional status operating along a continuum but there are continuums within and overlaps between political parties. There have been staunch devolutionists inside the Conservative Party and the SNP and staunch anti-devolutionists within the Labour Party and Liberal (Democratic) Party. But the party that is best described as the devolution party is Labour. Devolution became the official policy of the party in a way and to an extent it never has been in other parties. And for this reason, it is mainly to Labour thinkers that we turn to understand what it was they supported and why. Our approach is to focus on key individuals, partly to humanise the subject but also to emphasise evolving thinking. Devolution has always been a living idea, reflecting contemporary conditions.

So, who were the devolutionists? And what did they want?

The Devolutionists

The case for home rule had been well rehearsed long before a Scottish Parliament was established. The Scottish Home Rule Association (SHRA) was set up in 1886, largely with Liberal support. The *Scotsman* carried an editorial favouring home rule early the following year. While the issue never entirely disappeared, its salience waxed and waned over the decades. It would be wrong to think that the creation of a Scottish Parliament was inevitable. There is ample evidence that a Scottish Parliament was very much a fringe issue until the late 1960s.

The Liberals kept the flame alive over much of the 20th century. In the late 19th century, Gladstone's support for Irish home rule had been bedevilled by criticisms that it would involve Irish MPs having a vote on British matters in the Commons while no MPs would have a vote on equivalent Irish devolved affairs – essentially the problem that would later be called the 'West Lothian Question'. Various options were proposed – an 'in-and-out' option which would have prevented Irish MPs from voting on British matters that had been devolved to Ireland – essentially a version of English Votes for English Laws. The idea of excluding Irish MPs altogether while Ireland would still remain part of the UK was proposed but the experience of 'no taxation without representation', which led to the American Revolution, killed that idea. The response that would find lasting favour amongst Liberals was home-rule-all-round, what is now more commonly referred to as federalism, and indeed the founders of the

SHRA were supporters of this position. Liberal support for home-rule-all-round remained but was rarely given prominence and hardly developed beyond a sketchy outline.

There were, of course, many Scottish Liberals in the late 20th century who supported devolution. Scottish Liberals aligned themselves with federalism but, as with early Scottish nationalists and independence, Liberal federalism tended to be vaguely defined. They have generally been keener to make the case for Scottish home rule and treat UK-wide federalism as a longer-term objective. There have been Scottish Liberals who were probably little interested in a federal UK but were ardent Scottish home rulers. Many are best understood as devolutionists in practice who paid lip service to federalism in the knowledge that federalism was at best a distant prospect. John MacCormick, often seen as a Scottish National Party (SNP) figure, was an advocate of devolution and, after falling out with the SNP, became a Liberal home ruler. In his memoir published in 1955, MacCormick referred ambiguously to the 'ultimate goal of a free Scotland in a Federal United Kingdom'.

There were also a number of Conservative devolutionists. Alick Buchanan-Smith, Scottish Tory MP from 1964–91, was a principled supporter who had been Shadow Scottish Secretary but resigned when his party opposed devolution in 1976. He argued in a debate in 1976 that the UK was over-centralised, there was a feeling of remoteness in Scotland and that the Commons was over-loaded. Buchanan-Smith declared that opposing devolution was a 'betrayal of all I have stood for'. He became a Minister in Thatcher's Government but never reached the Cabinet and declined Ministerial office after the 1987 election with the intention of becoming the voice of anti-Thatcher Conservatism in Scotland and a committed devolutionist. His death in 1991 removed the last significant Tory devolutionist voice though a number of lesser-known Tories remained supporters against fierce opposition from within their party. Malcolm Rifkind, Buchanan-Smith's junior Shadow colleague, resigned with him in 1976 but soon fell into line on the Tories' anti-devolution stance. Rifkind became Secretary of State for Scotland in 1986 and had a more chequered record on devolution than Buchanan-Smith.

The SNP shares some credit with Labour for the creation of the Scottish Parliament. The SNP operated on the fringe of Scottish politics until the 1960s when it experienced an influx of new members bringing new skills and energy which, along with a more favourable context, saw it break through and have continuous, if often precarious, representation in the

Commons from 1967. The SNP election breakthrough forced Labour to rethink its position. The persistent threat from the SNP kept Labour committed to devolution through to the early 1980s. Thereafter, Labour's position became embedded and committed more in principle than out of fear of the SNP. Internal tensions caused the SNP difficulty. Hardliners were wary of, or opposed to, devolution but pragmatism ultimately triumphed when Alex Salmond led his party to campaign for the creation of the devolved Scottish Parliament in 1997 having previously been outmanoeuvred in his party on membership of the Constitutional Convention. He had opposed withdrawal from the Convention in 1989, when he was SNP Deputy Leader, but was defeated on the issue at that time.

Labour's support for devolution was erratic. Keir Hardie included Scottish Home Rule on his platform when he stood as the first independent Labour candidate in the 1888 Mid Lanark by-election. It is pointless now to read too much into that support. He was not espousing Scottish statehood. Would he support devolution, devo-max, independence or whatever today? The question is meaningless. And it would be ahistorical to prise him out of his time and place him into politics today. As the Keir Hardie Society has pointed out, Hardie's support for Scottish home rule had its roots in Irish home rule, as was the case with the Scottish Home Rule Association (SHRA) of which he was a supporter. Hardie was of his time and what he did support that has relevance today was a belief that Scotland was a distinct political community and that this should be manifested in the system of government. As Secretary of the London branch of the SHRA, Ramsay MacDonald wrote in support of Hardie in 1888, in preference to an

> obscure English barrister, absolutely ignorant of Scotland and Scottish affairs, and who only wants to get to Parliament in order that he may have the tail of MP to his name in the law courts.

Hardie's election address highlighted the number of landlords, lawyers and shipowners representing Scotland in the Commons and his main objection was the absence of the 'working men of Scotland'. His emphasis was unambiguously on class representation when it came to 'Scottish control of Scottish affairs'. Myths can be potent and Hardie as the progenitor of Scottish devolution is a powerful myth. But it is difficult to find references to his support for home rule beyond that first electoral contest.

The interwar years saw a group of radical Labour MPs returned to the

Commons committed to a Scottish Parliament. The 'Red Clydesiders' were strong advocates of Scottish home rule; they saw this as the best means of pursuing a radical socialist agenda. Jimmy Maxton told a home rule rally of 35,000 on Glasgow Green that being an MP had converted him to the need for a Scottish Parliament and in 1924 he told another rally that he saw no 'greater job in life [than to make] the English-ridden, capitalist-ridden, landlord-ridden Scotland into a Scottish socialist Commonwealth'. It was classic Maxton rhetoric. Labour's electoral advances in 1922 and 1923 in Scotland encouraged support for home rule and Bills were presented in the Commons over the following years. These proposals were broad in scope and had no prospect of being enacted. The failure to advance the home rule cause led to disillusionment and, for some, including Cunninghame Graham, to set up the National Party of Scotland. Graham, co-founder with Keir Hardie of the Scottish Labour Party following the Mid Lanark by-election, became a founding member of the National Party of Scotland and the first President of the Scottish National Party. Graham was a romantic in his socialism (he was returned as a Liberal MP in North West Lanarkshire in 1886 and became the first MP to describe himself as a socialist in Parliament) and in his Scottish nationalism. Exactly what he supported, however, was less clear. At this stage, the campaign was very much about the principle, with details left vague.

Gordon Brown offered important insights into the early 20th-century debates in an appendix on 'Home Rule and the Labour Movement' to his doctoral thesis on *The Labour Party and political change in Scotland, 1918–1929*. His insights remain pertinent. 'If Scottish sentiment was important in determining voting behaviour in 1929, it was Labour – not the nationalists – who could mobilise it.' That would remain true into the 21st century. Labour had a claim to be Scotland's national party, though not a nationalist party. Brown's other comment on home rule was particularly relevant and will be addressed later in this book:

> while Labour lost much of its initial enthusiasm for home rule and concentrated attention on economic and social questions during the twenties; the real problem for Scottish Labour was that it wanted to be Scottish and British at the same time. No theorist attempted in sufficient depth to reconcile the conflicting aspirations for home rule and a British socialist advance. In particular, no one was able to show how capturing power in Britain – and legislating for minimum levels of

welfare, for example – could be combined with a policy of devolution for Scotland.

That unresolved conflict explains Labour's abandonment of home rule in subsequent decades of the 20th century. The need to reconcile these conflicts remains an ongoing and unavoidable challenge.

The trade union movement and Communist Party of Great Britain (CPGB) played important roles in keeping home rule alive in the 20th century. The Scottish Trades Union Congress held a debate in 1968 at which miners' leader Mick McGahey argued that Scotland was a nation, 'Not a region of Britain, not a district, but a nation in its own right and entitled to demand a right to nationhood'. But there was more to his thinking than that Scotland was a nation. He believed the devolution of aspects of economic policy making would not undermine working-class solidarity. McGahey's ashes were buried in the foundation of the Scottish Parliament. Jimmy Reid would be another long-term advocate of a Scottish Parliament who had been a leading member of the CPGB and ended up a member of the SNP. His views too were rooted in a belief that Scotland was a nation and he adopted an instrumental view that a Scottish Parliament would be better placed than Westminster to deliver the kinds of policies he supported. The CPGB favoured a federal UK from the early 1960s. The strength of the CPGB in the unions and union links with the Labour Party ensured that a home rule voice would be heard during this period when Labour officially turned its back on devolution.

John Mackintosh was one of the most consistent advocates of a Scottish Parliament. He combined a deep understanding of national identity, government and the relationship between the two. He had been Politics Professor at Strathclyde University before becoming Labour MP for Berwick and East Lothian in 1966 and would later become Politics Professor at Edinburgh University while still a serving MP. In 1968 he published *The Devolution of Power*, making the case for major reforms across the UK. Many of his insights remain relevant. In an essay in 1974, weeks before the SNP scored its best result in elections to the Commons until 2015, he explained the 'new appeal of nationalism'. He noted that Scottish national identity continued to exist through the traditional carriers of nationality – the Church, educational system and local government system. He recognised too that Scots also had a 'British dimension' to their identity in which they had taken reasonable pride for over two centuries but that a 'gloom hangs over the country, a sense of failure'. This declining 'sense of self-esteem and self-confidence of the British' was undermining Britishness but there remained a 'residual hold' of the 'dual nationality'. He warned that Britishness would continue to decline 'so long as there is no pride in being British' and only a successful period of Government in London would halt this.

Devolutionists in the Labour Party were a diverse group. They included radical socialists and social democrats. Some supported devolution from conviction, while others supported it for reasons of electoral expediency. There was always a strong strand of Scottish national identity in Scottish Labour that transcended views on devolution. For some devolutionists, a Scottish Parliament was a means of making decision-making more accountable, more democratic. Alongside this was a view that it would permit Scotland to be bolder, more experimental in policy making. While Labour officially adopted devolution in 1974, it remained deeply divided and many who supported it then did so without enthusiasm. That began to change after 1979. The decision to hold a referendum on devolution in 1979 was a means of holding a divided party together. The inclusion of the 40 per cent rule, stipulating that the Government should move a repeal order on the legislation setting up a Scottish Assembly unless 40 per cent of the eligible electorate voted for devolution, created a major hurdle. In the event, while a slight majority of voters supported devolution (52 per cent to 48 per cent – notably the same margin that voted for Brexit across the UK in 2016) this amounted to only 32.5 per cent of the eligible electorate. This meant the issue returned to Parliament. Prime Minister Callaghan was caught between a rock and a hard place as Labour had lost its overall majority in the Commons and 38 Labour MPs signed a letter to Callaghan saying they would support repeal when a Government Minister moved such an Order in Parliament. Gregor Mackenzie, Rutherglen's MP who had been Callaghan's Parliamentary Private Secretary in the 1960s, told Callaghan on the morning of the referendum that he expected 39 per cent to vote for devolution but 'certainly a 36 per cent' vote. Callaghan acknowledged that 39 per cent would be much 'easier to deal with' than a 36 per cent. The 32.5 per cent proved well below expectations of supporters and what would be required to get Parliament to vote against repeal.

The SNP sought to call Callaghan's bluff by supporting a no confidence vote if the repeal order was not moved (and opposed by Labour). Callaghan calculated that it was better to face the electorate following defeat on no confidence than to move repeal knowing his party was divided. An election would have to be held soon anyway. Defeat on no confidence led to the 1979 general election. Margaret Thatcher's Conservatives were returned at the subsequent election. The legacy of bitterness between Labour and the SNP – the former blaming the SNP for causing the election of the Tories and the latter believing Labour had abandoned support for devolution – would cast a long shadow over Scottish politics. The Tories moved the repeal order in July 1979 and devolution was officially dead in this episode of Scotland's story.

Devolving and decentralising

Early in the century, John Wheatley had been an advocate of what has been described as 'socialism in one city'. But the tendency then as now was for all parties to be decentralist when out of office and centralist when in power at the centre. The tendency has been that those in office seek to hoard and enhance power. This is understandable, up to a point. Anyone who enters politics to do something, rather than to be someone, will want the tools to do whatever it is they believe in. And power is the key tool. Decentralisation is commonly seen as giving power away or at least sharing it, but as we will argue later, this is mistaken. Decentralisation is institutional scepticism, an acknowledgement that we do not know everything. Sharing power increases power, the ability to get things done, though does not come naturally, which is why it is important to create structures and practices that prevent power hoarding.

One of the great fears of many opponents of devolution in the 1970s was that a Scottish Assembly would suck up power from local authorities. For that reason, many councillors opposed devolution. There was a long and distinguished tradition of support for municipalisation throughout the 20th century. Conservative cuts to local spending and imposition of policies from the centre inclined many in local government who had previously opposed devolution to change their minds in the 1980s. This resulted in the Convention of Scottish Local Authorities (COSLA), under Labour control, to support the establishment of the Scottish Constitutional Convention, and provide assistance and the secretariat. The Convention document, 'Scotland's Parliament, Scotland's Right' stated,

> The Act will include a clause committing Scotland's Parliament to secure and maintain a strong and effective system of local government,

> and will embody the principle of subsidiarity so as to guarantee the important role of local government in service delivery.

Two of the most important figures in local government during this period were Rosemary McKenna and Jean McFadden, who served as Presidents of COSLA. Shortly after the 1997 election, Rosemary McKenna MP outlined her vision of a constructive relationship between local government and the Scottish Parliament. There should be discussion of the appropriate boundaries between functions of local government and the Scottish Parliament, she argued, and she did not envisage the Parliament sucking up powers. But important concerns were voiced by Jean McFadden. Writing in 1999, she noted that the devolution legislation was 'virtually silent' on local government with only two references in Schedule 5 (referring to the local election franchise as reserved and local taxes being excepted from reservation) and maintained that some councillors remained suspicious, fearing the Scottish Parliament would undermine local autonomy with policies that removed local discretion resulting in local councils becoming 'little more than agents of the Parliament'. At the time, this was seen as unduly pessimistic but with the passage of time it now appears to have been a warning that ought to have been heeded.

In so far as the case for devolved government was to democratise administrative devolution, it was important to recognise any unintended consequences of devolution. It was always going to be difficult to entrench local government autonomy. There was no doubt that the expectation had been that devolution would not stop in Edinburgh, nor indeed that the Parliament would become a centralising institution. But while 40 per cent of MSPs elected in 1999 had been councillors, not all brought localist assumptions with them.

Powerful local government, backed by an electoral mandate, can replicate the kind of innovation and ability to pursue policies tailored for its area that devolution was designed to do for Scotland within the UK. This has always created tensions between those who see a strong centre as a means of delivering equality and ensuring that all citizens and communities are given equal access to services and those who believe that citizen and community diversity requires different responses determined locally. Advocates of devolution had often been decentralisers, viewing the UK as too centralised and incapable of understanding or accounting for Scottish experience and expertise. One of the key early 20th century thinkers who deserves more attention was John Wheatley, as referred to earlier. Wheatley made a major contribution to the first Labour Government with his housing legislation. He had a history in local government and, as David Howell's classic comparative study of Wheatley, James Connolly and John Maclean, noted, Wheatley had been optimistic about the prospect of 'Socialism in One City' and had once envisaged the municipality having departments for home and foreign trade. The idea of cities engaged in such ventures well pre-dates current debates on whether the Scottish Parliament should operate on the global stage. This is a theme to which we will return.

Democratisation beyond devolution

As much of the debate leading up to the establishment of devolution had focused on the unrepresentative nature of the Scottish Office, we need to address some issues of representativeness. Representativeness has a number of meanings. At its simplest it means *re-presentation*, making present again. But how this is translated into practice presents challenges and options. Descriptive representation suggests that Parliament reflects the composition of the nation, or more accurately the electorate. This had been the dominant understanding of representative democracy that informed debates leading up to home rule. Trying to create a microcosm of the wider public involves many assumptions. Which characteristics are to be re-presented? Gender, class, ethnicity, age… the list goes on and the answer will always be contested. The extent to which Scottish politics was dominated by old white males is striking. As late as 1987 when Labour won 50 of Scotland's 72 seats, only one – Maria Fyfe – was a woman. That statistic now seems shocking but proved a radicalising moment in part due to Maria Fyfe's efforts and many other Labour women who linked the case for devolution with greater women's representation. Class representation has diminished from the days of the Red Clydesiders, especially more recently. The decline of working-class representatives has meant the decline of working-class interests. Scotland's ethnic and religious diversity has risen up the representativeness agenda. While the Parliament now gives votes to 16-year-olds, its membership is still heavily skewed towards the older end of the population spectrum.

Given the primary motivation of devolution had been to democratise administrative devolution, it was no surprise that rich debates on the form of democratisation would be central to debates in the Constitutional

Convention. No issue was given more attention by advocates of a Scottish Parliament. Discussions of the electoral system, gender equality and encouraging greater public participation were lively, well-informed and proved impactful. In a debate in the Commons in February 1998, Labour MP Rosemary McKenna warned that 'We shall never be forgiven if we wake upon the morning of 7 May 1999 and face the prospect of a small group of women in the Scottish Parliament'. Scotland's record in returning women to the House of Commons during the 20th century had been poor and, as Esther Breitenbach and Fiona Mackay, editors of *Women and Contemporary Scottish Politics: An Anthology*, remarked, had 'too often passed unremarked and unrecorded'. One of the most remarkable features of debates on a Scottish Parliament had been the way women had ensured that women's representation became linked to the establishment of the Parliament. A new Parliament created an opportunity to improve women's representation. Getting it right from the outset was important as otherwise shifting the gender balance once the Parliament was established would be much more difficult. A range of women activists injected the issue onto the devolution agenda with remarkable skill.

It would be up to the political parties to act but the devolution debates on representation ensured the issue was on the agenda as never before in the early 1990s. Labour led the way after fierce internal debates. They achieved 50:50 representation in the first elections by twinning constituencies with male and female candidates for each twinned pair of seats. The other parties were less pro-active, if active at all. The SNP responded with more informal and less successful efforts, returning 43 per cent women MSPs in 1999. The Liberal Democrats were committed in principle but ended up with only two women in its group of 17 MSPs. The Tories were a little better with three women in a group of 18 but objected to 'rules and regulations which create an artificial gender balance'. With 48 women in a Parliament of 129 MSPs returned in 1999, the Scottish Parliament had made a good start but with more work required. This achievement had been the result of campaigning by many activists inside Labour and other parties, the trades unions and a range of organisations. The question was whether increased women's representation would help women beyond the Scottish Parliament in Scottish society or whether these women would put party interests first.

Margaret Thatcher and the negative template of Westminster

Success, it is often said, has many parents and failure is an orphan. This is true of the establishment of the Scottish Parliament. Labour, SNP and Liberals (later Liberal Democrats) each has a valid claim to be a parent of the Scottish Parliament. So too, ironically, could Margaret Thatcher, though the Tory leader would have balked at the idea. Opposition to the Tories under Margaret Thatcher galvanised many who had been lukewarm supporters of devolution, converted many erstwhile opponents and gave impetus and urgency to the demand for a Parliament. Margaret Thatcher was perceived as threatening some of the very institutions that had contributed to a sense of Britishness amongst Scots. She undermined class solidarity far better than devolution ever could have with her anti-trade union legislation, sales of council housing and overseeing of an economy that saw the decline of manufacturing industries. Regional policies that had incentivised investment in Scotland, generous public expenditure in Scotland and the welfare state had been presented as evidence that the UK worked in Scotland's interests but that too changed after 1979 when many Scots believed that Tory Governments were undermining much that had made them want to be British.

There were many other arguments for a Scottish Parliament. For some, devolution was an end in itself, the political expression of the Scottish nation. For others, it was more of a means to an end. It was a stepping stone to independence for some, a bulwark in defence of the union for others. The language of the time stressed the need to address the 'Scottish democratic deficit' – a reference to Scottish Tory MPs being heavily outnumbered by opposition MPs in Scotland – which allowed Labour, SNP, Liberal Democrats and others to rally around the case for devolution after 1979.

Scotland was not alone in this. Wales and parts of England had similar experiences and, in some cases, had more grounds for complaint. There was a dimension in Scotland, shared with Wales, but absent across English regions: Scotland was a nation and a well-established political community. It was not just that decisions were being made for the whole of the UK that affected Scotland, opposed by a majority of Scots, but unpopular policies were being developed for Scotland that were the responsibility of the Scottish Office. A similar situation prevailed in Wales, especially after the establishment of the Welsh Office in 1964. Welsh Labour, it is claimed, has the longest uninterrupted winning streak of any party in the democratic world. This explains why support for a Scottish Parliament and Welsh Assembly rose up the political agenda over the course of the 18 years after the Conservatives came to office in 1979. Wales had decisively rejected devolution in 1979 but would very narrowly support it 18 years later. While the margin of victory was slight, the change from 1979 was greater than in Scotland.

In the wake of the 1979 devolution referendum, Jack Brand, one of the founders of the Campaign for a Scottish Assembly (CSA) and leading academic scholar of the Scottish national movement, had believed that it was vital to ensure that Labour remained committed to devolution. His fear had been that Labour might once more drift away from this commitment. The CSA would play an important role in keeping the idea alive and encouraging cross-party support. One of the clearest articulations of the case for a Scottish Parliament was found in a report by the Constitutional Steering Committee (CSC), established by and presented to the Campaign for a Scottish Assembly in July 1988. The CSC membership had members drawn from Labour, SNP and Liberal Democrats plus other figures in Scottish civil society. It was a remarkable document. The CSC report – *The Claim of Right for Scotland* – had been drawn up by a committee chaired by Robert Grieve, former Chief Planning Officer for Scotland, with the drafting done by Jim Ross. Ross had been an Under Secretary in the Scottish Office in charge of devolution in the late 1970s who took early retirement after the 1979 general election and became an active member of the Labour Party and a keen advocate of devolution. Devolution was very much unfinished business for him. The argument in the *Claim of Right* was that the team of Scottish Office Ministers created to provide Scotland with a distinctive government according to Scottish wishes 'cannot possibly do so' as the team was chosen from 'whichever political party has won a British general election' fought on British, not Scottish issues. It criticised Westminster Parliamentary procedures as ineffective, insufficient and a 'sop' to Scottish discontent.

The *Claim* referred to the 'English constitution' as an 'illusion of democracy' in which only one source of power – the Crown in Parliament – was recognised. Party discipline meant that Parliament was controlled by the Prime Minister, as head of the executive, rather than the other way around. Westminster, it maintained, was subjected to 'heavy pressure to conform with Government convenience'. This involved a 'unique concentration of power reinforced by a voting system' commended for providing strong government but allowing for a clear majority of voters to be crushed by a Parliamentary majority. The intention was to create a very different devolved system.

The critique pointed towards a different type of Parliament for Scotland, though the Committee did not see its function as drawing up such a scheme. It recommended that a scheme should be agreed by a Constitutional Convention. It considered different Convention models acknowledging that it 'must achieve acceptance by those on whose behalf it presumes to speak and act' and recognised the difficulties if, as was all but certain, the then Conservative Government opposed it. The challenge was achieving the highest level of legitimacy through broad support. The results of the 1987 general election gave impetus to the campaign. Margaret Thatcher was returned as Prime Minister for the third time to head a Conservative Government while losing 11 seats in Scotland reducing the governing party to only ten of Scotland's 72 constituencies and still in charge of the Scottish Office. The last piece of legislation passed in the previous Parliament had been the Abolition of Domestic Rates (Scotland) Act which created the community charge, quickly referred to by opponents as the poll tax. It would prove an important symbol of all that supporters of a Scottish Parliament saw as wrong with the then existing system of government.

The Constitutional Convention

The Constitutional Convention met for the first time in 1989. It had a difficult birth. The SNP feared that the Convention would be used to attack independence and decided not to participate. This was potentially a fatal blow given the importance attached to the breadth of support required for the Convention's legitimacy. But the SNP's absence helped the Convention achieve consensus and undermined criticisms that devolution would become a stepping stone to independence. There were no arguments about independence and less need to defend its proposals as a backdoor route to independence. The Convention's main achievements were providing momentum to the campaign for a Parliament, deepening the commitment of its members to a Scottish Parliament – especially the Labour Party – and providing a blueprint, albeit incomplete, for devolution.

While the SNP and Conservatives refused to participate, the Convention membership included 57 of Scotland's 72 MPs (49 Labour and eight Liberal Democrats), seven of the eight Scottish Members of the European

Parliament, all 12 regional and island councils, 47 of the 53 district councils as well as representatives of Labour, Liberal Democrats, Social Democrats, Cooperative Party, Communist Party, Orkney Movement and Shetland Movement. The Scottish Greens were initially involved but left when the their proposal for a multi-option referendum was rejected. Other key institutions that played important parts in deliberations and provided support were the trade unions, including the Scottish Trades Union Congress, and the Convention of Scottish Local Authorities (COSLA). In attendance at meetings were Scottish churches, the National Federation of Self-Employed and Small Businesses, An Comunn Gaidhealach and Comunn na Gaidhlig. Representatives of the Scottish Convention of Women and from ethnic minorities were also involved, contributing to debates on representation in the proposed new Parliament.

The Convention's proposals were patchy with considerable detail on issues of representation but less on finance, devolved competences and relations with London. James Kellas, doyen of Scottish political science, noted that the Convention was silent or vague on a number of matters that would require to be addressed: the West Lothian Question; revenue raising; entrenchment of devolution; the future role of the Secretary of State for Scotland; the number of Scottish MPs after devolution and initially, though this would be addressed directly later by the Convention, on the electoral system. Much detail was still required and there were a number of controversial issues that remained unresolved by the time Labour was returned to power in 1997.

Criticisms of the Assembly proposed in the 1970s informed debates in the 1980s and 1990s. Former Tory Prime Minister Alec Douglas Home had criticised Labour's 1978 devolution legislation a fortnight before the referendum vote in 1979 in an intervention widely believed to have influenced the result. Home, as a previous advocate of a form of devolution, had intervened with what he saw as five key flaws in Labour's proposals:

- the Assembly was unable to raise a proportion of its own revenue;
- Scottish MPs would continue to vote on English legislation while no MPs could vote on devolved Scottish affairs;
- the proposed 142 members of the Assembly was too large and he suggested 100 would suffice;
- there was no machinery to determine whether a Bill was purely Scottish before it was introduced into the Assembly;

- the first-past-the-post electoral system was a problem. Home favoured some form of proportional system.

Amongst the significant contributions responding to Home's critique was a speech in 1986 by Nigel Smith. Smith had been a long-term devolutionist and has been described as the 'most influential campaigner you've never heard of'. He chaired *Scotland* FORward, the 1997 pro-devolution cross/non-party referendum campaign organisation. He was determined that there would be no repeat of the 1979 referendum and sought to ensure that Labour and SNP cooperated. He acknowledged and addressed Home's five flaws. While much focus is given to politicians and parties in how devolution came about, there were many people outside party politics who were important in keeping devolution alive. Nigel Smith and Esther Roberton – the latter played a key role behind the scenes in the Constitutional Convention and wider campaign for a Scottish Parliament – were amongst such figures.

Over the next 18 years, many devolution supporters largely accepted Home's critique or elements of it and would reconsider the form devolution should take. Well before the establishment of the Constitutional Convention, Labour had moved towards supporting tax powers – articulated in the early days as 'tax raising powers' then later as 'tax varying powers'. The Convention did not address the West Lothian Question but there was a proposal to reduce the number of Scottish MPs following devolution in a report by the Constitution Unit at University College London (UCL) and in a chapter by Wendy Alexander (who would later become Donald Dewar's Special Adviser, MSP, Minister under devolution and Scottish Labour leader) and Jim McCormick, then working for a left-leaning think tank. Reducing the number of Scottish MPs in the Commons did not resolve the problem but diminished the likelihood of Scottish MPs affecting purely English legislation.

The size of the Parliament was linked to the electoral system, a subject debated at length in the Convention. The first major development in this respect was Labour's embrace of a more proportional electoral system, recognising that first-past-the-post was unacceptable to the Liberal Democrats and others. It also addressed one of Home's criticisms. But equally, the Liberal Democrats agreed that Single Transferable Vote, its preferred system, would not be acceptable to Labour. The mixed Multi-Member Proportional system was adopted – though Additional Member

System (AMS) would be the preferred and commonly used name. This involved electors having two votes – one for a constituency member and another for regional list Members. Labour had been considering electoral reform during the Thatcher years. Its 1990 conference passed a resolution calling for an inquiry into electoral reform. A working party was established under Professor Raymond Plant which initially reported in 1991 then produced a second report the following year. Plant candidly admitted that he knew little about electoral systems when he was appointed – he was a distinguished political philosopher – but understood that this was not a problem as Labour's leader wanted a genuinely open-minded approach to producing the report. Plant supported AMS for the Scottish Parliament but offered no firm advice on reform at Westminster. At the 1992 election, Labour's manifesto proposed to strengthen the Plant committee with an 'extended membership' and enhanced authority encouraging a 'wide and well-informed public debate on the electoral system'. A third report from the Plant Commission was issued in April 1993 which proposed a majoritarian Supplementary Vote for the Commons. It was a compromise as the group had been deeply divided. The proposed system involved keeping single member constituencies with voters marking their first and second preferences. Candidates needed 50 per cent of the vote to win. If no candidate achieved this then the third and lower candidates would drop out and their preferences redistributed to the top two. It was an odd system that was not proportional and would only have modified first-past-the-post. It was widely criticised. Plant himself had favoured a mixed system similar to that proposed for the Scottish Parliament. John Smith, Labour's leader when the third Plant report was issued, proposed that Labour should hold a referendum though he personally continued to support first-past-the-post. The 1993 Labour conference committed the party to upholding first-past-the-post, supporting a referendum but also supported AMS for the Scottish Parliament and a second chamber at Westminster elected by proportional representation. Labour was firming up its commitment to a Scottish Parliament elected using a more proportional electoral system but remained opposed to electoral reform for Westminster. This was an era in which a broad agenda for constitutional reform was influencing Labour thinking. Charter '88 brought together a broad cross-party body of opinion in favour of major reforms. Scottish supporters of Scottish devolution found common ground with this agenda.

David Butler, doyen of election and referendum studies in Britain, described the third Plant report as a 'revolutionary document' with wise observations but which 'ends with a silly answer'. The revolutionary element was that it envisaged coalition or minority government. Butler argued that the prospect of reform required a consensus around a new system but not the Supplementary Vote which he regarded as a 'bad one'. Perhaps even more revolutionary was the fact that Labour was looking at electoral systems across a range of different types of elections rather than in glorious isolation as much constitutional thinking tended to be conducted.

Given the mixed electoral system proposed for the Scottish Parliament involved a combination of the familiar first-past-the-post and a regional proportional element, the degree of overall proportionality would depend on the balance between the two elements. The relative proportion of constituency members to list MSPs would also influence the prospect of any party being able to form a government with an overall majority on its own. The total size eventually agreed was closer to that criticised by Home than what he proposed. There would be 73 constituency and 56 List MSPs. This was a compromise agreed between George Robertson of the Labour Party and Jim Wallace of the Liberal Democrats in a meeting in the Edinburgh home of future Liberal Democrat leader Menzies Campbell. The 73 constituencies would be based on the then existing Scottish seats in the Commons with one exception – Orkney and Shetland would be represented by separate Members, a gift agreed behind closed doors for the Liberal Democrats. The 56 would be based on the eight European Parliament constituencies that then existed. This was an example of the Convention operating in terms that it hoped would be adopted by the new Parliament, leading to cooperative, consensual compromise. The system was more proportional than AMS in Wales. In Wales, there would be a higher proportion of constituencies in the total number of seats than was the case in Scotland. Many in Welsh Labour concluded that this would usually deliver an overall majority for Labour. In the event, no party in Wales has managed to win an overall majority though Welsh Labour has won exactly 50 per cent of seats in three elections. It was in Scotland in 2011 that a party – the SNP – won an overall majority. Electoral systems influence election outcomes but ultimately it is voters who decide.

The Scotland Act 1978, the earlier devolution legislation that had not been implemented, had been an odd piece of legislation with the Assembly's powers based on lists of legislation in the schedules to the Act. This meant that the Act would have required regular updating and amendment even without changes to its competences. The UCL Constitution Unit, Wendy Alexander and Jim McCormick, proposed instead that reserved powers should be defined in law leaving all else to be devolved. Anomalies and omissions would become apparent, such as the failure to refer to retaining regulations governing Antarctica, but these were minor problems compared to the consequences that would have followed had the 1978 legislation been implemented. Delineating powers can never be done perfectly in a devolved system of government and there would inevitably be grey areas, but the system adopted made more sense than what had previously been proposed in the 1970s. However, what was left underdeveloped was the crucial question of how shared responsibilities and overlapping competences that inevitably arise in devolved systems, should be handled. And discussion of devolution took no account of how devolution might operate outside the EU.

John Smith, later Labour leader, argued in a lecture at Strathclyde University in October 1992 that three factors had convinced him that there was need for reform. The first was the experience of centralisation under the Conservatives. A series of pieces of legislation had disempowered local authorities. This strengthened Smith's support and converted many councillors who had previously opposed devolution. A Scottish Parliament, they came to believe, elected by the Scottish electorate would be more in tune, and therefore would work cooperatively, with local government. The second factor for Smith was the European dimension. Notions of subsidiarity were then in vogue and frequent comparisons with experience elsewhere in Europe were cited by home rulers as evidence of new, modern forms of government. These ideas remain relevant not least in the amendment of the UK Internal Market Act (discussed in chapters 3 and 4). The third factor was a 'discreet but significant sociological shift' from 'traditional perceptions of ourselves as subjects to a more modern view of ourselves as citizens'. The notion of Scots as citizens rather than subjects played a powerful part in the deliberations of the Constitutional Convention. This would be the underlying thinking of Labour's new commitment to devolution.

1997 Referendum

After 1979, Labour was initially committed to delivering a Scottish Parliament without a referendum. As late as February 1996, Labour's Shadow Scottish Secretary George Robertson had ruled out the need for a referendum. In June, along with Donald Dewar, Robin Cook and

Gordon Brown, Robertson announced that there would be a two-question referendum. The decision was taken without consultation with Labour's Convention partners but it spiked Tory Michael Forsyth's guns. Forsyth had become Tory Scottish Secretary the year before and had focused his attacks on devolution's tax powers – the 'tartan tax'. Labour had spent the previous few years seeking to dispel a reputation as a 'tax and spend' party so Forsyth's 'tartan tax' jibe hit a sensitive spot for Labour. But despite some internal turmoil, the decision to hold a referendum was accepted and allowed Labour to argue that any decision on whether the Parliament should have tax powers would be up to the voters. Voters would be asked whether they supported devolution in principle and separately if they supported tax-varying powers.

By the time the 1997 election came along, it was fairly clear that a Scottish Parliament would be created. The total wipe-out of Conservative MPs in Scotland and Wales only added to the sense of inevitability. There were doubters and a few opponents but support for devolution had become entrenched inside the Labour Party over the previous 18 years. This was very different from 1945 or 1979. There was no John Taylor type in Scottish Labour arguing that there was no need for a Scottish Parliament now that Labour was in power at Westminster. John Smith had referred to the 'settled will of the Scottish people' and there was evidence at that time that a substantial and stable majority amongst the public supported a Scottish Parliament. But campaigners took nothing for granted.

The Bill to hold Scottish and Welsh devolution referendums was the first proposed legislation published by the New Labour Government. It was another lesson from the experience of the 1970s. The 1979 referendum had come after a long, fractious debate on devolution legislation in Parliament. These Parliamentary debates had effectively been part of the long referendum campaign and contributed to public weariness with the issue and exacerbated divisions in the Labour Party. John Mackintosh, Labour's independent-minded MP, had warned that the public might get bored with devolution by the time it got to a referendum. The 1997 referendum would act as a kind of second reading, giving the public's endorsement of devolution in principle. It meant that opposition to the Scotland Bill would be relatively muted compared with the mutilation its predecessor had received in its passage through Westminster in the late 1970s. There would be no 40 per cent rule (requiring that 40 per cent of the eligible electorate as well as a majority of those voting should support devolution) in 1997. The rule introduced in the 1970s had created a hurdle that had not existed in the earlier or any subsequent referendums and had contributed to distrust of Westminster and referendums amongst many supporters of a Scottish Parliament.

A key issue was whether the SNP, which had stood aloof from the Convention, would lend its support. The SNP had become suspicious of Labour's devolution commitment – some seeing it as insincere and unlikely to be implemented, others seeing devolution as a means of undermining independence. Alex Salmond, SNP leader, had been trying to nudge his party towards supporting devolution and had met resistance. Opposition to devolution inside the SNP all but disappeared after the 1997 election. A special SNP meeting was held at which the party overwhelmingly agreed to campaign for Labour's devolution proposals in the referendum. One sticking point had been whether the Government would try to impose a glass ceiling on devolution, preventing further powers or the possibility of independence. Alex Salmond trusted Donald Dewar's assurance on this, an assurance made public on various occasions including during a debate on the Government's devolution white paper in July 1997. Salmond had asked Dewar to reiterate that nothing would 'interfere in any way with the sovereign right of the Scottish people to determine their own constitutional future'. Dewar replied that any effort to build barriers would be futile and that practical politics is what matters. This was agreed, though it had no formal constitutional status nor was it necessary, to assist Salmond in managing the SNP's internal politics. The SNP's governing body agreed to campaign for a 'Yes, Yes' vote in the referendum.

Between June and September, polls showed support for a Scottish Parliament never falling below 61 per cent and opposition never rising above 25 per cent. Support for tax powers was consistently lower than for devolution but always higher than opposition to tax powers. Only one poll recorded the gap between support for and opposition to tax power falling under 10 per cent. Ultimately, 74.3 per cent voted in favour of a Scottish Parliament and 63.5 per cent for tax powers. Sustained and significant support for a Scottish Parliament had been confirmed. Opponents accepted the result. This did not mean that there would not be future debate on details or that valid criticisms could not be made. Indeed, one lesson of the experience was that those on the losing side should not feel compelled to prostrate themselves before the victors and abandon all critical faculties. They must accept the result. The referendum showed that parties could cooperate in pursuit of a common goal, an experience that contrasted with the 1979 devolution referendum.

Implementation

Much work still needed to be done. The impression was created at times that Parliament was going through the motions, albeit strenuous and time consuming for Ministers and MPs, debating the legislation to create the Scottish Parliament. As Donald Dewar would note in his *Spectator* lecture in November 1998, the legislation involved 191 hours 43 minutes on the floor of the Commons, 2,025 amendments and amounted to around a million spoken words. It had been debated in a Committee of the Whole House given its importance as a constitutional piece of legislation. More important battles took place before the Bill was presented to the Commons. Some matters, as we have seen, remained unresolved and not all members of the government were reconciled to the decisions made by the Constitutional Convention. The Devolution Scotland, Wales and the Regions (DSWR) Cabinet Committee tasked with agreeing the details included some of the Labour Cabinet's most powerful figures, including devo-sceptics, and was chaired by the formidable Lord Chancellor Derry Irvine. As Robin Cook later remarked, Irvine's approach to chairing a meeting was to cross-examine the other members. Home Secretary Jack Straw and Education Secretary David Blunkett would prove sharp critics in the Committee. These weekly sessions were bruising for Donald Dewar who was a member of the Committee as Scottish Secretary. While he would return to Dover House, the Scottish Office headquarters in Whitehall, feeling despondent, his officials who had accompanied him to the meetings, would report on Dewar's successes in ensuring that there was no dilution of Scottish Labour's commitments despite powerful challenges. These internal government debates tested the proposed legislation and ensured that a better Bill emerged.

An important feature, further distinguishing 1979 and 1997, was the role of Whitehall, particularly the Treasury. There had been strong opposition to devolution amongst senior civil servants in the 1970s. Having a Chancellor of the Exchequer, who had cut his political teeth campaigning for a Scottish Assembly in the 1970s, taking office following a landslide election victory, made a difference. Apart from scepticism about devolution, there were officials who had doubts about the tight timescale for enactment and implementation. But the combination of an emphatic referendum victory, the more entrenched nature of Scottish Labour's commitment, having big Scottish beasts in the Cabinet who wholeheartedly supported the measure and a landslide majority, combined with a range of other constitutional reforms packaged together as 'modernisation', added up to unstoppable momentum.

By the time the Scotland Bill was debated at second reading in Parliament there was little prospect that any of its main provisions would be seriously challenged. Michael Ancram, as Conservative Shadow Constitutional Affairs Minister, moved an amendment at second reading 'accepting and respecting the clear decision of the Scottish people in favour of a devolved Scottish Parliament with limited income tax-varying powers'. But there was a downside. While the legislation was generally accepted to have been much better drafted with the more sensible retained powers model, the relative lack of scrutiny meant that the real debates had been left to the Cabinet committee away from public or media scrutiny.

Legislating for a Scottish Parliament would only provide a framework. Much more work needed to be done. A Consultative Steering Group (CSG) was set up, chaired by one of the authors of this book (Henry McLeish), two months after the referendum. It set out the principles that guided its recommendations:

- sharing power between the people, legislators and the Scottish Executive;
- the Executive should be accountable to the Parliament and the Parliament and Executive to the people;
- Parliament should be accessible, open, responsive and develop procedures making participation possible to the development, consideration and scrutiny of policy and legislation;
- Parliament should promote equal opportunities for all.

The report was explicit in seeking to 'avoid adopting procedures which are obscure or archaic'. The Scottish Parliament would be no replica of the Commons though there was a reference to recognising the 'need for the Executive to govern, including enacting primary and subordinate legislation and obtaining approval of its expenditure proposals'. Emphasis was placed on the role of committees which would 'initiate legislation, scrutinise and amend the Scottish Executive's proposals, and have wide-ranging investigative functions'. The committees would combine the roles of Westminster's Select and Standing Committees and be able to form ad hoc committees to address cross-cutting issues – and gave examples of public health, social inclusion and environmental sustainability – to ensure matters crossing conventional departmental boundaries were addressed. The combined roles were expected to allow Members to develop greater expertise. The CSG argued that equal opportunities had to be mainstreamed into developing policy, legislation, implementation and evaluation.

The parties geared up for the first elections in 1999. The constituency vote was likely to result in similar outcomes as the previous elections to the Commons, not least as Labour was experiencing an extended honeymoon. But the List vote was another matter. It was a novel system for both the voters and parties. Would it be seen as a second preference? To what extent would voters use the two votes to split preferences? To what extent would it perform its function of achieving a greater degree of proportionality? Would smaller parties unable to overcome the first-past-the-post hurdle manage to win List seats?

First came the selection process. In many constituencies the selectorate within political parties essentially decide on who would become Members of the Scottish Parliament (MSP). Candidates had to be placed high on the list to have a chance of being returned. The small size of the Parliament and likelihood that no party would win an overall majority inclined parties to be wary of more independent voices. Rebellions would potentially have more impact than in the Commons. Even before any internal contest, prospective candidates needed to be approved by the parties. On the one hand, this could lead to old-fashioned manipulation to get favoured candidates in place (or keep others out), but also allowed parties to work towards gender balance. A number of independent-minded MSPs managed to get through the process but tight control by whips was evident from the start.

Conclusion

It is difficult to capture the hopes and expectations of those who had campaigned for a Scottish Parliament over years, even decades. Donald Dewar provided context in his speech at the opening of the Scottish Parliament on 1 July 1999. It was a 'turning point: the day when democracy was restored' but it was 'about more than our politics and laws'. This 'new voice in the land' was a 'voice for the future'. The new First Minister described the 'proud moment' as we embarked upon a 'new stage on a journey begun long ago and which has no end'. Donald Dewar knew his history. It taught him that we cannot, and should not, imagine that the establishment of the Parliament was the end of Scotland's story. But it was a key moment in which many people had invested high hopes and expectations. The Parliament was, as he said, 'Not an end: a means to greater ends'. This would be open to a number of interpretations.

The establishment of the Scottish Parliament marked a major change in politics. It was different, but not entirely as expected or hoped for by many of its supporters. This does not mean that the hopes and expectations were naïve. The core principles of sharing power, increased accountability, greater participation and promotion of equality remain important. In the following chapters we consider the achievements, successes, challenges, weaknesses and failures but mostly seek to learn lessons from the experience of devolution and point towards what can be done as we look forward to the next 25 years and devolution's half century.

CHAPTER 2

Early Experience: Bedding Down, Challenges and Successes

There shall be a Scottish Parliament. Through long years, those words were first a hope, then a belief, then a promise... today there is a new voice in the land, the voice of a democratic Parliament. A voice to shape Scotland, a voice for the future.

Donald Dewar at the opening of the Scottish Parliament, 1 July 1999

Introduction

HAMISH MCDONNELL, A well-informed journalist and close observer of the Scottish Parliament, noted that the first decade of devolution had been 'momentous, exciting, extraordinary'. But looking back at these years today, they look like a period of relative quiet compared with what followed. What is most striking in retrospect is how quickly devolved government was taken for granted. The creation of a new Parliament is a complex business. While the focus was on the building project, it is what goes on inside the building – the debates, committee work, inquiries, processes, rules and regulations, standard operating procedures and crucially the relationships – that make a Parliament. The internal relations and those with other institutions and bodies – with the executive branch, civil servants, the range of non-governmental public bodies, local authorities, civil society organisations and other interest groups and of course Scotland's communities and citizens – are central.

Devolution was an opportunity to start afresh, a chance to innovate and create a modern institution, though it would inevitably inherit much from Westminster and UK Government. David Steel, as the first Presiding Officer, listed a 'dozen differences' that distinguished the Scottish Parliament from the House of Commons: fixed terms of four years; no annual sessions with Bills falling at a certain date in the calendar; a proportional element to the electoral system; a U-shaped chamber; more 'civilised' hours, rarely meeting after 6.00pm; a high proportion of female members; scrutiny before subject committees before debates in the chamber; a petitions committee; a weekly public 'time for reflection'; proceedings that were webcast; more accessibility with frequent visits from school children and young people; and a new modern Parliament building. But the creation of the Parliament also had unintended consequences, some foreseeable and some unforeseen.

Some of the differences outlined by David Steel were symbolic, perhaps trivial, but all reflected a desire for the Scottish Parliament to be different, more modern and effective. It created considerable interest beyond Scotland. In September 2001, Robin Cook, Leader of the House of Commons, and Lord Williams, Leader of the Lords, visited the Parliament to learn about its procedures. Cook returned with members of the Commons' Modernisation Committee two years later to consider the electronic voting system and Public Petitions Committee, though neither would be incorporated into reforms at Westminster. One Conservative MP remarked that,

> At Westminster you place a petition in a bag and it disappears and that's the end of it. I think you have a system here that appears to be very effective in looking at issues of genuine public concern.

Electronic voting was not adopted in the Commons for reasons explained by Cook, 'The Commons still sits in the design of benches that they inherited from the chapel Henry VIII gave them at the time the Commons walked out of the Lords' and there were too few seats for the MPs, making it difficult to provide a voting console for each.

The Scottish Parliament became an accepted part of the furniture of government, with only those on the far-flung fringes of Scottish politics calling for its abolition. The controversies that marked its early years were less existential so much as they concerned the escalating cost of the Holyrood building project. The building controversy had the greatest potential to undermine the public legitimacy of devolution. The Holyrood building was formally opened for business in October 2004 and the controversy has since receded in memory. The decision to build a new Parliament would in itself prove an object lesson in the gap between a policy decision and its implementation. The media played a significant part in how the Parliament was seen by the public and it would play an important role, as in any liberal democracy, in making it accountable to the Scottish public. It had been assumed that there would be more scrutiny of government decisions by elected Members but there would also be far more media scrutiny of government decision-making in Scotland. It was wholly legitimate to question Holyrood's rising cost, though at times this created tensions. Presiding Officer David Steel complained about the 'bitch journalism' in reference to the coverage of the issue. Journalists were only doing their job. Robust, even unfair, criticism is an inevitable part of democratic politics. The decision to hold a public inquiry into the Holyrood building project went a long way to drawing a line under the episode, though whether the inquiry resulted in substantial changes in how major infrastructural projects were conducted is less clear.

Sometimes a lack of controversy can be just as telling. The Church of Scotland General Assembly building was used as a temporary home until the new building was ready. A few decades before, such a temporary home would almost certainly have provoked opposition, but it was a sign of the times that nobody had a problem with the use of the Kirk's own Parliament as Scotland's temporary Parliament. Scotland is a multi-faith community, acknowledged in the weekly 'time for reflection' in the Parliament. This does not mean sectarianism has disappeared or racism no longer exists, but there have been efforts, notably across Scotland's main political parties, to recognise the importance of celebrating diversity.

New Politics

While an emphasis on 'new' emerged powerfully under Tony Blair's leadership of the Labour Party, it had appeared before in debates on constitutional change. The promise of 'new politics' following the establishment of the Scottish Parliament had been part of the rhetoric of the Scottish home rule movement during the 1990s. The nature of new politics was never precisely defined but some of its features can be discerned from statements made by senior figures in the campaign, the publications of the campaign groups and the 'Scotland Forward' umbrella organisation that campaigned for a tax-varying Parliament during the 1997 referendum. What was clear was that the new Parliament, with a new electoral system, was expected to create a more consensual political culture. The adversarial culture of the Commons was something many reformers wanted to avoid.

The experience of the Constitutional Convention, when Labour, Liberal Democrats and much of Scottish civil society had worked together, encouraged a belief that a different kind of politics was possible. The 1997 devolution referendum campaign, when Labour, Liberal Democrats and the SNP cooperated, amplified this sense that a model of constructive consensual politics could be achieved and contrasted sharply with earlier experience. The reasons each supported devolution differed: the SNP saw it as a stepping stone to independence, while Labour saw it as a way of consolidating the union and the Liberal Democrats saw it as a step towards a federal UK. Each saw it as an opportunity to democratise Scottish politics and wanted the same result. In October 1999, Donald Dewar, Labour First Minister, Alex Salmond, SNP leader, and Jim Wallace, Scottish Liberal Democrat leader shared a platform for the launch of the 'Scotland in Europe' campaign for the adoption of the Euro. Once more, this helped highlight the extent of cross-party support and the apparent marginalisation of the Conservatives in Scottish politics.

There were few differences between Labour and the SNP on a range of matters. Other than on the constitutional question, Labour and SNP had more similarities than differences. These parties would have made obvious coalition partners but remained adversaries pursuing disagreements confrontationally. It was not only the constitutional question that loomed large but that they faced each other directly in electoral competition. Labour and SNP were fishing in the same pond for votes and seats. Trust and good working relations had been developed between Labour and the Liberal Democrats in the Constitutional Convention. And there were fewer seats in which Labour and the Liberal Democrats were in direct contention than Labour and SNP seats. This made a Labour/Liberal Democrat coalition all but inevitable in 1999.

The probability that no single party would win an overall majority had implications for government. There had been scant attention to how Cabinet Government would operate. In a think tank paper written before devolution, Bernard Crick and David Millar, leading authorities on Parliamentary reform, had noted the 'silence of the [Constitutional] Convention on the structure of government'. There had been a limited debate on whether a different model might be possible but this was never developed. Something more akin to the operation of local authorities in which all MSPs, not just Ministers, would have direct access to civil service support, had at one point been suggested by a leading Liberal Democrat. Nor was there much discussion on how the executive branch and cabinet government should operate. The emphasis had been on the prospect of coalition with little concern for how that might operate. Collective Responsibility – the doctrine that Ministers might argue their corner privately within government but all Ministers must abide by and publicly support a decision once arrived at – was anticipated. Policy differences between Labour in Holyrood with UK Labour Government were permitted. It would have been possible for Liberal Democrat Scottish Ministers to disagree with party colleagues in the Commons who were critical of the UK Labour Government.

Any Cabinet will include people with conflicting views on a range of matters and it follows that not all differences will fall along party lines. Nonetheless, there are additional challenges when two parties coalesce in government and need to reach agreement on the broad outline of a programme for government. There were occasions when Collective Ministerial Responsibility broke down, though this did not prove damaging or leave the impression of a government in disarray. In 2002, Mike Watson as a Minister in the Scottish Executive, opposed hospital plans affecting his Glasgow constituency, though he voted with the Scottish Executive on the matter. Ken Macintosh resigned as a Ministerial Aide at the same time having voted against the plans. There were other examples but there is nothing to suggest that the approach under devolution diverged significantly from Westminster. Prime Ministers and First Ministers have been flexible in how they have dealt with Ministers who have spoken out, or more commonly been reported, though not directly quoted, disagreeing with a policy. Much depends on the importance of the issue and the strength of the Prime or First Minister. But the expectation is that Ministers would not vote with the opposition in Parliament. That this should be the same in Holyrood as in Westminster is hardly surprising in a system that relies on government coherence.

The implicit assumption had been that new formal institutions – notably the electoral system – would create new procedures which would break Scotland free of old-style, elitist, confrontational politics on show in the House of Commons. This gave too much weight to the role formal institutions play in politics. The new institutions and new practices proved incapable of overcoming adversarial politics and party competition, though could in some circumstances encourage different behaviour. It did not help that First Minister's Questions, replicating Prime Minister's Questions which encouraged theatrical adversarial politics, were imported from Westminster. There was an assumption that a hidden consensus existed in Scottish politics, frustrated by old institutions and practices. But changing the institutional structures would not be enough to change political behaviour and deeply instilled political culture.

There were critics of new politics from the start. Many opponents of devolution feared it would consolidate what they saw as an existing left-of-centre political consensus in Scotland. Most explicit in this respect was the view that emerged at *Scotsman Publications* under the editorial direction of Andrew Neil. *The Scotsman* had been a leading advocate of a Scottish Parliament for decades. Under Neil, the paper underwent a transformation. It became stridently critical of devolution but claimed it still supported devolution in principle. Its editorial columns carried arguments that Scotland needed to throw off the existing consensus. A *Scotsman* editorial following the publication of the Executive's first legislative programme complained that the new administration was too cautious:

> If there is to be a new politics in Scotland, then it must be the politics of fresh thinking, of good ideas celebrated and bad ideas shot down. It must be robust and full of life and invention, not dreary and consensual... (*Scotsman*, 17 June 1999).

There was also an odd view that imagined that including a broader range of society would somehow lead to consensus, ignoring the possibility that more diverse voices meant more interests and therefore more divisions and disputes. A higher proportion of women might be expected to mean more than an improved balance of representation. More women might want to raise or prioritise issues, not least regarding women's representation in other institutions, that had been neglected. More diverse representation meant that more voices would be heard. The German philosopher Jürgen Habermas characterised mass democracy as involving 'wild cacophonies'. The new Scottish Parliament proved to be a form of cacophony constrained by a strong whipping system.

Relative constitutional peace

For a period, it seemed that the constitutional question had been resolved. The 1997 devolution referendum campaign had seen a grand coalition of Labour, SNP and Liberal Democrats along with a swathe of Scottish civil society campaigning together. While the Conservatives had remained true to their opposition to the Parliament during the referendum, they largely accepted the result with good grace. The electoral system provided a path back for the Scottish Tories who had been wiped out in Commons representation in 1997. Two years later, the only Tories elected to the Scottish Parliament owed their success to the regional list.

But it was not only the Conservative Party that had to accept the result. The SNP recognised that it needed to give devolution a chance. In the first Scottish Parliamentary elections, the SNP paid lip service to independence placing it very firmly on the constitutional back burner. It was 14th in its list of 14 priorities and tenth in its list of ten pledges. It was committed to a referendum on independence within the lifetime of the Parliament if it formed a government, though was coy on how a referendum might occur. The referendum was a ploy taken from New Labour's playbook to decouple the commitment to independence from voting SNP. Just as Labour committed to a referendum to allow devo-sceptics and opponents to vote Labour in the 1997 general election by breaking the direct link between a Labour vote and devolution, so too the SNP hoped to attract voters who were sceptical or opposed to independence.

After the second elections in 2003, SNP front bencher Kenny MacAskill argued that his party should come to terms with the result. 'The electorate has spoken and has, for the time being, declined the opportunity offered by the SNP to move on to independence through a referendum.' The SNP, he argued, must persuade its core supporters that the Parliament can deliver tangible benefits as well as lead the way to independence. In 2004, he wrote a book in which he argued that there were many areas where shared responsibilities made sense. Did Scotland need a separate DVLA, Ordnance Survey, Commonwealth War Graves Commission, Civil Aviation Authority 'or other such institutions as opposed to exercising control from north of the border even if the institutions remain located south of the border'? It was a significant intervention at the time. He was not abandoning support for independence but seeking a more nuanced approach to the question. Mike Russell, who lost his seat as an SNP List MSP in the 2003 election, argued for a 'new union', language that was anathema to many in his party as it was to accept devolution. But it demonstrated a strand of pragmatism within the SNP and suggested a willingness to embrace devolution.

The constitutional question never disappeared; it just assumed less importance. The constitutional focus in these early years tended to place emphasis on tidying up the existing arrangements and started to focus on the need for fiscal powers. In 2005, for example, responsibility for railways, excluding safety and licensing railway operators, with accompanying financial support, was transferred to the Scottish Parliament. Alistair Darling, UK Transport Minister at the time, acknowledged that the Scottish devolved authorities were best placed to decide what was best for Scotland's railways. It made public policy sense.

A growing body of opinion across the Parliament began to look at fiscal powers. The argument for some measure of fiscal autonomy varied. In May 2001, a group of 12 economists wrote to the *Scotsman* making the case for 'full' fiscal autonomy as this would deliver greater 'accountability and responsibility', though some would later retract support. Support for some measure of fiscal devolution in broad terms would grow over the following years with voices inside Labour, SNP, Tories and LibDems in favour. There were few voices outside Scotland arguing that the Parliament should have fiscal responsibility. In 2001, David Davis, Conservative MP and then chair of the Commons Public Accounts Committee, called for the Scottish Parliament to have control of income tax, council revenue and a fair share of North Sea oil revenues. The Parliament, he argued, should take fiscal responsibility and accountability for money it spends. But that was very much a minority view in the Commons at that time. The problem with these proposals, especially for full fiscal autonomy, was the lack of detail. The relationship between fiscal responsibility and fiscal autonomy was too readily equated without consideration of potential problems.

The CSG principles in practice

The Consultative Steering Group principles provide an important framework to consider the operation of the Parliament. In 2006, Presiding Officer George Reid noted that the principle of 'sharing power between government, people and parliament' remained 'elusive'. The legislative process proved more like Westminster's than had been hoped. The rhetoric surrounding greater participation and empowerment had not sat easily with 19th-century notions of representative government. Greater access and participation proved difficult, though the Parliament's location in Edinburgh made access for Scots easier than the House of Commons. One of the quotes inscribed into Holyrood's walls is from Walter Scott's *Heart of Midlothian*,

> When we had a king, and a chancellor, and parliament-men o' our ain,
> we could aye peeble them wi' stanes when they werena gude bairns.
> But naebody's nails can reach the length o' Lunnon.

But try throwing a metaphorical pebble from the Highlands and Islands at a Parliament in Edinburgh. Devolution to Scotland needed to be accompanied by devolution within Scotland. The Parliamentary committees have tried to get out of the capital but a peripatetic Parliament has its limits. A more fruitful approach would be to devolve power from Holyrood as we discuss in a later chapter.

One innovation proposed by the Consultative Steering Group was the establishment of a Petitions Committee. The Committee acted as a conduit, considering petitions submitted to the Parliament and deciding what action should be taken and monitoring progress. One of the important functions of the system has been to open a channel for voices other than the 'usual suspects'. While there is always the danger that those 'usual suspects' and persistent petitioners might seek to take advantage of the Committee, this does not undermine its value as a point of access for a wide range of voices. Research has shown that this was achieved.

As we have noted, the Scottish Parliament has many parents. It is easy to identify the role of politicians and parties but support from across Scottish civil society was crucial. This contributed to the CSG proposing the establishment of a Civic Forum as a 'significant means of achieving an accessible Parliament within a participative democracy'. The hope was to reach beyond the 'usual suspects'. The Forum's funding ended in 2005 and was subsequently closed. This reflected a key change post-devolution. What had united much of Scotland had been opposition to Tory rule of the Scottish Office. The common 'enemy' was gone. The relationship between representative and participatory democracy was not so much resolved as assumed to have been adequately addressed through access to the Parliament's new committees, especially its Petitions Committee. But more work was required and technology would open up new opportunities.

There can be little doubt that the Scottish Parliament started well in terms of equal opportunities. More women were elected to the Scottish Parliament in 1999 than had been returned to the House of Commons from Scotland in the previous eight decades when women were first eligible to stand in elections. Scotland's first MSP from an ethnic minority community was only returned in 2007, Scotland's first blind MSP was elected in 2011 and its first wheelchair user in 2021. In 2021, 45 per cent of MSPs were women, six of the 129 MSPs were from ethnic minorities (two each from Labour, SNP and Conservatives) constituting 4.5 per cent of the total and more in line with population shares than previously. In 1999, just under

30 per cent of MSPs were under 40 years old (compared with under 10 per cent of Scottish MPs returned at the 1997 UK election). The average age of MSPs was 45 compared with 50 amongst Scottish MPs at that time.

The Parliament consists of more than its elected Members. Diversity monitoring of staff shows that by 2022/23, almost 60 per cent of 107 new appointments were men, though just over half the applicants were men and 14 per cent of appointments, though over a fifth of applicants, were from ethnic minorities. Of those with disabilities, 8.4 per cent were appointed and 9.3 per cent had applied. 17 per cent of LGBT+ applicants were appointed and 15 per cent had applied. Progress has gone well beyond pre-devolution experience though that is a very low bar and progress in these areas can very easily be reversed.

John McAllion MSP had criticised the strict whipping that went on in committees early in the life of the Parliament. He also saw a need for the committees to sit outside Edinburgh. There were occasions when the committee convenerships were held by party spokespersons: a step in the wrong direction, well beyond what happened in Westminster. This undermined the cross-party consensual nature of committees that had been hoped for. Early on, Donald Dewar noted that there was a tendency to see committees' main functions as summoning Ministers, narrowing the scope and purpose of committees. The committees had been envisaged as having a more powerful role than transpired. A review of Holyrood's achievements at the tenth anniversary found much to celebrate but also much work still to be done. Time and resource constraints had limited their impact, according to research by political scientists Chris Carman and Mark Shephard. Combining legislative and scrutiny functions, unlike in the Commons where these were split, with far fewer elected Members to fulfil committee work proved burdensome. This was soon acknowledged and addressed to some extent in reforms which reduced the size of committees and permitted substitute members with voting powers to attend when a member had other important commitments. A general restructuring and renaming also helped.

The committees did not manage to become the initiators of legislation but, as Carman and Shephard put it,

> engine rooms for the passage of majority-backed legislation from 1999 to 2007, or intensely partisan political squabbles and little actual legislation since 2007

The same interest groups with the resources to travel to London to lobby government can easily encamp in Edinburgh. But others with fewer resources would find Edinburgh more accessible. Interest groups have been described as weathervanes of power – focusing their activities where power lies. In a system in which the executive branch is dominant we would expect most effort would go towards accessing Ministers and officials rather than backbench Parliamentarians. But we would also expect groups, especially if access to governmental power is denied or difficult, to include Parliamentary lobbying. In each case, but especially with government, lobbying needs to be transparent. And we should not fall into the trap of assuming that the numbers of respondents to any consultation exercise is a measure of openness. It is not the number of responses but who is listened to that counts and that is more difficult to measure. Nonetheless, there is far greater transparency than existed pre-devolution.

The opening up of government was evident, with legislation on freedom of information passed in 2002 that came into force three years later and further regulations on environmental information in 2004. But this was felt by many to have been too limited and areas still remain obscure despite the appointment of a Scottish Information Commissioner to enforce the freedom of information. In 2017, a letter was signed by newspaper, online and broadcast journalists expressing concern about the behaviour of the Scottish Government and its agencies. There were repeated delays beyond the 20-working-day deadline without justification; requests for updates were ignored; information provided was often incomplete and required a further request, delaying the release of relevant information; requests were being screened by Special Advisers (SPADs) for any potentially politically damaging information. Once more, devolution involved a step forward but many more steps were still needed.

Pushing the boundaries

It would be wrong to imagine that everything was settled. One of the consequences of the retained powers approach was an understanding of devolved politics that drew a sharp distinction between devolved and retained matters (see Tables 2.1 and 2.2). Lists were drawn up defining devolved and retained matters and though a reasonable starting point, there remained much complexity and interdependency between UK, Scottish and local governments. Policy issues and problems cannot always be addressed discretely but require collaboration. This is particularly the case with 'wicked problems', the most complex, deep-rooted problems that are never completely solved and require cooperation and coordination across governments and with voluntary organisations, businesses and communities. One of the major lessons of the early years is that shared responsibilities cannot be avoided and there is a need for various institutions and a different type of politics to address such problems. This had been partially acknowledged as the devolution legislation had been making progress through the House of Lords. An amendment had been moved to create an Interparliamentary Consultative Commission. It would have been a cumbersome body, but motivated by a desire to include interparliamentary cooperation alongside proposed intergovernmental cooperation mechanisms. Instead, the responsible Minister in the Lords announced that there would be 'standing arrangements for the devolved administrations to be involved by the UK Government at ministerial level when they consider reserved matters which impinge on devolved responsibilities'. How this would work out in practice was left unclear.

When we consider problems, opportunities and policies, a more complex picture emerges. It is better to consider devolved government as involving some matters that are within the exclusive competence of Holyrood and others within Westminster's but with a substantial range of matters that are shared. This would prove important across so many issues and would be powerfully clear after Brexit (see chapter 6). Indeed, local government also plays a significant part in addressing problems, challenges and opportunities as well as having been an integral part of effective multi-level governance.

Table 2.1: Reserved matters under the terms of the devolution legislation

GENERAL RESERVED COMPETENCES		SPECIFIC DEVOLVED COMPETENCES	
Constitution	International relations, including EU and other international organisations	Financial & Economic Matters including fiscal (except devolved taxes); economic and monetary policy; currency; financial services and markets; money laundering	Social Security Non-evolved social security schemes; child support; and pensions
Crown	International trade and regulation of international trade	Home Affairs including misuse of drugs; data protection and access to information; firearms except air weapons; entertainment; immigration and nationality; scientific procedures on live animals; national security; official secrets and terrorism, betting; gaming and lotteries; emergency powers; extradition; lieutenants and access to non-Scottish bodies	Regulation of Professions Architects; health professions; auditors

GENERAL RESERVED COMPETENCES		SPECIFIC DEVOLVED COMPETENCES	
Union of Scotland and England	Civil service	Trade and Industry business associations; insolvency competition; intellectual property; import and expert control; sea fishing outside Scottish zone; consumer protection; product standards; safety and liability; weights and measures; telecommunications; postal services; research councils; designation of assisted areas; industrial development and protection of trading and economic interests; distortive or harmful subsidies	Employment Employment and industrial relations; health and safety; non-devolved job search and support
UK Parliament	Defence	Energy Electricity; oil and gas; coal; nuclear energy and energy conservation	Health and Medicines xenotransplanation; embryology; surrogacy and genetics; medicines; medical supplies and poisons; welfare foods
High Court of Justiciary & Court of Session	Treason	Transport Road transport; marine transport; and air transport	Media and Culture Broadcasting; public lending right; government indemnity scheme; property in satisfaction of tax
Registration and funding of political parties			

Source: House of Commons Library Research Briefing 2022.

Table 2.2: The Scottish Parliament website lists devolved matters to include:

agriculture, forestry and fisheries	environment	local government
benefits (some aspects)	equality legislation (some aspects)	planning
consumer advocacy and advice	fire services	sport and the arts
economic development	freedom of information	taxation (some aspects)
education and training	health and social services	tourism
elections to the Scottish Parliament and local government	housing	transport (some aspects)
energy (some aspects)	justice and policing	

Source: https://www.parliament.scot/about/how-parliament-works/devolved-and-reserved-powers

A diagram offers a more informative guide (Figure 2.1). Working together, these elements can achieve much but it if any one part is disruptive this can undermine the good work of others. Occasional re-engineering will be required. The system works best when each part pulls together with the others. And even this illustration is a gross over-simplification. Policy development and implementation involves a vast array of people and organisations – under each of these broad government headings lie a range of institutions not to mention Non-Departmental Public Bodies, third and private sectors, communities and citizens. Leadership in such a system is more like operating as a conductor of an orchestra or, rather, a series of conductors trying to conduct a number of orchestras to provide a coherent sound while playing simultaneously.

Figure 2.1: A truer picture of multi-level governance

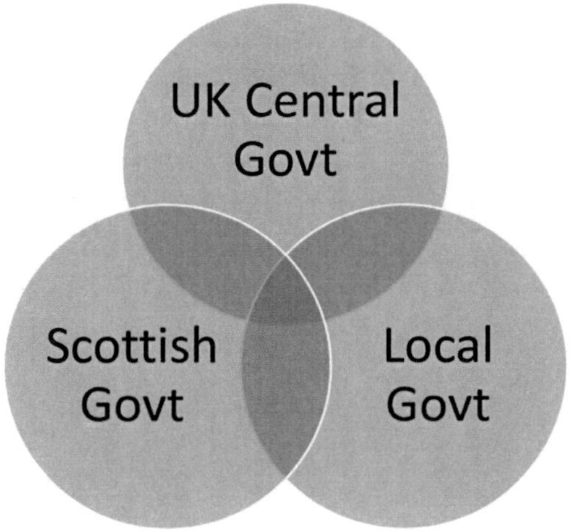

Given that part of the motivation behind having a Parliament was to improve relations between London and Edinburgh, it was not surprising that there was a hope that antagonisms and conflicts would be reduced. But Scotland's relations with the rest of the UK, and government in London particularly, will always be subject to tensions and difficulties regardless of Scotland's constitutional status, including if Scotland became independent. This is to be expected and in no sense a sign of failure. Conflict is an inherent part of democratic politics. The issue is how this is managed and agreement is reached. There was a tendency in many quarters to assume that more powers would solve problems without adequate attention to what might be done with those powers.

The Scotland Office replaced the Scottish Office in Whitehall after devolution. It was much reduced in authority, roles and competences compared with its predecessor. There would still be a need for a Scottish voice at the centre of UK Government. Relations between London and Edinburgh need not take place via the shrunken Scotland Office. How this would operate had not been a concern for most advocates of devolution; the Scotland Office's role would emerge through practice and much would depend on how successive Scottish Secretaries interpreted the role. This never became a major issue during the early years as controversies were limited and discussions were conducted largely constructively. There was a false sense that these matters were not a problem and that existing arrangements sufficed, though there were moments of tension even then. This ignored the highly favourable context that proved more important than institutional arrangements. The massive growth in public spending, along with administrations in Edinburgh and London keen to cooperate, hid potential problems.

John Mackintosh had written an important paper in the 1970s focused on intergovernmental relations after devolution. He was one of the few then or subsequently to give much thought to the arrangements required to ensure that a truly Scottish voice was articulated in the heart of government in London. Mackintosh identified six functions that would have been performed by the Secretary of State in relation to devolution as then proposed. This remains a useful guide. The Scottish Secretary's functions would include:

- operating as a UK Cabinet Minister;
- 'wet nurse functions' of fixing and running elections etc;
- 'vice regal functions' or 'continuity functions', inviting someone to form a government, formally ratifying changes in Scottish Government, appointing a caretaker government;
- 'veto' functions when legislation was *ultra vires* and a general power to declare a Bill unacceptable or even take over and undertake Scottish government;
- a channel for all communication with the EEC; and
- chief adviser to the UK Government on all aspects of Scottish affairs.

Mackintosh believed that even if the office of Secretary of State for Scotland was abolished there would be a need for some alternative means of feeding Scottish opinion into Whitehall. He saw the 'wet nurse' and 'vice regal' functions as easily relocated, reflecting his view that what was being proposed in the 1970s involved too many London controls. Communication with the European Economic Community (EEC) in the 1970s was not considered as significant as it would later become as European integration proceeded. At that time, Mackintosh's view was that the Scottish Secretary probably knew less about the EEC than any other British Cabinet Minister though it made more sense to allow Scottish Ministers to deal directly with the EEC on issues such as fisheries. Devolved/EU relations proved a major issue in later debates as the EU became increasingly important. The development of European regional and social policies, notably under George Thomson and Bruce Millan who served as European Commissioners responsible for Regional Affairs after careers as Scottish Labour politicians, ensured that there was a very clear Scottish interest at the heart of European policy making. Mackintosh was right to identify the need for robust arrangements and right to consider this in terms of functions rather than institutions. The key lesson from the early years was that there were functions previously conducted by the Scottish Office that were still required. How these would be catered for had been given inadequate attention.

There were, inevitably, disputes on policy and resources between London and Edinburgh from the start. Compromises were common and much debate took place behind closed doors, occasionally spilling out into public view. Arguments raged across a range of issues including handling of the Foot and Mouth outbreak, care for the elderly policy, police funding of the G8 summit at Gleneagles, whisky strip stamps and airguns. Communities Minister Malcolm Chisholm spoke out forcibly against Home Office policy on dawn raids to deport failed asylum seekers in Scotland. The suggestion in January 2001 that the Scottish 'Executive' should be renamed 'Government' was dismissed out of hand by London. It was not unknown for Ministers in London to assume pre-eminence on issues only to find that their colleagues in Edinburgh had a different view. There were occasions when UK Ministers sought to influence how Scottish Ministers allocated funding but found that, though they might be listened to, they had no authority. Views were considered but ultimately decisions on priorities were left to decision makers in Edinburgh.

Care for the elderly policy was a notable example of policy divergence in the early years (with one of the authors centrally involved). A Royal Commission on Long-Term Care chaired by Sir Stuart Sutherland, Principal of Edinburgh University, had recommended that caring for older people should be split between living costs, housing costs and personal care with personal costs paid for through taxation while living and housing costs should be selectively supported and jointly funded by the state and individuals. The Treasury insisted on clawing back Attendance Allowance following the introduction of the Scottish policy rather than allowing the allowance to stay in Scotland to help fund the policy. There were dire warnings that Scotland would become 'one giant nursing home'. As David Lipsey, who wrote a note of dissent as a member of the Sutherland Commission, put it in 2001, 'Older middle-class English people will flock across the border in unpredictable numbers to avail themselves of free care at the expense of the poor Scottish taxpayer.'

Hyperbole tends to be more a feature of public spats than the more considered exchanges that take place behind closed doors. This is not to suggest that internal debates were always refined and while private intergovernmental dispute resolution may be more reasoned, internal debates lack public and Parliamentary accountability and scrutiny. The Lords' Constitutional Affairs Committee in 2002 was amongst critics of the absence of scrutiny of these relations. In a report on 'Inter-Institutional Relations in the United Kingdom', the Committee expressed 'surprise by the limited extent of arrangements for the scrutiny of intergovernmental relations, not just at Westminster but also in the devolved assemblies and legislatures'. This would be reiterated over the following years. The Calman Commission, established in reaction to the SNP forming a Minority Government in 2007, was 'struck by how underdeveloped the intergovernmental and interparliamentary arrangements are'. It noted that Commons Select Committees can, with a few exceptions, exchange evidence with committees of the devolved legislatures but that this power had not been used.

Decisions made between governments may be scrutinised *after* the decision is announced. But information on how the decision was arrived at, what arguments had been used, how compromises were reached is absent. What is clear in the early years of devolution was that such battles – the bread-and-butter of relations – were often fierce but reasoned and invariably focused on differences of opinion on policy rather than part of a larger constitutional dispute. Labour and the Liberal Democrat Ministers in Edinburgh generally agreed on outcomes with Labour Ministers in London but might diverge on how these were to be achieved or the priority attached to different objectives. This meant that there was at least some consensus within which disagreements could be resolved. Central to requirements for the successful resolution of disputes was a desire to find agreement and the identification of existing common ground. Having a public policy rather than a constitutional framework within which differences were debated limited escalation, grandstanding and stalemates though this could never prevent disputes arising. Nor should they be prevented. Disagreements, constructively conducted, can be positive.

There were occasions when the threat of going public on a dispute was used when there was a stalemate in Edinburgh–London relations, as happened when Jack McConnell hit a brick wall over who should pay for policing of the G8 international summit at Gleneagles in Perthshire. This was a high-risk strategy as it could backfire, leaving the First Minister looking weak if unsuccessful and damaging future relations. It worked in this case. It was a tactic that needed to be used sparingly. The tendency to reach agreement behind closed doors could contribute to a sense that the Scottish Executive was not always standing up for Scotland in dealings with London. What is clear is that many battles were fought with Scottish Ministers robustly defending Scottish interests though often away from the public or media's gaze. Good relations could leave an impression that Scotland's interests were not being adequately pursued. Poor relations could suggest that devolution was not working.

Responsibility for external relations was a key area that would become contested but, again, had seen the Parliament push up against the boundary of devolved competences. The first sign of this came unexpectedly at the Scottish end. On a visit to Dublin in October 1999, Donald Dewar found he was treated like a visiting head of state, not what he would have expected had he still been Secretary of State for Scotland in the UK Cabinet. The motorcade from the airport, meetings with the Taoiseach and Irish President would not have been part of protocol in his previous role but the Irish authorities viewed Scotland's First Minister as having a quite different and more important status. It was also exceptional for Henry McLeish to be received by US President George W Bush on a trip to Washington DC. But even more significant was stretching the limits of devolution's competences to include supporting the developing world. While this was a retained matter in the devolution legislation, the Foreign and Commonwealth Office made agreement easier and led to a workable solution within the parameters of the legislation. Instead of requiring legislative change, it was agreed that a fund could be established allowing devolved government to make grants available to charities working abroad while not directly funding overseas governments or international aid agencies. It was a smart compromise, working within existing powers based on common values and beliefs and pushing at the boundaries of devolution.

Demographic trends were a concern and created a need to attract immigrants. This led to another policy development that required negotiations with London. *New Scots: Attracting Fresh Talent to Meet the Challenge of Growth* was a 2004 policy designed to allow overseas students from Scottish universities to stay on for two years after graduation and seek employment. There was opposition from English universities that feared the scheme gave Scottish universities a competitive advantage, but the policy gained the support of the UK Government. The Scottish Executive put in a joint bid with Ireland to host the European Football championships in 2008 and though the bid was unsuccessful it demonstrated the potential that existed for international cooperation.

For every public spat or even every private disagreement, there were always numerous examples of cooperation and agreement. The media focus was understandably on disagreements but considerable effort went into making sure that there was cooperation, though not necessarily uniformity, when possible. One of the most significant policy developments that affected local government and involved both Scottish and UK Governments was the decision in 2001 by the Treasury to write off Glasgow's £900m housing debt and provide financial support in the event of large-scale council housing transfer. The housing debt had hung like a massive financial albatross around Glasgow's neck. In April 2002, Glaswegian tenants then voted for stock transfer by 58 per cent to 42 per cent on a turnout of 64.4 per cent (higher than in the previous UK or Scottish Parliamentary elections).

One of the most notable achievements of the early years of devolution was the joint effort by UK and devolved governments to tackle poverty. A series of measures, largely emanating from London, as it had relevant powers, ensured that child and pensioner poverty declined in absolute and relative terms significantly. But, as the Institute for Fiscal Studies noted at the time, it was not just the amount of money spent but how it was spent that mattered. The achievement arose due to increases in spending on benefits and tax credits. Understanding what is effective, evaluating and avoiding policy initiatives designed to get a headline proved vital in improving outcomes. There were areas where policy was less successful – notably amongst poorer working-age adults without dependent children. But the fact that administrations in London, Edinburgh and across much of local government worked reasonably well together in pursuit of improving outcomes was a testament to the available success when devolution is understood as a partnership.

Furthermore, not all policy initiatives required spending. An early decision was taken to remove parts of legislation that prohibited 'promoting' homosexuality in schools. Apart from the homophobic nature of the provision introduced in the 1980s, it was poorly drafted and left teachers unclear as to what they could and could not say and do. Was it possible to mention anything to do with gay issues or give support to a young person who questioned their sexuality? It gave a green light to those who promoted homophobia. Wendy Alexander, Cabinet Minister for Communities, led the case for the removal of the section and was supported by a broad range of civil society. Strong opposition came from other elements in Scottish society, including the Catholic Church, with businessman Brian Souter establishing the 'Keep the Clause' campaign and contributing £1 million to fund a private referendum. Less than a third of electors returned postal ballot papers and while 86.6 per cent of those returned supported keeping the clause, this meant that just over a quarter of Scottish electors signalled support for retaining the clause. It proved a bruising experience and a reminder that there was a significant minority who did not agree with progressive measures. The Scottish Parliament voted overwhelmingly for repeal; a reminder that it takes much more than legislation to change attitudes.

These were good times for devolution in two important respects. Labour was in office in London until 2010 and Labour was the largest party in coalition with the Liberal Democrats until 2007. The other factor that meant that devolution operated in relatively good times was finance, as we discuss below. There were tensions between the two parties in the coalition, especially in the run-up to elections when each party sought to distinguish itself from its partner and claim exclusive credit for popular policies. While consensus is likely to exist when the same party is in office in Edinburgh and London at the same time, consensus is not the same as total agreement though it does go some way to ensure at least broad common ground on which relationships can be built. However, this alone does not prevent disputes. Indeed, relations can be more strained within the same party as was often evident in relations between central and local government in Scotland. Internal battles can be poisonous in any party.

One important development which saw Holyrood lead the way in UK health policy was the decision to ban smoking in public places. Initially proposed in the first session of the Scottish Parliament by Kenny Gibson, a backbench SNP MSP who lost his seat at the next election, the issue was then picked up by one of his SNP colleagues. Labour Health Minister Tom McCabe became a strong advocate and the Scottish Executive brought forward its own legislation. The Chief Medical Officer, the Health Committee and work of health professionals promoting a smoking ban proved a powerful combination. Ireland's experience encouraged the introduction of the policy in Scotland. The initiative was bold, preventative and addressed a major issue of poor health. Legislation was passed in 2005 and came into force the following year. There had, of course, been opposition, not least from John Reid. Reid was not only a Scottish MP but Health Secretary for England (itself an interesting appointment given that health was largely devolved). Smoking was one of the few pleasures left for the poor in sink estates and in working men's clubs, he maintained. But his colleagues in Holyrood disagreed and saw the enormous long-term value in addressing this cause of poor health. There was an attempt to challenge the legality of the ban by a hotel group but this was dropped when it became clear that the challenge would fail. The policy was a gamble and there had been fears that banning smoking in public spaces would be ignored and could not be adequately policed. In the event, the public, including smokers, supported the ban. One study found that the number of children admitted to hospital with asthma decreased by 18 per cent in the three years after the ban, having been growing by an average of 5 per cent in previous years. A major study published in 2009 concluded that the Scottish law had been a success. Second hand smoking exposure was dramatically reduced, there was strong support for the law and there had been no adverse impact on pubs and restaurants or a major displacement of smoking from inside to outside of premises or to homes.

Even with the massive injection of money, provided due to the Barnett consequentials resulting from Tony Blair's decision to massively increase health expenditure to reach EU health spending averages, it became clear that the NHS was in need of urgent treatment. Professor David Kerr, an eminent oncologist in Oxford, chaired an expert group that began work on this which included a series of meetings with patients and medical staff in Scotland. Town hall meetings were held allowing the public a say in what emerged in the Kerr Report, a 20-year plan for reform. It offered a critique of the health service and proposed an alternative model. It was a bold vision but it ran up against strong opposition.

Success or otherwise will often lie in the eye of the beholder. A supporter of land reform may point to reforms as success or at least improvements, while opponents of land reform will see this differently. What all can agree on is that the post-devolution land reforms would almost certainly not have happened without a Scottish Parliament. There was ample evidence that the new devolved system had a significant impact on public policy.

Years of plenty

The public finances were, if anything, more important than having the same party in office in London and Edinburgh in embedding devolution. The early years of devolution were a period of almost unprecedented growth in public expenditure. The Blair Government had committed itself to its Tory predecessor's spending plans for the first two years after coming to office. But that commitment came to an end at the point when the Scottish Parliament was first elected. There followed a period of massive growth in public spending across the UK. Devolved Scotland was as much, indeed more, a beneficiary as any other part of the UK. As a consequence of the Barnett formula, Tony Blair's announcement in January 2000 that health spending should increase to the European average by 2006 meant that Scotland would share in this commitment. Past commitments to increase NHS spending had been made conditional on real growth in the economy but there was now no such condition.

The UK Labour Government's spending on health and education together constituted a substantial part of devolved spending, and thereby subject to the Barnett formula, meant that there was rapid growth in real terms devolved spending. There is nothing like growth in public spending to oil the wheels of intergovernmental relations. Due to Barnett consequentials, the Scottish block grant more than doubled in cash terms and increased by 60 per cent in real terms between 1999 and 2010, the equivalent of an average annual real terms of over 5 per cent over this period. It is difficult to underestimate how significant this growth in public expenditure had been but equally difficult to emphasise the impact of the crisis on public spending. It might not have been of Biblical proportions – seven years of plenty followed by seven years of famine – but the growth came to a halt creating a different climate around the same time as there were changes in parties in office in London and Edinburgh. It was easy to get a false sense of stability, notwithstanding the odd skirmish in this earlier period of rapid growth in spending. The real test of devolution lay ahead. The impending banking crisis, creating what has been described as the 'Great Recession', triggered by the US housing bubble bursting, would have a major adverse effect on the Scottish economy and public finances. It was the first external shock. Another was to follow with Brexit.

One consequence of the good times tends to be that less care is taken as to how money is spent. It was much easier in this period to commit to policies that involved increased expenditure, with less thought to opportunity costs than would later be required. The Agreement reached between Labour and the Liberal Democrats had largely involved combining commitments made by each party into a programme for government without the need to negotiate and prioritise that would be required in more fiscally strained times. The agreement included over 460 specific commitments. Sir John Elvidge, who would take over as Scottish Government Permanent Secretary a few months after the 2003 election, later remarked that a 'managerialist' style of government was intensified as a consequence and this stifled innovation on the political and civil service side of government. More importantly, it led to a failure to prioritise. There was also a tendency to assume that any lack of progress in improving outcomes was due to implementation failures rather than the policy itself or the resources made available. It did not matter which party was in office. All parties are inclined to be fiscally lazy when money is awash in public spending rounds. And there was little preparation for the almost inevitable end of the good times.

McIntosh and multi-level governance

With devolution imminent, Donald Dewar had established a Commission under Sir Neil McIntosh, former chief executive of Strathclyde Regional Council, to consider relations between the Scottish Parliament and local government. The McIntosh Commission reported in June 1999 with a long list of recommendations. It called for a Covenant between the Scottish Parliament and Scotland's 32 local authorities, the creation of a Joint Conference where Parliamentarians and local government representatives could hold dialogue on the basis of equality, the introduction of a power of general competence for local government, a formal working agreement between local government and Scottish Ministers and an independent inquiry into local government finance. In addition, it recommended reform of the electoral process to simplify and make participation in local elections more accessible, four-year fixed-term councils with elections to take place mid-term in a Scottish Parliament and the use of a more proportional electoral system with an immediate review of the existing one. This would signal a major change in Scottish central–local relations. Efforts should be made, it insisted, to ensure wide participation and access to decision-making of a wider cross-section of the public. It suggested that Community Councils should undertake 'renewal' and consideration be given to engagement with young people including the possibility of extending the vote for Community Councils to 16-year-olds.

Over the following years a number of these recommendations were introduced. The introduction of the Single Transferable Vote for local elections, following a further major inquiry headed by academic and former councillor Richard Kerley, resulted in more councils with no single party having overall control. Reforming local finance proved politically difficult. A review under Sir Peter Burt, issued in 2006, rejected a local income tax or local sales tax and proposed a local property tax charged as a percentage, suggested at 1 per cent of the capital value of each property each year. Property was seen as a proxy for wealth. But the idea was rejected by the Scottish Executive. This was neither the first nor last time an inquiry into alternative sources of local government finance had been conducted resulting in a well-argued report. The problem with reform was not an absence of ideas but the political will and understandable fear of the political consequences of reform.

Creeping centralisation occurred and local government voices were increasingly heard complaining about ring fencing – money allocated to local government but tied by central government to specific purposes. Relations could be strained, though eased by local authorities sharing in the significant growth in public spending in the early years. But this would not last. Non-Departmental Public Bodies (NDPBs) had been criticised pre-devolution as lacking accountability and a perception grew that membership of such bodies was often party political. Research found that expenditure on NDPBs had grown from under £3 billion in 1979 to over £10 billion in 1993. A series of studies had identified a growth in such bodies over devolution. An effort to have a 'bonfire of the quangos' had limited success though 52 were abolished or merged. This included replacing 43 NHS trusts with 15 boards. These reforms were not likely to attract public attention even if they could have a positive impact on public services.

Multi-level governance (MLG) became a fashionable idea in the years before devolution and played into debates in Scotland. The idea of subsidiarity, drawing on wider European developments as John Smith had acknowledged in 1992, was frequently invoked. Much of this European thinking had focused on the complex relationships between local government, member states and the European Communities/Union. It did not simply mean layered government. It involved a multi-faceted phenomenon with overlapping processes and jurisdictions, with collective efforts of civil society, government and public bodies as well as private institutions and the third sector working towards common goals. No single 'level' is able to deliver services and improve outcomes for citizens on its own. This does not mean that there must be total agreement. Local, devolved, UK central government and the EU pushed and pulled against each other but so long as this did not lead to stalemate then positive outcomes could be achieved.

Under devolution, however, most attention has been paid to bilateral relations – between local and devolved governments; local government and the EU; devolved and UK governments; UK Government and the EU. When seen as multi-level, we begin to appreciate the complexity of the system, though even this can over-simplify governance arrangements. It is hardly surprising that the focus tends to be on simple binary relationships as these are easier to understand. Multi-dimensional relationships are more complex but they are essential in providing public services. These complex relationships can make or break policy outcomes. During the early years, the new devolved institutions acted as important nodes in these webs of relationships. Many of those involved in devolved decision-making had previously had experience in local government of engagement with the EU as well as UK central government and of course with local communities and third sector organisations. Local authorities well understood that decisions made in the EC/EU had a direct impact locally, not least as far as structural funds (created to develop economic, social and territorial cohesion), additionality (the principle that European money should go to projects that would not otherwise have gone ahead), public procurement and rules governing the transfer of undertakings (whereby employees' rights were transferred when a business or undertaking was transferred). Freedom of movement, including the harmonisation of qualifications and the growing area of European social policy not to mention vital economic implications of European integration were well appreciated. Scottish local authorities had been early in establishing offices in Brussels and recognising the impact that European decisions had in Scottish communities. This experience proved useful.

Europe had featured significantly in debates in the lead up to devolution linked to the growing significance of the EC/EU in everyday public policy. Scottish Office civil servants had been seconded each year to Brussels ever since the UK joined the EEC in 1973, building up expertise and contacts. The question of how devolved institutions should engage with European policy making had been a difficult issue for devolutionists. The SNP had adopted 'independence in Europe' as its policy in 1988 and made great play of Scotland having direct Scottish–Brussels relations. The Scottish (and later Scotland) Office might represent the UK on occasion in EU negotiations but it would be bound by UK policy positions. A devolved administration would not necessarily feel bound in the same way, especially if the governing parties in Edinburgh and London differed. A fudge was agreed whereby the Scottish devolved position would feed into Whitehall 'as directly and fully as possible in decision-making on EU matters which touch on devolved areas'. But decisions on who should lead in Council of Ministers meetings would be taken by the UK 'lead Minister'.

An intense debate on whether a Scottish office, supported in some way by the UK Government, should be based in Brussels had been conducted within the Scottish Office and UK Government in the late 1980s. The case for and against was presented in a paper by a Scottish Office civil servant that was subsequently leaked. On the one hand, a Scottish office in Brussels would provide a more effective lobby for Scottish economic and business interests if left to the variety of Scottish interests. It would raise Scotland's profile and, from the Scottish Office's perspective, offer an alternative profile from one that might be pursued by sectoral interests (the Scottish Office was concerned that the local authority offices in Brussels were not articulating Scottish Office interests). It would improve the flow of information and allow Scottish Government bodies to take a more active role in European matters. On the other hand, the official noted that Scottish activity might cut across and undermine UK central government positions and would likely be opposed by the Foreign and Commonwealth Office and other government departments, including the UK's representation in the EU. They warned that it might also be an excuse for junketing. But in the event, Scotland Europa was set up as a membership organisation in May 1992.

Similar concerns would continue to be expressed about how devolved government might behave. The devolved Scottish Executive established Scotland House, which incorporated Scotland Europa. The office would provide information, assist with visits to Brussels by Parliamentary committees and raise awareness of Scottish interests amongst European decision-makers, feeding these interests early on in the policy making process. It would develop links with regions and member states across Europe. On becoming First Minister, Henry McLeish explicitly included 'Europe and External Affairs' in his colleague Jack McConnell's portfolio of responsibilities. Soon after its establishment, the Scottish Parliament embarked on an investigation into European structural funds and how these interacted with funding from the UK Treasury. The Parliament, as indeed the UK Parliament, struggled with scrutiny of EU policy affecting devolved areas and the establishment of a European officer in Scotland House in Brussels was short lived. The Secretary of State for Scotland and Chancellor, both Scottish MPs, were asked to provide evidence but declined. This would continue to be a source of tension between London and Edinburgh.

Conclusion

Devolution had bedded down well during its first decade. While there were debates on policy and differences over whether more powers were needed, there was nonetheless remarkable acceptance of devolved government. The economic context to these first years helped provide relative stability. The downside was that some of devolution's weaknesses were less apparent and would become all too obvious in the next phase when money was much tighter, different parties were in office in Edinburgh and London and the constitutional question started to loom large. Differences with London were more frequent than publicly appreciated in these early years, leaving an impression that Scottish Ministers were not standing up for Scotland in their relations with Ministers in London.

A range of policy initiatives had been possible that would have been unlikely without devolution. In part, this reflects different preferences but also capacity. The devolved Government was able to develop policies and pass legislation and the Parliament able to scrutinise executive branch decisions to an extent that had never been possible before devolution but Parliament's role in policy development was negligible. Such achievements were soon taken for granted. In the years leading up to devolution there had been many references to a 'democratic deficit' and questions raised concerning the legitimacy of decisions made by a Scottish Office headed by politicians who were not representative of Scotland. It was more accurate to refer to a legitimacy deficit rather than a democratic deficit but the latter term had more political bite. That the legitimacy deficit had been addressed with devolution did not mean, nor could it ever mean, that the will of the Scottish people had been settled indefinitely. Each generation would be able to revisit the system of government as and if it so wished.

CHAPTER 3

More Challenging Times

...this is not Westminster. This Parliament is a proportional Parliament. It is a Parliament of minorities where no one party rules without compromise or concession... The Parliament will be one in which the Scottish Government relies on the merits of its legislation, not the might of a parliamentary majority. The Parliament will be about compromise and concession, intelligent debate and mature discussion... My commitment today is to reach across the parties and try to build a majority, issue by issue, on the things that matter to the people of Scotland. I will do so through necessity certainly, but also through a genuine belief that it is the right and best way to govern Scotland.

Alex Salmond, 16 May 2007

Introduction

MICHAEL FORSYTH USED to warn that 'devolution is not just for Christmas'. There is little doubt that devolved government was born into favourable times and that there would be more challenging times ahead. John P Mackintosh's warning in one of his last *Scotsman* columns before his early death in 1978 was prescient,

> To put it at its simplest, the best conceivable conditions for a massive revival of the SNP would be a Conservative Government which faced, but could not handle, Britain's endemic economic problems and which clearly did not give a fig for Scottish affairs.

As it turned out, the return of a Tory Government in 2010, albeit one moderated by coalition with the Liberal Democrats, did not, at least initially, create the conditions Mackintosh envisaged. At first it looked as though devolution would continue to work constructively with a Tory Government in Westminster and an SNP Government in Edinburgh. The SNP, as the above quote suggests, did not set out to undermine devolution but had no choice but to take account of the views of others. A changing context eventually contributed to increased tensions. An independence referendum became all but inevitable when the SNP won an overall Holyrood majority in 2011, even though independence had not featured highly in the election campaign. Labour struggled to come to terms with its position as an opposition party in Holyrood and more so as no longer Scotland's dominant party. The Tories, on the other hand, saw an opportunity. David Cameron recognised that devolution was here to stay and promised to respect the new devolved system. As a result, his colleagues in Holyrood, led by Annabel Goldie, whose personal support exceeded that of her party, engaged constructively with the SNP. Devolution was making odd political bedfellows.

SNP Minority Government

The electoral system made it very difficult for any single party to win an overall majority. Labour and the Liberal Democrats had formed coalitions from 1999–2007. In 2007 the SNP won one more seat than Labour and claimed victory. No other party was willing to enter coalition with the SNP though the Tories had been clear during the election that they would be constructive in their dealings with the governing party, whether SNP or Labour. The SNP governed as a minority from 2007–11 with Conservative support on key votes. Its Programme for Government would involve compromises and the abandonment of some manifesto commitments. A more consensual politics emerged by necessity.

The 2007 elections were remarkable in other ways. Local elections had been held on the same day as elections to the Scottish Parliament in 1999, 2003 and 2007. But Single Transferable Vote (STV) was used for the first time to elect local councillors in 2007. The SNP share of first preferences was 27.1 per cent (an increase of 3.8 per cent compared with SNP votes in 2003) while Labour's share was 28.1 per cent (down by 4.1 per cent). But the allocation of seats after other preferences were taken into account and quotas were reached, resulting in the SNP increasing its number of councillors by 182 to 363, 15 more than Labour, which lost 161 councillors. The result tended to be lost in coverage of the SNP becoming the largest party in Holyrood. But it had significant implications. Councillors provided an important base of activists across Scotland's communities.

Voters were faced with a new electoral system in which choice was expressed numerically. In addition, the Holyrood ballot paper was changed and instead of separate papers for voters to record their constituency and list votes, a single paper was issued on which voters recorded each vote expressed with an 'X' for constituency member and list choices. And to add to it all, new electronic voting was used for the first time to speed up the count under STV. Taken together, it created a perfect storm. There were more spoiled ballot papers than normal. The overnight count was disrupted and counts were postponed until the next day.

Labour conceded defeat in the Holyrood elections 19 hours after the polls closed. Alex Salmond, SNP leader, insisted that his party was the winner even though it had won only 36 per cent of seats with less than a third of the vote, 'It is very clear indeed which party has lost this election, and the Labour party no longer has any moral authority left to govern Scotland,' he insisted. It reflected a Westminster-style 'winner-takes-all' understanding of the formation of a government that ignored the multi-party nature of Holyrood. It was conceivable that a majority could have been constructed that did not include the SNP but it was not just the SNP that understood that government formation required that the largest Holyrood party should form the government. This view was shared across the Parliament.

The challenge for the new Scottish Government was to work out what it could feasibly get through Parliament given the election outcome. With only 47 of Holyrood's 129 MSPs, the SNP would have to build coalitions within Parliament or, as it soon learned, govern with less recourse to Holyrood. The main focus was on the annual budget – which could not be avoided. Committees chaired by opposition Members often focused on calling Ministers to account, scrutinising the government rather than holding enquiries. Less primary legislation was passed than during the previous Parliament (see Figure 3.1 below). The Tories with 17 MSPs embraced this new politics and supported each SNP budget during the Parliament and gained some concessions for doing so. The Greens, with two MSPs, signed a 'Cooperation Agreement' with the SNP, having been in discussions with the SNP for over a year before the election. Green MSPs would support the SNP in votes for First Minister and other Ministerial appointments. The SNP would consult the two Green MSPs on its legislative programme and budget and would nominate a Green MSP as Convenor of a subject Committee. Minority government works best when the governing party is able to construct majorities in Parliament with different combinations of opposition parties' support and is more vulnerable when it has to rely on one party. And the two Green MSPs would not be near enough to provide an overall majority.

Figure 3.1: Primary legislation passed by the Scottish Parliament, 1999–2024.

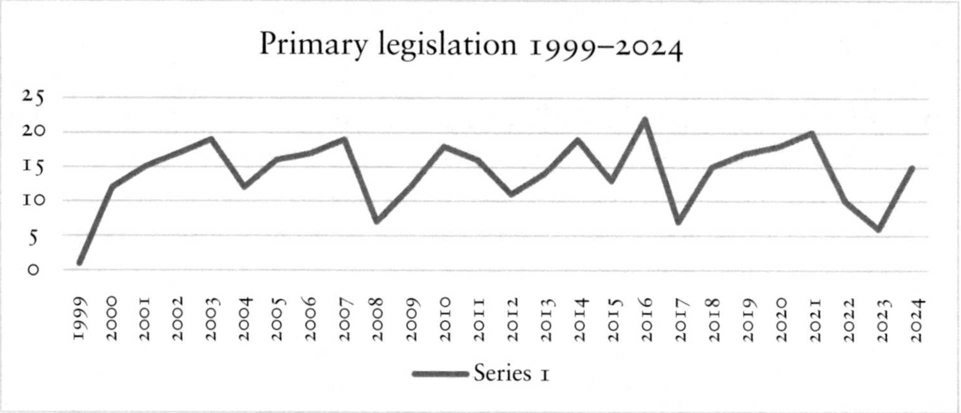

The 2003–07 Parliament had seen the rise of smaller parties and independents. The Greens won seven seats in 2003; the Scottish Socialist Party won six; Dr Jean Turner won on a Save Stobhill Hospital platform in Strathkelvin and Bearsden; Dennis Canavan was once more returned as an Independent MSP in Falkirk West having previously been Labour MP for the same area since 1974; and Margo MacDonald won a seat as an Independent on the Lothians list having been an SNP MSP in the previous Parliament until she was effectively deselected. At every previous election when the SNP had posed a threat, its opponents presented the prospect of an SNP victory in apocalyptic terms to frighten voters away from supporting the nationalists. The SNP, they insisted, would constantly pick fights with London, would focus exclusively on independence, and was not interested in everyday issues. This was captured in a line frequently invoked by Labour politicians describing the SNP leadership – they woke up each day thinking about independence while Labour leaders woke up each day thinking about how they could improve the NHS, education system, protect working families. The SNP struggled to counter this. The 2007 result for the SNP was aided by the unpopularity of Labour at Westminster due to the

UK's involvement in the Iraq War. The SNP focused heavily on governing competence rather than constitutional change and this became the leitmotiv of the SNP Minority Government under Alex Salmond. Within four years, its opponent's depiction of an SNP Government needed revision. The sky had not fallen in after the SNP took office. It had not picked fights with London. It offered a series of populist measures and was perceived to be competent by voters. This made the SNP's task in facing the electorate in 2011 much easier than ever before.

Primary legislation is only the tip of the iceberg when it comes to policy making. Ministers can make policy even if a Parliamentary majority disagrees. Legislation often empowers Ministers to make decisions and while these may be subject to Parliamentary approval, this is more easily achieved than trying to pass primary legislation. There had been occasions when Ministerial decisions were made which the Parliament voted against but where the Government decision still held. The SNP was quick to point out that its predecessors had also taken advantage of this when necessary. What became clear during this period was that Holyrood's role as a policy maker was limited in much the same way as the House of Commons. Parliament might limit what the Scottish Government did but the opposition majority struggled to propose alternative legislation. The other parties were too divided to offer much of an alternative to the SNP.

A number of SNP manifesto commitments were ditched as the SNP lacked a majority in Holyrood. Its commitment to replace the council tax with a local income tax had to be abandoned. This policy would have run up against formidable implementation problems had it been pursued even with an overall SNP majority. SNP campaign literature on replacing the council tax was particularly targeted at older voters, claiming that nine out of ten pensioners would pay less with a local income tax. Pensioners had been amongst the least likely to vote SNP in the past but the SNP vote increased considerably amongst older voters in 2007. Similarly, a populist commitment to introduce a £2,000 first-time buyers' grant had to be abandoned, which was fortunate as it would have contributed to inflating house prices.

Another policy commitment, focused more on winning votes than improving outcomes, was the decision to reverse proposals set out in the Kerr report on the health service referred to in the previous chapter. Kerr had proposed a 20-year project of reforms. Entitled *Building a Health Service Fit for the Future*, it sought to ensure a sustainable health service involving a redesign to emphasise prevention, local service delivery and greater integration of the NHS with other public services, and better use of technology, including telemedicine. There needed to be greater targeting of health support in poorer communities and a need to address the implications of the growing elderly population. The NHS had to change if it was to meet the challenges ahead. The shift involved was as much cultural and behavioural as it was institutional. The recommendations were an application of principles which the Christie Commission on the Future Delivery of Public Services would recommend six years later. But changes of this type involve some difficult decisions which would be unpopular, at least in the first instance. Short-term political costs were required for long-term health gains and created an opportunity for opposition to make political capital; electoral calculations could not be ignored. Nicola Sturgeon, as SNP Health spokesperson, proved adept at beating a populist drum and presenting the proposals as removing local health services. It helped the SNP win power but undermined a serious effort to reform the NHS. Fifteen years later, David Kerr reflected on the consequences of allowing campaigning to stifle mature policy making. He noted that avoidable mortality had plateaued and the gap in mortality rates between the poorest and wealthiest was widening in Scotland. His message was clear and consistent with his original report – there was a need for cohesion, collaboration and cooperation – and he emphasised the lesson from the pandemic that 'all levels of government' needed to work together when faced with a deadly common threat. Despite all this, overall, the period between 2007 and 2011 was one of calm with little policy innovation.

The SNP had authority and access as the governing party. This meant its voice would be heard. A statement or speech from the First Minister, and often as not from other senior Ministers, would be widely reported. Setting out the government's objectives and priorities, even if unable to do much else, would at least be heard. The authority vested in the Scottish Government allowed it to build capacity in underperforming areas. Two key areas became central during this period of minority government – the economy and energy, reflecting Alex Salmond's background and interests. While devolved competence in these areas was limited, there was recognition that a vibrant economy would reduce demand for some public services and ease a transition to independence. The establishment of an impressive Council of Economic Advisers, including Nobel Economics Laureates, contributed to the image of the SNP as serious on economic affairs, though the Council's impact is more difficult to discern. In comparison, Salmond's successor, Nicola

Sturgeon, showed scant interest in the economy despite the additional fiscal competences that meant that Scotland's economic performance would become important as never before in determining Scottish public spending.

The SNP became expert in the politics of symbols, often allied with substantive reforms. It moved to restyle the Scottish *Executive* as the Scottish *Government*, a move that had been supported by the civil service. Officials had wanted an immediate change but the SNP sought to make the change only when Parliament was about to return after the Summer Recess to avoid giving the sense that they were more interested in symbols than policy substance. The change was more than symbolic in that the Government was restructured. It had originally been structured largely around the old Scottish Office model, geared as it was to administration and lobbying. The intention was to be more about governing. The reaction of Ministers in London to the name change had been hostile when it had first been proposed in January 2001, as we have seen, and Holyrood's Procedures Committee had rejected a similar proposal in May 2006. While 'Scottish Executive' would continue to be used in legal documents, as this was the designation under the terms of the legislation establishing devolution, 'Scottish Government' was otherwise adopted. The formal legal change would come about in the Scotland Act 2012. For the SNP, this represented an important symbolic change but also, as seen by senior officials in Edinburgh, a sensible change that removed public confusion – though there remained a tendency to confuse Government and Parliament when devolution was discussed. The SNP was showing early evidence of understanding the importance of symbolic politics.

Challenges and responses

With money tighter and lacking an overall majority, the Scottish Government had to be more imaginative in its use of available policy tools. Policy tools come in different forms and though the Scottish Government's toolbox might not have been as full as it wanted, especially lacking the fiscal tools it desired, it was not empty and there was still plenty of money to spend. It took a few years before the impact of the Great Recession fed through to cuts in Scottish public spending. Real terms increases peaked a couple of years after the SNP came to office, allowing it to follow past practice of making generous financial commitments. But the writing was on the wall. Spending fell from 2010/11 through to 2017/18. Over the course of devolution, a gradual shift had occurred in the allocations of spending. Local authorities suffered cuts and ring fencing, limiting how they could spend shrinking budgets. This proved short-sighted as it undermined efforts to improve outcomes.

Evidence had been mounting even before the banking crisis of 2007/08 that difficult public finance decisions would have to be made. There could be no certainty that funding increases of the order experienced in the earlier years would continue. The Scottish Executive had been warned in a study under a group chaired by Bill Howat, a former civil servant who had also served as a local authority chief executive, that difficult decisions would have to be made as pressure on public services increased. The group's report was completed in 2006 though only released after the 2007 election. Howat was – or ought to have been – a wake up call. The report noted an array of priorities that compromised the ability to plan and set out clear outcomes. There needed to be greater clarity on how outcomes would be delivered. It argued that the Scottish Executive needed a 'more formal and rigorous process to assess how effectively it performs'. Better financial discipline was essential, especially, it maintained, in a period of financial constraint. These warnings were made before the economic shock caused by the banking crisis. Policy initiatives needed to be challenged more, with clearer evaluations of policies. It noted the need for 'exit strategies' or transferring short-term funding to core funding. Howat maintained that too much focus was on spending available budgets rather than clearly defining what needed to be provided. The group called for more strategic thinking with less detailed interference in delivery. It noted the 'complex and costly web of public bodies and agencies', the 'crowded landscape' that required review and concluded that it was time for a 'systematic re-assessment of the relationships between the Scottish Executive, its Executive Agencies and Non-Departmental Public Bodies'. Howat felt there was the potential for spending realignment to save about £1 billion or 4 per cent of relevant budgets.

In 2009, in his first report on Scotland's public finances, Auditor General Bob Black noted that the Scottish economy was in recession and the public sector was under the greatest pressure since devolution. Existing levels of public spending would be difficult to maintain to meet new demands. He urged the Parliament to use its scrutiny role to consider the relationships between spending costs, activities and service performance with a rolling programme of performance reviews. In evidence to the Commission on the

Future Delivering of Public Services two years later he noted the growing pressure: an ageing population; shrinking workforce; recession-related demands for places in post-school education; local government and third sector pressures due to rising unemployment and reforms to the welfare system; capital commitments such as PFI projects. He also observed the 'daunting maintenance backlog' in the public sector estate that had built up over decades. The Scottish Parliament had inherited a stock of assets – schools, colleges, universities, hospitals, police and fire stations and many other public bodies as well as roads – that had been well used but were being 'passed on to our children in a worse state because of our failure to maintain them properly'.

The good times were at an end. Hard choices are never easy and tend to be avoided even when postponing decisions only increases problems and ultimately costs more in the long run. The publication of the Howat report, *Choices for a Purpose*, highlighted the challenges the new SNP Government faced and, alongside the 'Great Recession', contributed to lowering public expectations. John Swinney, the SNP Finance Minister, released the Howat Report in 2007 but little action followed. The SNP Minority Government did a better job at managing expectations but continued to introduce measures, designed more to win electoral support than address deep-rooted social problems, which added to financial pressures. On one level this is understandable. Parties can do little in opposition other than make it more difficult for the governing party or parties to make hard choices. Appeals to older, middle-class electors with a higher propensity to vote only add to the problem. Inter-generational injustice began to mount and will be addressed in a later chapter.

A further review of budgetary matters was one of the concessions made for Conservative support in annual budgets. The Independent Budget Review (IBR) group, chaired by Crawford Beveridge, former chief executive of Scottish Enterprise, reported in July 2010. The key difference in the four years between the two reports was a worsening financial situation. The IBR report set out a series of options but warned that many people would find it 'uncomfortable reading'. It argued for an 'outcomes-based' approach to replace an 'input-based' approach to tackling challenges. Though not stated explicitly, the underlying message was that spending decisions were too often based on promises designed to appeal to voters rather than concerned with improving outcomes. While it made no firm recommendations, it offered a list of options. It noted that the Parliament had expanded the provision of free or subsidised public services on a 'near universal basis' under devolution in an 'increasing and buoyant public spending context'. But the changed context, according to the IBR, meant that this was unlikely to be affordable in future. It further noted that decreases in the Scottish Government's capital budget would be 'far greater' than other expenditures and that capital expenditure has an impact on growth and jobs. In response, it argued that sustained borrowing and investment was of paramount importance. While universality was attractive and commendable, it was no longer affordable across so many areas and raised questions as to whether concessionary travel, free prescription charges, eye examinations, free personal and nursing care and tuition fees could be sustained under the existing fiscal arrangements.

The IBR suggested that there was a plethora of institutions for a small country – 32 local authorities, 23 NHS bodies, eight police forces, 20 universities, 43 colleges and over 100 other public bodies. It warned against an immediate wholescale restructuring though recommended a strategic review of the future delivery of public services. In the interim it suggested joint action between public bodies. Strong leadership would be required. Overall, it was a sobering report that went to the heart of challenges ahead. But once more the report attracted little attention and, to borrow the words of the great Enlightenment philosopher David Hume, it 'fell dead-born from the press' (though Hume's work was at least eventually recognised). Some recommendations were followed up. The eight regional Scottish police forces and eight regional fire and rescue services were reorganised into a single Police Scotland and one Scottish Fire and Rescue Service. The motivation was to make financial savings, which quickly happened, and to facilitate the rapid transfer of staff and resources in response to major emergencies and incidents across Scotland. There were early concerns that services locally were disrupted in the implementation process. Lessons could be learned on how to achieve amalgamations and improved functioning of public services from this limited exercise in public service reform.

The 'Great Recession' would have ramifications across the globe. This occurred around the time that there was awareness of the growing challenges in public service delivery. In June 2010, Bob Black warned that Scotland faced a 'long hard financial winter, which will require very difficult choices to be made about priorities'. One of the few politicians during this period to engage seriously with these issues was Johann Lamont, leader of Scottish Labour. In a speech in late 2012, she argued that resources ought to be focused more on those in need, suggesting that many existing policies were populist and failed to have the impact that policies focused on tackling disadvantage and poverty would have. Her message was blunter but similar to those in the Howat and IBR reports. These reports were stuck in a drawer and 'Not to be opened until after the [independence] referendum', she maintained. The drawer remained firmly closed even after the referendum.

One of the IBR's recommendations that was easily actioned was the establishment of a Commission on the Future Delivery of Public Services. The Commission was chaired by former STUC General Secretary Campbell Christie and reported shortly after the 2011 Holyrood elections. It called for radical changes in how services were delivered after taking extensive evidence and was encouraged to be bold by all major political parties. There was a consensus that change was needed. The Commission complemented the IBR report but also had a similarly limited impact. The Commission operated against a background of a number of related analyses. A report – *Joining the Dots* – by Susan Deacon, former Labour Health Minister, on early years noted the 'masses of research and evidence and heaps of good practice' and argued that there was no need to invent any of this but that there was a need to 'work together to connect it up – in short "to join the dots"'. Her call for a radical shift in energy, time and resource from analysis and process to getting on with the job of helping people was an indication of frustration that would only grow.

Efforts were made to encourage shared services, including plans for greater collaboration across the Clyde Valley and a review of ICT infrastructure in public services to reduce fragmentation and duplication. Reports and ideas proliferated but action tended to follow slowly if at all. All of these developments pointed towards similar conclusions captured by Christie's critique and conclusions. There was a sense that public services had been paternalistic, delivering for and to people rather than listening to citizens and giving communities a voice in policy making and delivery. John Smith's 1992 call for recognition of the shift from subjects to citizens had not taken off as many had hoped. Public institutions had grown up and operated in silos with too much concern for institutional interests and insufficient attention to citizens' needs. All too often individuals, families and communities would find themselves having to navigate a morass of organisations to get assistance. Process was prioritised over outcomes. It was difficult to estimate how much resource went into tackling avoidable problems, though Christie estimated it at over 40 per cent of local public service spending. As one former Health Minister remarked, the health service was great at putting bodies back together that have fallen off a cliff but Scottish society was poor at preventing them falling in the first place. All this led to waste, duplication, inefficiency and, more importantly, it resulted in poorer services for citizens. The report noted the 'inconsistencies and tensions between national targets and local outcomes which have constrained local partners' ability to work together' and prevented 'working towards shared outcomes, keep them and their resources in silos, and miss opportunities to improve local outcomes and efficiency'.

Christie suggested reforms with four key objectives: empowering citizens and communities; greater partnership and integration of services; a radical shift towards prevention; and a whole system approach. There had been previous efforts in this direction with the establishment of Community Planning Partnerships (CPPs), which initially brought together public bodies in each of Scotland's 32 local authorities to agree priorities and work collaboratively. This constructive development took statutory form in legislation passed in 2003 with guidance on their operation the following year. An Audit Scotland review in 2006 noted that the 'different geographic boundaries, accountability and financial regulations' inhibited collaboration. Greater agreement on setting priorities amongst partners and the Scottish Executive was recommended. CPPs would develop further over the following years. One area that the Scottish Government addressed more than any of the others was public engagement and empowerment. But it did so inconsistently and only where it was relatively easy. Demands were placed on local authorities and others to a far greater degree than on the Scottish Government itself. Collaboration, prevention and efficiency were much more challenging and there was little progress, though plenty of lip service was paid to each. The Scottish Government's reaction was to treat the report's recommendations as a menu from which it would pick and choose and for others to deliver.

Two former Scottish Government Permanent Secretaries offered reflections on devolution after leaving office. Sir John Elvidge was head of the civil service in Scotland between 2003 and 2010. A year after his retirement he observed that less transferable learning was taking place than devolution ought to have offered. He maintained that a 'radical new model' of Scottish Government had been emerging from 2007 in which government sought to operate as a single organisation with a single purpose based on outcomes. Partnership lay at its heart, not only across the public sector, but with civil society. Departmentalism had been rejected, he maintained. That may have been how it was seen in Scottish central government but it was not how it was experienced by citizens, families or communities in Scotland. He noted the 'high degree of consensus between all political parties about most aspects of social policy and the performance of the UK economy'. But if there was a consensus, then it was around vague, general principles and certainly not about delivery. Sir Peter Housden, Elvidge's successor, developed thinking on the 'Scottish model'. He noted that the rise of New Public Management in Britain had resulted in centralism and national standardisation 'with little space for partnership'. The Scottish approach, according to this view, was different. There was some evidence of this difference though not quite as much as many imagined or hoped for.

On coming to power in 2007, the SNP did more than change the name of the Scottish Executive to Scottish Government. It acknowledged some critiques of how devolved government had been operating. It set out to reduce the number of priorities, noting that if everything was a priority, then nothing was a priority. It saw the need to improve monitoring of progress on outcomes. Reforms were included in the SNP manifesto and drew on the 'Virginia Performs' model in the USA. Some of its thinking was shared with senior officials in the Scottish Government. It established a National Performance Framework (NPF) to monitor progress in improving outcomes, a matter that Howat had raised. Various indicators and targets in 'Scotland Performs', its online tool, would be used. This would be updated periodically. But while mechanisms for monitoring outcomes had improved, not all outcomes were improving. Monitoring was important but insufficient. The age-old problem followed. The NPF had been too top down and became an end in itself. Efforts would subsequently be made to rectify this with greater involvement of COSLA.

Centralisation continues apace

Devolution confirmed what many in local government had feared. In 1999, as discussed in chapter one, Jean McFadden, who had served as leader of Glasgow City Council in the 1980s and 1990s and as COSLA President, had warned that devolution might suck power up from local authorities. Fears that Scottish central government would reduce grants to local government to spend on its own priorities looked prescient at the end of the financial good times. Local authorities were increasingly becoming agents of central government but with fewer resources. It was a far cry from the promise of subsidiarity many devolution advocates had envisaged. As we saw in the previous chapter, the McIntosh Report back in 1999 had proposed a 'quantum change in the character and quality of local government' and a new relationship between central and local government based on 'mutual respect and parity of esteem'.

While the SNP won more council seats than Labour in 2007, Labour still retained overall control of Glasgow, North Lanarkshire, East Ayrshire, West Dunbartonshire, South Lanarkshire and North Ayrshire. The SNP was only in overall control of Angus. A range of coalitions were formed across much of Scotland. As a new government, the SNP needed to build a constructive relationship with local authorities, not least as money was going to get tight in the years ahead. The SNP negotiated a 'Concordat' with the Convention of Scottish Local Authorities (COSLA) in 2007. The Concordat was a deal in which COSLA agreed to a council tax freeze, which had been in the SNP's manifesto for Holyrood, in exchange for a reduction in ring fencing, allowing local authorities more autonomy in how they spent their money. There was also a commitment to greater cooperation. Single Outcome Agreements would be reached, replacing the 'myriad of existing systems' for each Community Planning Partnership (CPP) based on agreed outcomes. The council tax freeze lasted until 2016/17 and then again in 2021/22 with an agreement on capping increases. There was an initial expectation that central–local relations would improve but relations deteriorated over time as ring fencing and centralisation were increasingly imposed.

For a very brief moment in 2023 it looked as if a new era of constructive engagement in Scottish central–local relations was again emerging. When Nicola Sturgeon resigned as SNP leader, her chosen successor Humza Yousaf outlined what he described as his 'vision to hand more powers to local councils' and more flexibility for council budgets. On becoming First Minister, Yousaf signed an agreement with COSLA for a 'New Deal with Local Government'. This Verity House Agreement (VHA) (named after COSLA's Edinburgh headquarters) was signed at the end of June 2023 and was similar to the 2007 Concordat in claiming to promote parity of esteem and mutual respect, principles outlined in the 1999 McIntosh Report. In a newspaper article, Yousaf stated that local authorities would be involved in decision-making processes 'at the earliest opportunity'. In September, Yousaf addressed the annual COSLA conference and insisted it was 'not just an agreement on a piece of paper' but, more importantly, put forth what it meant 'in terms of implementation'. This commitment was short-lived. Less than a month later he announced a council tax freeze at the SNP's annual conference without any consultation with local authorities, including his own SNP councillors. The VHA would have been a major improvement if only the Scottish Government had been serious.

The 'National Conversation' and Calman

The election of the SNP in 2007 might have been expected to lead to Scotland's constitutional status rising up the agenda. But the constitution became less salient amongst voters between 2007 and 2011 elections and support for independence flatlined. This was the phoney war period in the constitutional battle. The SNP Government launched a 'National Conversation' upon first coming to office. This was essentially a conversation amongst nationalist friends. The lack of an SNP majority in Holyrood meant that there was no prospect of a referendum. A white paper produced by the Scottish Government in August 2007 discussed the current arrangements, extending Scottish devolution, independence, the changing nature of the UK constitution and whether changes could be brought about by legislation or a referendum. It was more of an options paper than a straightforward case for independence and proposed a three-option referendum. While the Minority Scottish Government launched its 'Conversation', the Parliament voted for an alternative approach. A resolution moved by then Scottish Labour leader Wendy Alexander proposed the establishment of a Commission to 'improve the financial accountability of the Scottish Parliament' and 'continue to secure the position of Scotland within the United Kingdom'. This was passed with the support of Labour, Conservative and Liberal Democrat MSPs while Scottish Green MSPs abstained on both an amendment moved by the SNP calling for a referendum, as well as on Labour's motion. The UK Labour Government provided a secretariat; Sir Kenneth Calman, former Chief Medical Officer of Scotland and later of England, was chosen as its chair. The focus of debate over the next few years was largely on more fiscal autonomy. While the SNP's National Conversation had little direct impact, the election of the SNP had pushed the issue of more powers onto its opponents' agenda. But the parallel developments signalled the stirrings of an unresolved debate that would explode in the next Parliament.

The Calman Commission produced reports in 2008 and 2009 setting out new devolved competences which would lead to the Scotland Act 2012. The Scottish Parliament would have new fiscal powers. It could change income tax by up to 10p in the pound across all tax bands, have control of stamp duty, aggregates levy, air passenger duty and landfill tax. Its borrowing powers would be increased and control of drink driving limits and air guns would be devolved. Some of this required the establishment of new institutional infrastructure – Revenue Scotland became Scotland's tax authority. As the Calman Commission noted, taken together this would result in real financial responsibility. More importantly, it would inevitably introduce an element of risk. Under the fiscal arrangements that prevailed in the early years, devolved public services were almost entirely financed by grant from London. So long as the UK economy as a whole was prospering and UK Government was generously funding equivalent public services in England, then devolved government received a generous share of public expenditure. Transferring significant responsibility for taxation meant that the performance of the Scottish economy became more important in terms of Scottish devolved spending. Scotland would need a growing economy to have a strong tax base to fund the growing demand on public services. Fiscal devolution therefore meant that the Scottish economy – and crucially the Scottish tax base – became much more important. An underperforming economy meant a reduced tax base, which in turn would mean less money for public services.

The respect agenda

Important as these matters were, the issues failed to capture the public imagination. In large part this was due to the subdued nature of the debate, certainly compared with the debate that would follow after 2011. The SNP had come to office on a commitment to govern competently. It did not want to be seen to be constantly picking fights with London or pursuing its constitutional objective at the expense of other policies. The SNP went out of its way at this stage to appear constructive. Its leadership believed that convincing voters that independence was attractive first required evidence that the party of independence was capable of governing effectively. Similarly, the Conservative Party in office in London from 2010, initially in coalition with the Liberal Democrats, needed to show that it accepted devolution and would not seek to undermine it, having campaigned against its establishment over the long years leading up to and during the 1997 referendum. Prime Minister David Cameron proposed a 'respect agenda', seeking to signal a shift in Tory attitudes. This was just one part of Cameron's attempt to detoxify the Tory brand that had included his trip to the Arctic to be photographed with huskies to highlight his environmentalist credentials and his 'hug a hoodie' call to project a more caring image. Theresa May's comment that the Tories were seen as the 'nasty party' had its Scottish counterpart in its anti-devolution image which opponents presented as evidence that the Tories were 'anti-Scottish'.

Cameron appreciated that the debate over whether Scotland should have devolution was over and that the Tories' best hope was to be seen to have accepted devolution and to engage constructively with the Scottish Government. The SNP and the Tories, with diametrically opposed views on the constitution, found themselves cooperating, working to make devolution effective; it was in neither party's interest to be seen to undermine devolution. It was also clear that there was nowhere near majority support for independence, hence the SNP arguing for three options on the ballot paper in any referendum. There had been polls early in 2007 suggesting that support for independence was over 50 per cent but few, including the SNP leadership, took these seriously.

For a brief period between 2010 and 2011 it looked as if devolution was working even better than many supporters expected given the circumstances. This was notable given the challenging context of having a Tory Government in London and an SNP Government in Edinburgh, combined with the economic shock that started with the sub-prime mortgage crisis in the US. Efforts were made to see if agreement could be found on extending devolution during this period but the Cameron Government proved unresponsive; no doubt in part due to a belief that the SNP's days in government would soon be over. All but one opinion poll suggested that Labour was ahead of the SNP between June 2010 and late March 2011. There was little reason to compromise with the SNP when it looked like Labour would soon be returned to power. The window of opportunity for the continuation of constructive relations effectively closed when the SNP won an overall majority in the Holyrood elections in May 2011.

The accidental referendum

All changed with that election result. The SNP won an overall majority despite, not because of, its commitment to independence. Independence support may have given the SNP its base but the support that provided the overall majority came from perceptions of SNP competence in government. The 2011 Scottish Election Study had found support for independence at 24 per cent, the same as in 2007, when three options were offered to voters. 'More powers' and the status quo each had the support of 38 per cent. This meant that in a binary choice between independence and the status quo, the 38 per cent who wanted more powers would be forced to abstain or vote for something that was not what they really wanted. The core support for independence that surveys and polls had recorded provided the classic nationalist base of support. Support for independence built on that base by attracting many who became convinced that a better Scotland was possible when forced to choose between independence or the status quo.

The SNP was judged top amongst voters across the range of devolved responsibilities while support for independence remained under 30 per cent. A commitment to a referendum had been in the SNP manifesto again. The overall majority meant it could not be ignored even though it had not featured as a major item in the campaign. The central issue was whether London would agree to a referendum. In the event, Prime Minister David Cameron agreed, no doubt influenced by the polls and expectation of an easy win and how that might impact on the SNP. If the referendum resulted in the level of support then being shown in polls for independence, then there was a real possibility that a devastating defeat would destabilise the SNP. The SNP had been prioritising increased economic powers – and had identified a number of specific powers – and its leader and key spokespersons were clear that they did not want a referendum until well into the second half of the Parliament when asked about timing. But its objectives changed as the results became known and an overall Holyrood majority had been won.

The Tory Prime Minister had previously conceded a referendum on a new electoral system for the Commons as part of the agreement with the Liberal Democrats and got the result he wanted when 68 per cent of voters rejected the Alternative Vote system. The experience of that referendum, held on the same day as the Holyrood elections, may have helped confirm Cameron's belief that conceding a referendum did not bring any dangers he could not overcome. But he had misread the public mood in Scotland. He ignored the potentially dynamic effects of a campaign and the implications of insisting on a binary choice. Cameron's unionist fundamentalism would prove a major mistake.

The SNP were just as aware of the polls on independence. Had the SNP been confident of victory then it is unlikely that they would have proposed a referendum with three options. The proposal for a three-option referendum was understandably viewed with suspicion in London. The SNP wanted to hedge its bets. While independence was its first preference, if Scots voted for some variant of 'more powers' then the SNP would portray this as a step in the right direction. It would be easier to spin such a result as a partial victory than suffer what might prove to be an unmitigated defeat. Refusing a third option became a red line for London. But there were problems even without Cameron's opposition to a third option. The SNP could hardly be the advocate of both independence and a third option and no other party was willing to take the lead on the latter. Various ideas had been canvassed over the previous years but all were underdeveloped and lacked a clear institutional champion. Various formulations had been suggested – More Powers, DevoMax, Fiscal Autonomy, Full Fiscal Autonomy – but as Michael Moore, Liberal Democrat Scottish Secretary, remarked in 2012, 'DevoMax is really a brand without a product, a concept of more powers for Scotland without any detail about what that entails.'

The 2012 Edinburgh Agreement between the UK and Scottish Governments set the terms of referendum and overshadowed all else in Scottish politics over the next two years. The Agreement meant each would respect the result. It is easy to ignore this document but it proved one of the most important examples of agreeing to disagree. Loser's consent is important in any decision-making, to avoid ambiguity or challenges to a result from the losing side. Tensions would have mounted without this Agreement and would likely have resulted in angry stalemate. But losers' consent did not last, as we explain below.

Those who were active in the referendum tend to view the experience very differently. Despite losing, campaigners for independence tend to view it as a democratic renewal in which the public engaged enthusiastically and positively. Opponents, despite winning, more often see it as a heated, angry and unpleasant affair. Each perception has some validity. The campaign witnessed remarkable levels of public engagement, fun and festival-like campaigning but it also had a divisive and bitter side. The duration and intensity of the campaign were unprecedented. Debates ranged long and wide concerning the kind of society and economy people wanted as much as about Scotland's constitutional status. Leaving aside the merits and demerits of the case for and against independence, the 'Yes' campaign was upbeat, offered hope and inspired enthusiasm. The 'No' campaign was, perhaps inevitably, negative and often came over at times as sullen and gloomy. The status quo was all too easily portrayed by independence supporters as a defence of a Tory Government in London.

While the Conservatives and SNP each saw their interests best served through cooperation and making devolution work prior to 2011, the two parties came to see electoral advantage in the polarised binary choice posed by the referendum. Labour would be squeezed out as a consequence. Without having a clear alternative in this binary battle, the Labour Party and those who had long voted Labour were forced to take sides. The referendum would be an opportunity for both the Conservatives and SNP to make incursions into Labour support. Labour was left stranded as the political agenda shifted onto the constitution.

Politics is an expectations game and there was more relief than celebration amongst opponents of independence when the result was known. Independence supporters were disappointed but far from demoralised when 45 per cent on a remarkably high turnout of 85 per cent voted for Scottish independence. A third option may not have been on the ballot paper but the option was forced onto the agenda in the final days of the campaign with the 'Vow'. The Vow was signed by the Conservative, Labour and Liberal Democrat leaders and essentially meant that some vague version of 'more powers' for the Scottish Parliament was now on the agenda. It acknowledged that 'People want to see change'. Much debate would ensue over subsequent years as to whether the Vow had been kept and whether it played a decisive part in the referendum outcome. While social science quantitative analysis might suggest it was not as important as many imagine, few people involved on either side of the campaign believe it had no impact. And most importantly, it ensured that more powers and responsibilities would come to Holyrood. The Vow was vaguely worded, allowing each side to claim it has or has not been kept. It promised that the Scottish Parliament was 'permanent and that extensive new powers' would be delivered; it hoped that the people of Scotland would be 'engaged directly' in this process; and the UK would ensure 'opportunity and security for all by sharing our resources equitably'. Each of these commitments left considerable room for interpretation. A more precise commitment was the 'continuation of the Barnett allocation for resources' and the power to raise revenue and that 'we can state categorically that the final say on how much is spent on the NHS will be a matter for the Scottish Parliament.'

Businessman Lord Smith, respected by both sides in the referendum, agreed to 'convene cross-party talks and facilitate an inclusive engagement process' to produce 'Heads of Agreement' and recommendations for 'further devolution of powers' by 30 November 2014. The timescale made any prospect of a truly inclusive engagement process all but impossible, which might anyway have simply invited a resurrection of the referendum campaign. The reference to 'Heads of Agreement' acknowledged that the timescale meant that the details would be left to negotiations between the UK and Scottish Governments. It also meant that there would be arguments over whether the 'Heads of Agreement' had been implemented. The members of the Smith Commission included two members from each of the parties represented in Holyrood. These were people who had just come through an intense and lengthy campaign and were expected to come up with an agreement on more powers within this short period of time.

Even though debate during the referendum had been very broad in scope, discussion of some form of fiscal autonomy had been brewing for some time. Twelve economists wrote to the Scotsman in 2001 in support of fiscal autonomy to deliver 'accountability and responsibility'. New fiscal powers had been a theme in Wendy Alexander's proposal to set up a Scottish Constitutional Commission in November 2007. Ruth Davidson, Scottish Tory leader, had proposed that Scotland should set its own income tax in the event of a 'No' vote during the independence referendum. After the referendum, the National Institute for Economic and Social Research think tank argued that to make the Scottish Parliament fully accountable, MSPs must be able to 'take decisions on which they can succeed or fail' and referred to the reliance on grants from the Treasury as 'pocket money'. A consensus had long been emerging around this aspect of more powers though had never been put directly to the wider public.

What emerged was the Scotland Act 2016. Further fiscal and welfare responsibilities would be devolved and Holyrood would be able to extend or reform a range of welfare benefits. The Scottish Government announced its intention to 'create a Scottish social security system based on dignity, fairness and respect, which will support those who need it, when they need it'. This conformed with the language and aspirations that had animated the Yes campaign. But how deliverable this ambition would be depended on a range of interconnected factors. The Smith Commission had proposed a 'no detriment' clause, meaning that there should be no detriment due to fiscal devolution or resulting from policies of either Scottish or UK Governments. It was an odd declaration. If fiscal responsibilities were devolved then risk was devolved and 'no detriment' depended on how the new powers would be used by a Scottish Government and the performance of the Scottish economy, not only on action by the UK Government. It would be to Scotland's detriment if the Scottish Government failed to use its powers well. In its narrower sense, no detriment meant that the UK Government grant to the devolved administration would only be altered to take account of the increased tax powers and to provide for equitable funding for the new devolved welfare responsibilities. But these matters were inevitably subjective and contested.

Once more, the focus of much discussion was on the proportion of revenue spending that would be covered by new taxes raised in Scotland. Less attention was paid to the other important side of the equation. Greater fiscal and welfare autonomy also meant greater economic and fiscal responsibility. In the early days of devolution, the growth in devolved public spending was a direct consequence of growth in UK public spending. As we have seen, when Tony Blair had announced in January 2000 that the proportion of UK Gross Domestic Product (GDP) spent on health was inadequate and would rise to the European average, he was not only committing to significant real terms increases for health in England, as this had consequences for the devolved administrations, though Scottish Ministers need not have spent the additional money on health. But the new powers meant that paying for more generously funded public services would now rely on the performance of the Scottish economy.

The new Fiscal Framework gave Holyrood more fiscal autonomy but added complexity to relations with London. Scottish devolution is financed with a mix of a block grant from the Treasury, some devolved taxation, some shared tax revenues, block grant adjustments and borrowing powers with a number of rules governing the operation of the Fiscal Framework. It thereby involves a number of moving parts that have added to the opaqueness of the system. Complexity tends to blur accountability and open the door to blame games and this has certainly been the case with the Fiscal Framework. The notion that devolving more taxes would increase fiscal responsibility has proved much more challenging than advocates had expected or claimed.

The devolution of income tax powers as well as considerable welfare powers in 2016 was accompanied by the non-statutory Fiscal Framework negotiated and agreed between HM Treasury and the Scottish Government with little parliamentary scrutiny or public consultation. It was updated in August 2023. The Fiscal Framework aims to provide a mechanism for adjusting the Block Grant, which HM Treasury provides the Scottish Government annually on the basis of the Barnett Formula. This annual adjustment is necessary to take account of a) a substantial proportion of the Scottish Government's Budget now coming directly from tax revenues raised in Scotland and b) additional revenues to the Scottish Government to reflect expenditure no longer incurred by the UK Government as a result of the devolution of 11 social security benefits. Limited borrowing powers were also devolved.

The framework is highly complex and not very well understood either within Holyrood or beyond, thus limiting the intended objective of increased accountability of Scottish Ministers for raising the money they spend. The Scottish Fiscal Commission (SFC) has referred to the 'economic performance gap' – the extent to which the Scottish budget now depends on the performance of the Scottish economy and its relationship with the wider UK economy. The SFC has estimated that Scottish taxpayers are paying £1,676 million more in income tax despite the Scottish budget only benefiting by £838 million in 2025–26. The devolved social security benefits are inevitably demand-led creating more uncertainty. Any increase in demand for such welfare benefits need to be met either by increased devolved taxation or cuts elsewhere in spending.

The demand for responsibility to allow for increases in welfare benefits had been stipulated by the SNP but Ministers had not taken into account the complexity of this transfer and the initial timescale proved unrealistic. The difficulties alerted the party's more thoughtful members to appreciate that further powers in future and the prospect of independence would involve vastly more complexity than they had appreciated. But one major success was the Scottish Child Payment (SCP) launched in 2021 by the Scottish Government. Low-income families in receipt of a range of benefits (universal credit, child tax credit, working tax credit, incomes-based job seekers allowance, pension credit, income support and income-related employment and support allowance) with children under 16 were eligible. It has been expensive – Scottish Fiscal Commission forecasts published in January 2025 suggest the cost will rise to over £500 million by 2027/28 – but the impact has been considerable. The Scottish Government has estimated that it will keep 60,000 children out of poverty. The SCP is one of the most successful policies of the last decade under devolution.

A number of economic 'strategies' have been launched since devolution, each focused on promoting growth with recurring themes of investment, skills and innovation running through each. In recent times, there has been greater emphasis on inclusivity and wellbeing in the rhetorical of Ministers and Government publications. However, there has been little innovation and a tendency to exaggerate differences with policies pursued by government in London. The financial system has become ever more complex and poorly understood. The Barnett formula still exists but is affected by these changes. Changes from one spending round to the next must take account of increased responsibilities for welfare payments on the one hand, but also having greater power to tax on the other. Many assumptions have to be built into calculations and these assumptions are reviewed and corrected. But insufficient attention was paid to the economy in the intense campaigning that came to dominate Scottish politics. Similarly, insufficient attention was paid to public services.

Policy stagnation and the rise of performative politics

In 2018, Audit Scotland warned that the NHS's position was not financially sustainable and had long noted pressure on Scotland's local authorities. The 2018 Audit Scotland report maintained that the NHS urgently needed to move from short-term fire-fighting to long-term fundamental change. The challenges of the ageing population required faster change. Audit Scotland noted that none of Scotland's health boards had met all key national targets and that waiting lists continued to increase. Six years on in another report, Audit Scotland observed that demand for NHS services was rising, costs were increasing and 'significant service transformation' was needed. The NHS was unable to meet the growing demand. The pandemic had exposed and exacerbated problems. But there was 'no overall vision'; there was a need for greater emphasis on preventative measures and putting 'patients at the centre of future services'. New powers without new policies would not help. An assumption appeared to have been made that having new powers was itself the answer to Scotland's public service challenges. The balance in considering institutional and policy reform had become skewed in favour of the former, neglecting policy development.

Amongst many reports and warnings, in November 2024 Audit Scotland warned that spending pressures had become more acute. There was no evidence of large-scale change and the Scottish Government had failed to establish effective arrangements for reform, did not know what additional resources would be needed to support reform and had not provided enough leadership to help deliver change. It noted the lack of transparency about medium-term risks and that there had been delays in strategy and financial plans.

Political rhetoric ran away with itself with the commitment to closing the attainment gap in education. As Professor Lindsay Paterson, Scotland's leading education policy expert, noted, the Scottish Government had 'never had a coherent strategy for dealing with the educational effects of poverty'. While the SCP is an important element in tackling child poverty, much more thought, resource and effort will be required if there is any serious prospect of closing that gap. This was part of a tendency to deliver speeches without adequate attention to implementation. An example of this performative politics included a commitment to altering legislation governing gender. Predictably, this provoked a battle with the UK Government which the Scottish Government may have assumed would have the support of majority opinion in Scotland. If so, it backfired, as the public majority agreed with the UK Government. Evidence of problems that would arise had been ignored or dismissed by Ministers.

The Scottish civil service and relations with London

The civil service is a reserved matter under the terms of the devolution legislation. The Scottish civil service is part of a unified British-wide civil service. This differs from the system of devolved government established in the 1920s in Northern Ireland where a separate Northern Ireland Civil Service (NICS) was then established. The unified British civil service has contributed to coordination and cooperation between Edinburgh and London. Numerous communications occur frequently between the two. It is striking how little concern there was and continues to be, even from the SNP, that we have a unified civil service. This may reflect recognition that civil servants working for the Scottish Government effectively owe allegiance to the Scottish Government, much as Scottish Office civil servants had been keen advocates for Scotland in dealings with Whitehall colleagues. It may also reflect a recognition that a unified civil service with Scottish officials with strong links to Whitehall provides the best of both worlds. *Scotland's Parliament*, the devolution white paper issued in July 1997, maintained that there would be a need for the devolved administration to 'keep in close touch with Departments of the UK Government'. Mutual understandings were required, covering 'appropriate exchange of information, advance notification and joint working'. It was anticipated that the vast majority of matters would be dealt with routinely by officials but if further interventions were needed then the Cabinet Office in London and Scottish counterparts in Edinburgh would 'mediate' and if necessary Ministers in Edinburgh and London would intervene'. John Sewel, leading the devolution legislation through the Lords at the time, repeated the point that concordats would be drawn up that would cover a 'range of matters, such as procedures for the exchange of information, advance notification and joint working'.

However, while a common civil service exists it would be wrong to infer that this meant that officials owed an allegiance to the UK Government. Inside any government there will be divisions and differences with departments often becoming advocates for 'clients'. Before devolution, civil servants in the Scottish Office saw their role as defending Scottish interests. Over decades, Scottish Office civil servants proved adept at making sure Scotland did well in public spending and that Scottish needs and interests were well articulated in Whitehall. These civil servants tended to be Scots, though this was not a qualification and not always the case. The same applied after devolution and civil servants continued to be well networked across Whitehall. These networks proved invaluable and ensured continuity when changes of government occurred.

There is always the suggestion after a party has been in power for a long time that the civil service has become too close to the governing party. It is notable that when the SNP came to office in 2007, the professionalism of the civil service ensured a smooth transition. Senior appointments are not imposed on a Scottish First Minister. The First Minister is involved in these decisions. Peter Housden was appointed Permanent Secretary in 2010 after a career in English local government and Whitehall, with no significant experience of Scottish government. He had to navigate the challenges of heading the civil service in Scotland during the independence referendum, in which his political leaders were arguing for independence while his colleagues in Whitehall were assisting their political leaders in arguing against independence. All the while, officials in Edinburgh and London ensured that everyday public policy decision-making continued. Housden found himself accused of abandoning impartiality and becoming an SNP supporter by leaders of Scottish Labour, Tories and Liberal Democrats who complained to Sir Gus O'Donnell, head of the UK civil service. O'Donnell rejected the criticism. The accusation said more about the heated nature of the debate than the Permanent Secretary's professionalism. Civil service impartiality is defined in the Civil Service Code as 'acting solely according to the merits of the case and serving equally well governments of different political persuasions'. Civil servants cannot 'act in a way that is determined by party political considerations, or use resources for party political purposes'. There have been senior appointments, including Housden's at Permanent Secretary level, of individuals with little experience in Scotland, but balanced by other relevant and more important experience. John-Paul Marks, appointed in 2022, had previously worked in the Department of Work and Pensions in Whitehall, bringing that experience to the Scottish Government at a point when considerable welfare experience was needed given the expansion of responsibilities in this policy area. His appointment as Permanent Secretary and Chief Executive of HM Revenue and Customs means that the head of this important body will have had intimate knowledge and experience of Scottish devolution. The ability to draw on this wider pool, with strong connections in Whitehall, has worked well for Scotland.

In a debate in the Scottish Parliament in October 1999, Donald Dewar explained the purpose of Memoranda of Understanding and supplementary agreements between UK, Scottish and Welsh administrations. These set out how relations should work. Detailed concordats were produced to deal with the coordination of European Union matters, international relations, statistics and financial support for industry. These were not legally binding; they could not be 'enforced through litigation or in the courts' but outlined 'sensible working practice'. They built on relations that had existed between Scottish Office civil servants and colleagues in Whitehall. Discussions with officials in the early days of devolution confirmed that these new documents essentially codified past practice and indeed few senior officials needed to refer to the Memorandum or similar documents. The issues addressed in the documents concerned communication, consultation, information exchange, confidentiality and monitoring of decision-making. These had always been important principles prior to devolution and had become embedded in relations between the Scottish Office and the rest of Whitehall. The problem that arose was that devolution resulted in more detachment from devolved Scottish business across Whitehall with greater likelihood of insensitive or ill-informed decisions being made.

Joint Ministerial Committees (JMCs) were also established after devolution. The JMCs operated in different formats. A plenary JMC was anticipated to meet at least annually at which the Prime Minister and heads of devolved administrations would discuss relevant issues and resolve differences. Separate JMCs would meet focused on subject areas on, for example, health which would involve Health Ministers from devolved administrations and the relevant UK Government Minister. But the JMCs largely fell into disuse. The only one that continued to meet regularly was JMC (Europe). On its election in 2007, the SNP asked for the reinstatement of JMCs, including plenary meetings. As Alex Salmond explained before the Commons Scottish Affairs Select Committee in 2010, there were many issues on which there was broad agreement between London and Edinburgh Governments. There was no need to manufacture fights as there were 'enough of these legitimate political differences in terms of aspiration for the future constitutional status of Scotland without having to invent disagreements over other things'. Salmond placed emphasis on dispute resolution, in particular over finance, as he felt the Treasury adopted a high-handed attitude when differences arose. In this, his view was shared with many Labour members. Rhodri Morgan, First Minister of Wales 2000–2009, led the successful case for devolved bodies receiving a Barnett share of regeneration expenditure associated with the London Olympics (not to be confused with expenditure on the Games themselves). But that had taken considerable effort and campaigning.

There was a sense amongst many politicians and officials in London that formal procedures and institutions were unnecessary and that differences could be managed informally between Labour Ministers in London and in devolved administrations. Private resolution of disputes was more manageable than dealing with differences which became public. However, various individuals and Parliamentary committees expressed concern that the JMCs were not being used in the early years. Alan Trench, then of University College London, was the foremost authority on the dangers of disuse and argued that more formalised and more frequent meetings should be held. This became the orthodox view amongst commentators repeated rather unthinkingly even when circumstances changed.

In a debate in the Scottish Parliament within six months of its establishment, SNP MSP Alex Neil argued that it was important to recognise the problem of Ministers in London operating as both English and UK Ministers and asked why the JMCs could not be chaired on rotation amongst the devolved and UK Government Ministers. This, he argued, would represent 'real devolution'. Proceedings of each meeting of the JMC were regarded as confidential to allow for 'free and candid discussion' though they might issue a public statement on outcomes. One question raised in that debate was how intergovernmental relations, necessarily often taking place in private, could be scrutinised. The answer provided was that relevant Parliamentary committees could call witnesses. It was the classic tension heard in debates on freedom of information. There needed to be transparency but also conditions that allowed for serious discussion rather than grandstanding with a view to the next day's headlines.

Brexit

Scotland's relationship with the EU has gone through dramatic change over time. Half a century ago, Scotland was the most Euro-sceptical nation in Britain. The SNP joined with many key figures in the Labour Party to campaign to leave the European Communities in the 1975 referendum. Scottish Secretary Willie Ross, amongst other leading Scottish Labour politicians and the Scottish Trades Union Congress (STUC), campaigned against EEC membership. In 2016, Scotland recorded the largest vote in favour of remaining in the EU. There were key moments in that journey from scepticism to support and a number of reasons for the change. The European Communities came to be seen as an ally rather than a threat in Scotland though by no means by everyone. Scotland, including its local authorities, benefited from structural funds. Many Scots became strong supporters when French Socialist Jacques Delors was President of the European Commission. Delors' address to the Trades Union Congress (TUC) in Bournemouth in 1988 was a significant moment. The STUC became a strong supporter of membership. The SNP's gradual conversion to the European cause, formalised in 1988, was important. As Margaret Thatcher became more hostile, majority opinion in Scotland became more positive. By the time of the 1992 general election, being pro-Europe became associated with support for a Scottish Parliament. Voters who supported devolution tended to support EC membership.

Brexit was not considered likely when the devolved Parliament was established – indeed the term 'Brexit' was only coined in 2012 – and its implications for devolution were unanticipated. Brexit would be a major test of devolution. The Brexit slogan had been 'take back control' but where was power being taking back to? To Westminster or devolved government or what balance between the two? Michael Gove, co-chair of the Vote Leave campaign in the 2016 Brexit referendum, had said that Holyrood would gain new powers as a consequence of Brexit, including new powers over immigration. Member states were bound by EU policy. EU policy constrained policy divergence between but also within member states. While Brexit was presented as allowing the UK to diverge in its policy preferences from the EU, the question was whether such divergence would be permitted within the UK after Brexit. The UK Government wanted divergence from the EU but opposed divergence within the UK.

Brexit was never going to be a straightforward exercise, more a complex disentanglement of numerous links and relationships. There was never any possibility of a clean break. The vote for Brexit was only the first step in a long process that involved detailed negotiations between the UK and EU. The issue for devolved bodies was what role, if any, they would have in that process. The answer became clear early on. The devolved administrations, including the Scottish Government, were hardly consulted and not centrally involved in the negotiations. Their preference for the softest of soft Brexits and desire to maintain as many links as possible was unacceptable to the UK Government. Theresa May's Government was focused on dealing with divisions on Brexit within her party and maintaining the support of the Democratic Unionist Party, on which her Government relied after the Tories lost an overall majority in the 2017 general election. May's failure to negotiate her way through tricky Parliamentary politics led to her demise, allowing Boris Johnson to become Prime Minister. Johnson's contempt for devolution and lack of interest in serious policy making was all too obvious. Both May and Johnson, in their different ways, ignored the Scottish and Welsh devolved administrations.

In 2017, the UK Government issued a white paper stating that on leaving the EU the 'powers which the EU currently exercises in relation to the common frameworks will return to the UK' and that whether any such matters should be devolved would be decided later. Devolved administrations in Edinburgh and Cardiff complained about a 'power grab' by London and argued that there should be a presumption that EU competences should, at least in the first instance, be devolved. According to the legislation creating the Scottish Parliament, matters that were not specifically retained at Westminster would be devolved. The UK Government took the view that EU affairs had been retained under the devolution settlement. This meant, as it saw it, that control was being taken back from the EU to Westminster, at least in the first instance. There was no meeting of minds between the UK and Scottish Governments, nor much of an effort to find agreement.

The UK Government argued that transferring formerly EU competences to devolved bodies opened the door for potentially troubling policy divergence. It sought to maintain a common market and free movement in goods, services, capital and people across the UK to replace the free movement across the EU. These free movements had been the cornerstones of the European Single Market. But this was a blanket policy. There had been scope for divergence in how policies were implemented under EU policy in many areas. EU principles of subsidiarity and proportionality were not replicated in the UK Internal Market Act, 2020 (UKIMA) designed to remove internal trade barriers within the UK post-Brexit. The UKIMA was passed but without the consent of the Scottish Parliament or Welsh Senedd. New institutions were established but the question was not simply institutional but how the governments would behave. The challenge was reaching agreement on what should be devolved, what needed to be held at the UK centre and what should be commonly agreed as well as how agreements should be determined. It once more raised the issue of relations between devolved and UK governments. Brexit led many to believe that devolution needed to be rethought.

Brexit contributed to a further deterioration in Scottish–UK Government relations. The absence of meaningful discussions and the gulf in views on what Brexit meant, plus the revival of demands for another independence referendum, made for tense politics. In the immediate aftermath of the Brexit referendum Nicola Sturgeon saw an opportunity to reignite the referendum campaign. Though the SNP played a very limited part in the Brexit referendum, it was quick to see the campaigning opportunity when 62 per cent of Scottish voters supported Remain while a slim majority across the UK voted for Leave. Nicola Sturgeon insisted that these changed circumstances legitimised the demand for a second independence referendum. Losers' consent to the result of the 2014 referendum was abandoned on the basis of a statement, though not a major item during the campaign, in the SNP's 2016 election manifesto. It stated,

> We believe that the Scottish Parliament should have the right to hold another referendum if there is clear and sustained evidence that independence has become the preferred option of a majority of the Scottish people – or if there is a significant and material change in the circumstances that prevailed in 2014, such as Scotland being taken out of the EU against our will.

While a claim can certainly be made that Scotland had been taken out of the EU against its will, there was far from 'clear and sustained evidence' of majority support for independence. Inevitably, the UK Government refused this. Political trench warfare ensued. Opinion polls followed advances and retreats in support for independence and the union.

The constitutional 'upas tree'

Most people had made up their minds during the independence referendum but considerable collateral damage was done to public services through neglect as everyday policy concerns took a back seat. Government business in Scotland was all too often seen through a constitutional lens and challenging problems were neglected. The transformation from the brief period after 2010 when the Conservative–LibDem coalition took office was complete. As the SNP's reputation for competence in government declined, it relied heavily on appealing to supporters of independence. Even when independence support was less than support for the union, it was high and salient enough to ensure the SNP would remain the largest party when translated into votes at elections. The Scottish Greens might support independence but the SNP took the lion's share of independence support, whereas the Tories, Labour and LibDems competed for a share of unionist support.

Peak support for the SNP had come in the immediate aftermath of the 2014 referendum. Scotland's constitutional status had dominated the political agenda and the issue would not disappear. In 2015, seven months after the referendum, the SNP won 56 of Scotland's 59 seats with 50 per cent of the vote, crushing its opponents and leaving Labour, Tories and the LibDems with one seat each. The SNP explicitly campaigned on a promise that the 2015 election was not a campaign about independence but benefited from the reverberations from the referendum regardless. In the following year's Holyrood elections, the SNP lost its overall majority and only made a slight recovery in 2021. A deal was agreed – the 'Bute House Agreement' – with the Scottish Greens. This was not a formal coalition but the co-leaders of the Greens became Government Ministers. In 25 years, Scotland had experienced coalition; minority government in which a loose agreement was reached with a minor party; minority government and another loose deal with a minority party but with two members given ministerial office; and single party government with an overall majority.

In 2017, the SNP lost 21 seats in elections to the Commons, leaving it still the largest party; it then recovered 13 seats two years later but well short of the high point in 2015. Support collapsed in 2024 when Labour returned as Scotland's largest party in the Commons, winning 37 seats and leaving the SNP with only nine. There had been plenty of intimations of these electoral developments. Voters were tiring of the constitutional question, the cost of living was taking priority and the SNP's record in office was tarnished. Nicola Sturgeon had failed to take advantage of remarkable levels of goodwill, including amongst those who opposed independence, to use devolved powers to address Scotland's social and economic problems. Her preference was to focus on performative politics and short-term populism. The SNP leadership continued to insist on another referendum but ran up against an immovable UK Government. Another referendum was a distant prospect and the SNP leadership must have known that had one been conceded it was far from clear what the outcome would have been.

The SNP's focus on independence had become Scottish politics' 'upas tree'. The fabled version of the upas tree reputedly kills every living creature within ten miles due to its poisonous vapours. It was an exaggeration, but with an element of truth to it, just as it would be an exaggeration to say that the independence referendum killed off all other debates but there is an element of truth to that too. The SNP's strategy of proving it was capable of governing competently to showcase what independence might be like had meant parking the immediate demand for independence between 2007 and 2011. That had worked well for the SNP and the independence cause. The reverse occurred when independence came to dominate the political agenda. Just as everyday public policy takes a back seat during an election campaign, the same happened during the referendum. The difference was the intensity and duration of the independence referendum. It would have been irrational had the SNP done anything other than use its position in the Scottish Government as a tool in the campaign; the UK Government did the same. It was a unique situation in which the machinery of two governments were mobilised against each other. But the referendum did not settle the issue.

In the early 1980s Sidney Blumenthal identified what he described as the 'permanent campaign' in American politics. It involved remaking government into an 'instrument designed to sustain an elected official's popularity'. Public policy becomes subservient to the needs of the campaign. This happened in Scotland after 2014. It had been hoped that the Scottish Government might revert to governing mode when the referendum was over. Margo MacDonald, who had committed so much of her life to independence, died before referendum polling day and her husband Jim Sillars told those attending her memorial service that Margo knew there would be 'harsh statements on both sides, the debate will be fierce, there will be verbal wounds inflicted' but her message was that 'At a minute past 10, whatever the result, she wanted those divisions to end, and this nation to seek a unity of purpose'. There was a long tradition of fractious and adversarial politics in Scotland and it was never likely, nor would Margo have expected, that a new style of consensual politics would emerge. What she had hoped was that they would focus on issues affecting working people, their families and communities. Nor would she have abandoned her support for independence but would have reflected on the result and sought to learn lessons. For a brief period after the referendum her advice seemed to have been heeded. Then, a combination of the resurrection of the independence campaign and increasing pressure on public services contributed to the deterioration in relations between the Scottish and UK Governments. Under Nicola Sturgeon, the SNP adopted the politics of constitutional campaigning at the expense of the business of governing. This was mirrored in London by UK Governments, most notably pursuing a hard Brexit out of the Single Market despite the very narrow UK-wide result (with a share of support in favour of Leave almost exactly the same as the vote for devolution in 1979 in Scotland). David Cameron's 'respect agenda' and the SNP's emphasis on governing competently were replaced by blame games. The UK Government presented itself as an immovable object while the Scottish Government saw itself as an unstoppable force. Deadlock was all but inevitable.

Conclusion

Scottish politics entered a new phase after 2011. Social and economic challenges were used as political footballs. There were times when the criticisms and warnings of anti-devolutionists appeared to be justified. Devolved government was never going to be perfect and there was ample evidence that government in London could not be portrayed as a paragon of competence and integrity focused on improving outcomes. But neither was the Scottish Government such a paragon. John Swinney, who had led the SNP in the early years of devolution, was called back into service after Humza Yousaf's difficult period as First Minister. His task was to stabilise his party. His approach was more professional than his predecessor but it seemed his brief period on the backbenches was insufficient time to reflect on his long years as a Minister at the heart of the Scottish Government. Centralisation and short-termism with a good dash of populism persisted though independence was quietly demoted in significance. The timing of his leadership – two months before the UK election and with another Holyrood election within sight – meant that he would not have the opportunity to develop policies that might have short-term political costs but potential long-term benefits for citizens.

The operation of the Scottish Parliament was affected by the adversarial constitutional turn in politics. Issues would be viewed through a constitutional lens which ought to have been viewed through a public policy lens. In their 2014 book, *The Spirit of Compromise*, Amy Gutmann and Dennis Thompson distinguished between campaigning and governing mindsets with reference to contemporary US politics. Campaigning, they maintained, involves distrust between parties, antipathies and wilful lack of empathy but governing requires constructive engagement, mutual respect, trust and compromise. The Parliamentary Committees were affected though some operated reasonably when the media spotlight was elsewhere. But major issues of contention became embroiled in the constitutional debate and battles within the governing party. The most damning indictment of the committees came when a special committee was set up to investigate the Scottish Government's handling of complaints against the former First Minister Alex Salmond. This was not so much hyper-partisan as a bitter intra-partisan problem. The issues involved remain unresolved, obscured and controversial and the committee did little for Holyrood's reputation. The SNP MSPs on the committee proved inadequate for the task and failed to leave their loyalties to the new leader at the door on entering the committee. It is difficult to imagine so many elected representatives in a governing party in Westminster behaving in such a manner.

SECTION TWO

The Next Twenty-Five Years

CHAPTER 4

Devolution: The Next Generation

What we must try to get is a unique system of devolved government, something which will reflect Scotland's own unique position in the UK... The UK is undoubtedly becoming more divided politically... This polarisation makes devolution more urgent in my view... It is only if that relationship were to be constantly denied and frustrated, if Scotland were to be ignored that things would get very much worse.

John Smith, *Bulletin of Scottish Politics*, 1982

Introduction

IN HIS 2001 study of *Democracy in Europe*, the philosopher Larry Siedentop asked, 'where are our Madisons?' Siedentop felt that the European Union needed the kind of thinking from first principles that had informed the American Constitutional Convention at the end of the 18th century. Institutional development tends to occur piecemeal with little reference to principles so occasionally there is a need to pause and reflect, challenge and reform. The Scottish Constitutional Convention, meeting from 1989, was an example of a constitutional moment informed by principles. It produced rich debates on issues of representation. The Consultative Steering Group (CSG) produced a report and recommendations informed by key principles. We again need similar thinking on Scotland's future having had a quarter of a century's experience of devolution. But we also need to think harder about how these new institutions and attendant powers should be used. The tendency to assume that a competence or power is the solution needs to be replaced by greater awareness that competences and powers are tools and it is what we do with the tools, whether these are appropriate tools, that matter. It is not our intention to offer a blueprint for a new constitution or to resolve the UK's many anomalies but to address some of the unfinished business of devolution. It is our contention that the principles that informed the Constitutional Convention and set out by the CSG should still apply. The thinking of many of those who played a significant part in the long debates and eventual establishment of the Parliament remain relevant. The challenge is translating these principles and that thinking into a different political and economic context, with devolution's expanded powers and responsibilities in mind.

Ever since the 1707 union, there have been Scots who feared that Scotland was being marginalised or that Scotland might even cease to exist as it became assimilated into a greater England. Sir Walter Scott is often cited as an example of someone who feared assimilation. Scott's 'Letters of Malachi Malagrowther' attacking attempts to prevent Scottish banks from issuing their own bank notes in the early 19th century is one of the most celebrated campaigns to retain something distinctly Scottish. His biographer and nephew told how Scott, on another occasion, had been agitated in reaction to those who had not taken seriously his fear that proposed reforms in the Scots legal system would 'destroy and undermine, until nothing of what makes Scotland shall remain'. This would be a recurring fear over subsequent decades in campaigns to save some manifestation of Scottishness perceived to be under threat.

Fears of assimilation were almost invariably due to insensitivity rather than to conscious efforts to eradicate Scotland or Scottish identity. A Royal Commission on Scottish Affairs, chaired by Lord Balfour, was set up in response to the Scottish Covenant movement that had campaigned for a Scottish Parliament after the Second World War. Balfour reported in 1954 and concluded that history taught that misunderstandings due to 'thoughtlessness, lack of tact and disregard of sentiment' could lead to discontent aggravated by 'needless English thoughtlessness and undue Scottish susceptibilities'. There was a 'widespread feeling that national individuality' was being lost and that the Treaty of Union was 'no longer remembered as a voluntary union of two proud peoples each with their own distinctive national and cultural characteristics and traditions, but rather as the absorption of Scotland by England' and that this was 'no new fear'. As Balfour insisted, 'recognition by United Kingdom and Great Britain Ministers of Scotland's national status' was essential and that misunderstandings should be openly discussed as otherwise they would grow. From an English perspective, Scots might often seem over-sensitive, a view that inspired PG Wodehouse to create a character in one of his novels who suggested that it has 'never been hard to distinguish between a Scotsman with a grievance and a ray of sunshine'.

The message from the Balfour Commission 70 years ago needs to be constantly repeated. There is reason to believe that the creation of the Scottish Parliament means that the Scottish nation is now under less threat and is less likely to be dissolved into a greater England. The Scottish Parliament has become a very significant institutional expression of Scottish identity, more important than those historical representations of Scottishness – the Kirk, the Scottish educational system, local government system or Scots law. Its decisions have an immediate, understood and daily effect on all who live in Scotland. It is tempting to assume that recognising Scotland's national status has been devolved and thereby any associated problem solved. Assimilation now looks very unlikely but the notion that devolution has solved the problem Balfour diagnosed is mistaken. The danger of needless thoughtlessness and insensitivity at the centre remains and may even have grown, especially amongst those in government in London who assume that the Scottish 'problem' has been solved through devolution. Scots will continue to seek to distinguish themselves from their nearest and much larger neighbour and will feel aggrieved when 'England' is used when 'Britain' or the UK is accurate. Decisions may be made in London affecting Scotland with little heed for Scottish interests or sensibilities.

Recognition of Scotland's national status in London will be necessary, regardless of Scotland's constitutional status, because Scotland will always remain England's neighbour. If Scotland became independent it would still serve Scotland ill should such thoughtlessness and insensitivity occur in London. The difference is that Scots would have less reason or opportunity to complain or, in Balfour's words, discuss 'thoughtlessness and insensitivity'. The problem that remains is how Scotland is viewed and heard in London. One lesson we have learned is that since devolution there is less, not more, appreciation of the need to acknowledge Scottish distinctiveness in London. Something similar to the 'two solitudes', to borrow the title of a famous Canadian novel that explored differences and misperceptions between English and Canadian identities, has arisen post-devolution. The lack of communication between neighbours encourages misunderstandings, grievances and tensions. There is a need for greater respect and appreciation of Scotland in London and of London and the rest of the UK in Scotland, and for this to be manifested institutionally as discussed later in this chapter.

In this chapter we discuss the impact devolution and subsequent events have had on identities and interests. What does it mean to be Scottish or British and how do national identities relate to other identities? We pay particular attention to England and English identities as this has become more salient over the last quarter century. We then consider the kind of state the UK has become and may yet evolve into. Finally, we turn to the centre of government in London, which we argue has been neglected and needs much more attention. Debates on intergovernmental relations have become rather stuck in a rut, with recommendations made in the early years of devolution simply being repeated as though nothing new could be learned from the last decade. There are dangers that are now clearer which need to be taken into account. We will consider Holyrood and governance *within* Scotland in the following chapter.

Identities and interests

An identity is formed in contradistinction to some 'Other' or 'Others'. In saying we are Scots we are also saying who we are not. The 'Other' for those who see themselves as Scots in political terms has usually been some variant or combination of England, London, Westminster and took on a sharp political form in the 1980s as the 'Other' became conflated with 'Thatcherism' for many Scots. Asking if people are British or Scottish forces a false dichotomy. Being Scottish need not be incompatible with being British. Every individual has multiple identities. Not only might we feel Scottish and British but we have other identities. Class, age, ethnic, gender, religious, language, regional and cultural identities may be more important to an individual than national identity and the importance of each identity may wax and wane over time. Many advocates of independence understood this well. They linked national and other identities in the 2014 independence referendum campaign. *Women for Independence* was a case in point. They sought to contrast these linked identities with what they presented as reactionary, backward-looking Britishness. To be Scottish was presented as being in favour of a fairer, more equal society in which people had multiple identities. The SNP under Alex Salmond promoted the idea of prefixed Scots – New Scots and Asian Scots for example – and he and others acknowledged having a British dimension to their identity. Opponents might understandably object that they were at least as progressive as any on the Yes side. In reality, while each side sought to caricature the other, the referendum was essentially a contest between two sides that were both predominantly progressive and civilised and with politically uglier elements on both sides too.

There has also been a determined effort to remove the close association of Scottishness and Scottish nationalism with Presbyterianism which had been prevalent well into the 20th century. There had always been Irish-Scots, people who had Irish roots, but the past strong association of Scottish identity with Presbyterianism meant this prefixed Scots identity had not been given a name or recognition. This association weakened over time. In 1998, Cardinal Tom Winning made a speech in Brussels entitled 'A New Scotland in the New Europe' in which he described Scottish nationalism as 'mature, respectful of democracy and international in outlook' signalling a change in outlook amongst Scottish Catholics to Scottish national identity, not to mention Scottish nationalism.

Identities vary in intensity over time. If we ask people whether they are Scottish or British we are making a number of assumptions. We assume a binary choice – either Scottish or British. We assume that these identities are important at the time of asking. But identities are shapeshifters, difficult to pin down though powerful. John P Mackintosh argued that Scots had a 'dual nationality', they could be both Scottish and British. Fifty years ago, he referred to Scotland's distinctive culture 'compounded of history, accents, football, deprivation and reactions to English condescension'. He later offered a further glimpse into this thinking, 'Some of the institutions that matter are peculiar to Scotland and create a sense of identity while others – such as the tradition of parliamentary democracy – are purely British'. There are problems with a focus on institutions, though institutions are 'carriers of nationality' as he noted. The monarchy is often cited as the institutional embodiment of Britishness but many Scottish nationalists are monarchists and want to remain part of a United *Kingdom*. This is the formal position of the SNP. It is the union of Parliaments, rather than the union of Crowns, that the SNP opposes. And there are many republicans who identify as British. Few politicians in the post-war period were more critical of the monarchy than the former Fife Labour MP Willie Hamilton (predecessor of one of the authors of this book) who was also determinedly British and emphatically unionist.

Values are often invoked in discussion of national identity. But distinguishing Scottish values from British values or British values from European values is problematic. There is a tendency for individuals to associate their own values with the national identity with which they most closely associate. But liberal democratic values cannot be the exclusive property of any national identity. And nations are collectives not individuals. And within any nation there will be a multitude of competing, conflicting identities as well as multiple competing and conflicting values. To refer to a national character or national values is meaningless.

The more worrying form identity can take is when it becomes exclusive. As Mackintosh saw it, the SNP's exclusive nationalism in the 1970s left little room for British or European identities and was one factor that prevented him from supporting the nationalists. This was an unfair assessment, at least as far as applied to most of the then SNP leadership. Whether ascribing exclusionary nationalism to the SNP then was fair, many in today's SNP and advocates of independence present an image that is far from exclusionary. Mackintosh was a strong supporter of European Community membership and could not have foreseen the SNP's later conversion to the European cause. As he stated, we have only to recognise and add the 'European dimension to the dual nationality to fit the realities of modern political life'. The European question teaches us that our identity is not only plural but there are different types of identity. A sense of belonging may have a strong emotional element or may be transactional. Old notions of community and identities remind us that a community of interest need not create a strong emotional bond. There are elements of emotional and transactional bonds in both British and Scottish cases. And, ironically, as we noted in the first chapter, many Scots came to support devolution as a means of protecting what were British institutions – the NHS, welfare, regional policy interventions and generous levels of public expenditure.

Anthony Smith, one of great scholars of national identity, once rhetorically asked, 'who will feel European in the depths of their being, and who will willingly sacrifice themselves for so abstract an ideal? In short, who will die for Europe?' It may be contended that the lack of emotional depth in the largely transactional relationship that is the European Union makes it more fragile, less durable. This may help explain Brexit. Trade with the rest of the UK is quintessentially transactional and there is a danger that this makes the relationship that is Britain fragile too, though much less so than European identity. The 'dismal science' of economics does not lend itself well to emotions, at least until economic decisions are taken that really hurt and, crucially, are perceived to have caused hurt for citizens and communities. Transactional relationships do not automatically lead to emotional commitment even when the transactions are mutually beneficial.

But it is too simplistic to suggest that Scottish identity is emotional while British or European identities are transactional as there are emotive and transactional elements in each and all relationships can result in emotional bonds.

Memory plays a part in identity formation. Memory is not history. Memories are subjective and often faulty. The memory of the collective endeavour of the Second World War has resonated across the UK since the end of the war and though this appears to have waned it is often re-awakened at notable anniversaries. Scottish regiments encapsulated the duality of this memory. It was not only a memory held by those who had lived through that war but later generations brought up on recalled memories through stories, films and myriad forms of memorials. But the raw emotion has faded. The Second World War no longer holds the same place in the public's imagination that it once did. The UK's foreign interventions in recent times have had the opposite effect. Previously, the British Empire offered Scots great opportunities through the exploitation of the pink coloured parts of old Imperial maps. It has long been suggested that the decline of Empire contributed to a weakening of Britishness in Scotland and indeed in England. Greater recognition of the pernicious exploitation of the Empire has further eroded what had once been a solid foundation of Britishness.

The welfare state is similar, though positive and much more enduring. The National Health Service has long been cited as evidence of a great British achievement with shared British, including distinctly Scottish, origins. The welfare state has long been recognised to have contributed to a sense of Britishness both transactionally and emotionally. The Scottish citizen was provided protection by the state. The emotional commitment to the NHS was illustrated powerfully in the opening ceremony of the London Olympics in 2012. But perceived threats to the NHS by UK Governments in the 1980s, subsequently undermined Britishness in the eyes of many Scots and gave rise to the paradoxical situation of many supporting a Scottish Parliament in order to save this British institution. It is no surprise that independence support rose towards the end of the 2014 referendum when the SNP focused on what it presented as the threat to the NHS if Scotland voted No.

What it means to be Scottish will differ from person to person and cannot nor should be pinned down. The nature of Scottishness remains and will always be irresolvable. That does not mean it is unimportant. One development over the last generation, starting before the Parliament came into being, was the greater appreciation of the varieties of Scottish identity. This is evident geographically, linguistically and ethnically. Scottish identity is an umbrella encapsulating an array of interconnected and shifting identities, just as British identity does.

Britain, Britishness, England and Englishness

Bookshelves that once heaved with works on Scottishness and what it means to be a Scot are being replaced with shelves of works on Britishness and Englishness. England and Englishness, as well as Britain and Britishness, are now the source of much debate. In a book published over 40 years ago, political scientist Richard Rose noted, 'One thing is for certain: No one speaks of the *UK*es [sic] as a nation'. The official name of the state is the United Kingdom of Great Britain and Northern Ireland which makes 'British' a common short-hand but strictly speaking inaccurate and exclusive. This did not matter so long as the issue was uncontested. Most people in Britain are oblivious to the issue and more likely to respond with slight bemusement when this is pointed out, much as people in England would often respond when Britain and England were commonly, though inaccurately if innocently, conflated.

There has been a growing significance in popular politics of England's 'Other'. Europe became important as England's 'Other'. And for many in England, and not a few in Scotland, the 'Other' includes immigrants and refugees. There has been a tendency amongst some Scots to identify with Europe and with immigrants as a way of distinguishing being Scottish from a caricature of their 'Other'. It has become the political equivalent of well-behaved Scottish football fans distinguishing themselves from (the small contingent) of English fans who behave badly. We should not pretend an absence of negative stereotyping and 'Othering' of minorities amongst Scots and encourage an open, inclusive idea of being a Scot.

Scotland will be England's 'Other' and vice versa when two national sports teams meet. But otherwise, Scotland is rarely England's 'Other', though devolution and the growing perception that Scots were getting their cake and eating it occasionally made Scotland the 'Other' for some in England. There have been accusations that Scotland gets more than its fair share of public expenditure with often crude, ill-informed references to the Barnett formula but this has had limited impact on the English public. The first election to the newly created office of London Mayor in 2000 saw candidates from all parties seeking to outbid the others in claiming that too much public spending was lavished on Scotland. One newspaper referred to a debate on whether London lost out at Scotland's expense as the 'Battle of Barnettburn'. In 2001, the first UK election after devolution, the Barnett formula was sporadically raised in campaigns across the UK. All the while there were claims in Scotland that a 'Barnett squeeze' was an attack on Scotland. All of this signified an increase in the 'territorialisation' of UK politics with greater emphasis on competition for limited resources. But it failed to create much of a backlash against Scotland. When everyone is gaining then those gaining least are unlikely to make a fuss. It is when all are losing and perceptions grow that one area and people are suffering more than another that trouble starts brewing. Growth in expenditure across the UK dampened perceptions and criticisms that Scotland was getting more than its fair share. A well-leavened system of intergovernmental financial relations helps.

There are other forms of Englishness. Senior Labour politician David Lammy wrote thoughtfully about identity in his 2021 book *Tribes: How Our Need to Belong Can Make or Break Society*. Identity politics, he argues, is 'not intrinsically right or wrong' but has the 'potential for good as well as for abuse'. He noted the multicultural and diverse nature of football players and celebrities but it was the British Caribbean football fans in most Premier League stadiums that were 'far more illustrative of England' for him. He avoided the dismissive tones of those critical of identity politics who fail to acknowledge their own identities. He wrote,

> The premise that underpins identity politics is that there is some deep similarity, or essential continuity, between the experiences of different individuals within one oppressed group. It suggests there is something unique about the experience of being black, female, disabled, a refugee or LGBT. I am unashamed to admit that in recent years many of the issues I have campaigned on – from Grenfell to Windrush, fair access to universities and even in part my opposition to Brexit – have been linked to my identity as one of very few black UK politicians from a deprived social background.

Identity formation need not of course require oppression. Professor David Olusoga of Manchester University noted the 'hyper diverse' nature of the young English football team in the 2024 Euros and suggested that England manager Gareth Southgate was building a 'new, workable version of English identity'. The portrayal of Englishness by many Scots is just as caricatured as the Wodehouse character's portrayal of Scots.

Lammy made a further notable point. England had been left out of the constitutional reforms of the Blair years.

> England's separation from the new project of devolution, while every other constituent nation's identity was encouraged, has been an important factor in causing a kind of national identity crisis... English men and women are not decided on whether to call themselves English, British or both.

An Englishness that turns its back on Scotland or sees the Scots as 'Other' may seem unlikely though there is evidence that many people in England feel at best ambivalent about the union. Much can change over time with prejudices stoked by populists. There are various options available and this is a matter that has widespread implications.

When we look back to debates on devolution from the 'Geordie Revolt' in the late 1970s – when Labour MPs in the North East of England opposed Scottish devolution, fearing it would give Scotland a greater advantage over their region in the battle for investment and spending – we see misdirected inter-territorial competition. There is a need to address these perceptions especially as they are wrapped up in easily mobilised national or regional identities. There is now greater appreciation that people in the North East of England have many interests in common with Scots. This understanding came earlier in the North East than it has in Scotland. Professor John Tomaney, who led the unsuccessful North East devolution campaign in 2004 and one of the leading authorities on regional government and policy in the UK, became a strong supporter of a Scottish Parliament well before 1997, seeing the potential of shared interests for common campaigns operating alongside Scottish and English regional autonomy. His view has become more common since then and opportunities now exist to build on this perception.

Care should be taken not to abandon one 'Other' for another. The 'Other' across much of the UK is 'London'. Polls show that people in the north of England, Scotland and Wales were the most anti-London areas of the UK. A poll in 2014 found that two-thirds of voters agreed that 'too much of England is run from London' and another that more than four in five people living in cities other than London felt that Westminster and

Whitehall were unresponsive to where they lived. 'London' is as vague as any 'Other' and can include some mix of Westminster/Whitehall/the City. What is often framed in territorial terms hides other tensions. While there is ample evidence that major investments have been made in infrastructure in London, the cost of living in the UK capital is much higher than elsewhere. This has little impact on the super-rich, whereas London's less well-off suffer excessively. The 'Other' for many Londoners lies not outside London but within it and they would find common cause with many people across the rest of the country. Class identity has declined with great significance for British politics over the last couple of generations. It is not that objective class – based on wealth, income, education, occupation or access to material, cultural or other resources – has become unimportant or that differences have disappeared in a more equal society. It is subjective class, the sense of belonging to or associating with a socio-economic class, that has declined. Identity politics has filled the gap left by the decline of class politics. The building blocks of 'working class solidarity' that contributed to a fairly united labour movement and to a sense of unity across Britain, and was a barrier to support for devolution in the 1970s, have been undermined. Gone are so many of the large-scale unionised industries and the large public sector housing estates that created solidarities. Too little effort has been made to reinvigorate and create alignment with other progressive alliances across Britain or the United Kingdom.

We return to the public policy aspects in a later chapter but here we want to emphasise the importance of the interactions of different types of identities. There is much misunderstanding and considerable myth-making that can easily be exploited by unscrupulous populists. Identity matters, for good or for ill. David Lammy was right to point out that identity is not some antediluvian force in politics. Britishness or Scottishness can be seen as umbrella identities under which an array of other identities exist. One identity may become first amongst equals for a period but always exists alongside other identities. Acknowledging the existence of and celebrating the good in an identity is necessary while avoiding exclusivity. Forging and maintaining alliances across geographies amongst those who feel aggrieved, left behind or have a common interest is vital. In this respect, much may be learned from politics in London, which has seen important cross-community collaborations and a sense of a common identity being built. Research shows that residents in London identify most strongly as 'Londoners' ahead of being British or English and the growth in the number of Londoners who were born outside London or abroad has not reduced that sense of being a Londoner. London identity is inclusive and easily acquired, as Jack Brown noted in his 2021 book *The London Problem*.

What kind of UK?

In 1959, the journalist and home ruler JM Reid wrote that Scotland was not a state in the American or European sense, it was not a unit of a federation, it was not a unit of local government and nor was it similar to an English region. The eminent political scientist Richard Rose described the UK as an 'intellectual puzzle' in a paper published in 1977. Rose's concerns were both practical as well as intellectual. The puzzle was not just how to describe the UK and Scotland's position within it but to consider how it should operate. It was then commonly and uncritically asserted that the UK was unitary, it was 'one and indivisible'. By definition devolution is incompatible with a unitary state. But the UK has never been a unitary state in which all parts are treated the same and in which all policies were applied uniformly. Devolution involved a break with what had gone before though this did not mean there had never previously been some measure of policy diversity as we discussed in chapter one. The nature of the UK and Scotland's position within it cannot be dismissed as a matter of only academic interest or that the 1707 union has no relevance in the 21st century.

When we refer to the state we are referring to both the geographical entity but also what happens within its boundaries. The geographic boundaries of the UK have changed since 1707. It incorporated Ireland at the start of the 19th century then lost most of Ireland in the early 20th century. But it is in the second sense of the state that change has been most significant from a Scottish perspective. The influence and relevance of the Kirk, the institutional embodiment of Scottish distinctiveness from before the 1707 union, has withered from the days when its influence was felt in every corner of Scotland. But there has been no withering away of Scotland. The nature of the union has changed but Scotland has retained distinct features despite the manifestation of that distinctiveness changing over time.

The British state, formed through a union of Scotland and England, accommodated the component nations within a loose union. The centre of the new state initially had a very limited role in the lives of people in Scotland or England but over time the state's remit, and thereby the centre's, grew – especially from the late 19th century. That growth was largely welcome as it brought security and opportunities without stifling diversity. Scotland's place in the union developed piecemeal creating a Heath-Robinson-type arrangement over time. While the establishment of the Scottish Parliament was an important and positive development it added some new anomalies. There is nothing new in constitutional anomalies and attempts to remove these must take account of unintended consequences of seeking uniformity and symmetry. The UK is asymmetrical because it recognises diversity.

Public expectations and the rise of the interventionist welfare state fundamentally altered the UK. New responsibilities required government machinery and as the state's reach increased into society and economy, decisions needed to be made on what was decided by whom and where This took account of the state as a union of nations. Richard Rose noted that there were at least three different ways of making policy, each with territorial implications and that different ways of making policy are required for different policy areas. For each policy there are places on the continuum where decisions would be most appropriately made, from highly centralised and uniformly applied policies at one end, to permitting considerable latitude for discretion at the other. Unitary policies 'could only be made by central government' and included 'military defence, diplomatic representation and control of money'. Autonomous policies could apply in only one part of the state. Cooperative policies were a 'two-way street'. The problem with shared policies, as John Sewel pointed out in evidence he gave to the Calman Commission many years later, is that of accountability,

> Shared powers lead to murkiness of accountability. It's hard enough for the individual citizen to know what the Government is doing and would be harder if two Governments both had powers to act. Accountability is essential.

But shared powers are inevitable in many areas of public policy.

As discussed in chapter two, devolved government involves a mix of unitary, autonomous and cooperative policy making. Institutional reforms alone will not help. More frequent and regular meetings of Ministers in an environment of blame games and mutual hostility can add to problems. There are options on how to address the accountability of the perceived deficit in intergovernmental relations. In the long run, a radically reformed second chamber in Westminster representing the regions and nations of the UK could have a role. Additionally, recommendations made by the Calman Commission to create an interparliamentary Committee with members drawn from the Commons and Holyrood and with the power to call witnesses from Scottish and UK Governments is needed. But fundamentally, the focus on institutions has created more problems than solutions. Form should follow function and the function in this case refers to tackling socio-economic problems rather than creating institutions as an end in themselves. If the form simply aggravates problems by creating constitutional battlegrounds then it is not serving a useful purpose.

Rose gave orthodox examples for each category of policy type but there are at least shadings between these three types. When we consider health, for example, we are referring to a vast array of decision points, as well as a range of other policies affecting public health. One of the standard texts, *Making Health Policy*, notes the role poverty, physical environment and working conditions play in public health. A range of policies on 'education, food, transport and urban planning directly impact on health and disease' as well as economic and fiscal policies that have important health implications. Health policy decisions are never the exclusive domain of UK or Scottish central governments even if overall framing and funding is decided by these governments. A vast array of decisions, including everyday clinical decisions, are made by doctors, nurses, health workers, local authorities and many others. The panoply of institutions and decision points is unavoidable and means that different decisions are made from the very local all the way to Cabinet.

More thought needs to be given to Scotland's relationships with the rest of the UK but also relations within Scotland. The easy answer would be to let the Scottish or UK Parliaments decide on all the big framing policy decisions. That would be neat and clear-cut but would also create problems. More thoughtful advocates of independence have long understood that there are matters that are better shared across the UK or Britain. For many years the SNP started to take this seriously. Its support for EU membership was motivated in large measure by a desire to ease the transition to independence within common European, including the rest of the UK, frameworks. A wide range of matters would need to be shared to mutual advantage though where the line would be drawn is disputed and would change over time. But the stirrings of respectful discussion came to a juddering end in the shadow of a binary constitutional battle. As the prospect of constitutional trench warfare recedes it may be possible to resurrect a serious debate.

Fundamentalist nationalism may be in retreat on both sides of the binary divide, creating space for those who might have felt inhibited or simply saw contributions drowned out by the fundamentalist noise from both sides.

The issue is as much about how change should occur as what change should happen. The starting point is the legal definition of competences. But legal understandings have limited impact when it comes to public policy. Issues, problems and policy agendas do not fit into neat legal frameworks. Nonetheless, legislation defining what is reserved and thereby what is devolved is necessary. Over the last 25 years changes in devolved competences have been brought about inconsistently, especially when we compare the situation in Scotland and Wales. Perhaps this anomaly is just part of UK constitutional practice but we need to be aware of creating anomalies that in turn create grievances. The right for people in Northern Ireland to determine their constitutional future while similar rights are denied in Scotland has created understandable criticism. Welsh devolution has undergone very significant change since the Wales Act 1998 when the Welsh National Assembly was unable to pass primary legislation. Major reforms occurred after a referendum in 2011 when Welsh voters gave strong support to primary legislative powers. In Scotland, new competences have been devolved in the Scotland Acts 2012 and 2016 with little or no direct recourse to public opinion. Neither piece of legislation required a referendum though the latter occurred following the independence referendum that had formally excluded an option on more powers. The 2016 Act followed a cross-party Commission that worked to a very tight timescale and made recommendations that were then the basis for negotiations between Scottish and UK Governments. The absence of consistency in how competences are decided is anomalous. Agreement needs to be found on how reforms to devolved competences are made that should be applied consistently across the state including how Scotland's theoretical right to become an independent state should be tested. There are now tried and tested ways of engaging with citizens but there needs to be agreement on when and how these should be operationalised consistently. But before such ideas are adopted we need far more thought on the relationship between such initiatives and representative democracy.

It would make sense to agree a process for change – and this could involve not only extending devolved competences but also, if so desired and agreed, returning competences as well as agreeing new institutions to facilitate and determine cooperative policy making. It might seem odd to include the possibility of returning competences but it would be advisable to be open to different scenarios no matter how unlikely they may seem at the moment. Such decisions are classic constitutional issues – or 'rules of the game' – with agreed processes to decide how reform might occur. This is not to suggest that every change in devolved competence should be the subject of a referendum but some principles might guide when a referendum is required and/or alternative means of public engagement occurs. There is now a considerable body of scholarly practical evidence and advice that can be drawn upon to ensure that changes have citizen legitimacy.

Past devolution debates took little account of the rest of the UK or government at the centre. While devolution enhanced the sense of Scotland as a nation, the UK remains a puzzle. There has been little attempt to formulate a new understanding of the UK post-devolution. In some respects, the creation of the Scottish Parliament was a small 'n' nationalist project. The focus had been on the creation of a representative democratic institution that would make existing administrative devolution more accountable, provide more time to debate, legislate and scrutinise government in Scotland and allow for more autonomy in policy making. Less attention was paid to wider implications and relations – with either the rest of the UK, with Whitehall and Westminster, or with the European Union. And there was little enough attention paid to relations between what would become the new Scottish central government and local and regional institutions within Scotland.

The relations between the component nations and regions of the UK and their relations with the centre help us understand the UK today but this requires an understanding of relations between state, society and the economy. An interventionist state requires very different and more complex territorial structures than a 'nightwatchman state'. The latter leaves the provision of public services to the market and civil society. The idea that a 'Big Society' will provide services when the state does not intervene or has departed is fanciful. The state has far greater capacity to ensure that all citizens have access to necessary services but requires elaborate institutions throughout its length and breadth.

The UK may be slowly evolving into a form of federalism, though Brexit and the UKIMA have set that process back considerably, but it is unlikely to become a symmetrical federation in which all parts are treated the same in the foreseeable future. The component nations and regions may have different internal institutional arrangements and pursue different policies and hang together more loosely than in the past. The end point, if such is even meaningful, or direction remains uncertain, not least, to invoke Thomas Jefferson as quoted in the introductory chapter, the 'earth belongs to the living, not to the dead' and 'one generation is to another as one independent nation to another'. We could invert the objective of 'ever closer union' in the preamble to the 1957 Treaty of Rome that created the European Economic Community. The UK may move towards an 'ever looser union' but how loose cannot be written in stone.

Scotland and the wider world

An argument can be made that diplomatic representation need not be unitary, as Richard Rose suggested, but that it could be cooperative, as indeed has been experienced under devolution as discussed in chapter two. The boundary between domestic and foreign policy has always been blurred and Scottish representation abroad existed before devolution. Cities, regions and components of federations have long engaged in external relations, directly seeking inward investment and developing relations with external organisations and polities. The most obvious examples lie in the European arena. Scottish local authorities developed links with European institutions well before devolution. Strathclyde Regional Council set up an office in Brussels in the early 1980s and Lothian, Fife Central and Tayside regions combined forces to promote joint interests in Brussels. This east coast consortium, for example, had recognised a common interest in developing ferry links to northern Europe.

How Scotland's voice should be heard in European institutions post-devolution had been one of the most challenging questions when Labour came to power in 1997. While Scottish Office civil servants and Ministers might attend European institutions, they did so as UK representatives and had not been able to strike out on their own to pursue solely Scottish interests. But, under devolution, Scottish civil servants and Ministers with their own Scottish electoral mandate created a wholly new situation. This was not a problem so long as common policy positions were agreed in advance but the possibility of tensions are likely to increase when the governing parties in Edinburgh and London differ. The Scottish voice would continue to be articulated via UK institutions or would operate around the margins of EU decision-making. In a St Andrews Day lecture in Brussels in December 1997, Donald Dewar set out how he hoped this would work. He recounted exchanges with representatives of German Länder and Spanish

Autonomous Regions who were very clear that relations with their federal governments worked harmoniously on EU matters, though that had not always been the case. German Land governments had campaigned to be able to represent Germany and reportedly congratulated the UK for allowing Scotland to lead for the UK in 'appropriate cases'. They acknowledged that differences would occur but this was regarded as 'healthy plurality'. Dewar's vision had been predicated on respectful and cooperative relations between Edinburgh and London. Alan Trench, leading scholar on intergovernmental relations in the UK, noted in evidence to the Calman Commission in a more charged political context, that the many norms and values that were once taken for granted were 'no longer common and certainly cannot be taken for granted'.

The current nature of the UK precludes a model, comparable to what was possible in Germany and other federal states, in which a commonly agreed regional position is arrived at across the various components of the federal state and articulated directly where appropriate in European institutions as occurred after the German Länder reacted to the Single European Act by demanding a greater voice in European affairs. Land members of the second chamber of the German Parliament coordinate views, if necessary by majority vote, to be articulated for Germany as a whole in areas that fall under the components of the German federation. The UK's highly asymmetrical system of devolution means that there are no obvious English components or means of coordination with which Scottish, Welsh and Northern Ireland administrations could form a common position at present. Much depends on developments in England and the creation of an Assembly or Senate of Nations and Regions in the UK if this is to happen.

The main public policy aims of devolved government engaged in international relations will concern trade and economic affairs. It is incumbent on the Scottish Government to demonstrate that money is being spent wisely on offices and activities abroad. Careful monitoring and learning from activities and achievements, including attracting inward investment, is necessary. In addition, there needs to be cooperation with the rest of the UK to avoid bidding wars to attract inward investment and evidence that international activities do not undermine UK-wide activities. There should be no problem with the humanitarian activities that have already been successful. So long as this continues or is extended after consultation with the appropriate UK Government then such parallel (or para-) diplomacy can only enhance Scotland and the UK's reputation internationally.

A distinction can be made between para-diplomacy, when sub-state governments engage in international relations in parallel with central government usually focused on trade and economic affairs, and proto-diplomacy, when a sub-state government operates as if it is a separate state and seeks consciously to undermine central government. There is, inevitably, a fine line between para- and proto-diplomacy and much will come down to perceptions. Para-diplomacy will include moments of conflict and disagreement but this should not be reason to adopt a blunt binary approach in which external relations should be within the absolute competence of the centre. Conflict and disagreement are the essence of politics and democratic politics involves the pursuit of resolving differences. Differences will always arise but become more acute when the Scottish Government seeks to present itself as an independent state and is keen to play up any differences – this is proto-diplomacy. It also becomes a problem when any attempts by the Scottish Government pursuing para-diplomacy are portrayed as a form of illegitimate proto-diplomacy by UK central government. In other words, differences move from the realm of normal political differences requiring the usual respectful negotiations and compromises into the realm of public squalls in which battles are the end in themselves.

There is a case for representatives of devolved institutions participating with UK Government in negotiations with the EU in relevant policy areas. But this can only work if devolved bodies behave responsibly and do not use such participation to further constitutional aims or to score political points. Such negotiations involve trade-offs and difficult choices and once agreement is reached then acceptance by participant devolved bodies – indeed a willingness to help sell any agreement – is essential. If any devolved representative was to abuse such participation then it would be necessary to exclude them from future negotiations. But Scottish politics will need to move firmly out of the shadow of the 2014 independence referendum before such a proposal should be implemented.

The welfare state

The comment by Gordon Brown in an appendix on 'Home Rule and the Labour Movement' in his doctoral thesis, referred to in chapter one, remains relevant today and requires much more attention. Brown noted that

> No theorist attempted in sufficient depth to reconcile the conflicting aspirations for home rule and a British socialist advance. In particular, no one was able to show how capturing power in Britain – and legislating for minimum levels of welfare, for example, – could be combined with a policy of devolution for Scotland.

There is a respectable school of thought that believes that redistributive policies should be the prerogative of central government. The centre alone is in a position to ensure that citizens are treated equitably regardless of where they live. The centre provides equalisation through grants and ensures that poorer areas with weaker economic bases do not suffer poorer quality public services. From this perspective, much taxation and welfare payments are often seen as necessarily the prerogative of the centre. The assumption is that the centre would be more favourably disposed to redistribution and crucially able to redistribute within the state as a whole. Decentralising responsibilities for welfare to poorer areas can simply involve devolving penury, leaving less well-off areas with the greatest need for state support to fend for themselves without adequate means of doing so. This partly reflects the influence of American thinking on federal-state relations where states' rights in the USA are often associated with conservatism. But in the UK we have often experienced greater demands for redistribution from below.

How much diversity in welfare is acceptable? One response is that any difference involving more generous allocation of resources should only be permitted if it is provided from the devolved or local body's own resources. But without central support this would mean poorer areas would be unable to provide the same level of services as richer areas. The principle of 'leeway' was used in discussions of financing devolution in Northern Ireland in the 20th century. Leeway recognises circumstances when additional resources are needed, greater than provided elsewhere, to help an area which may not be in a position to provide adequate support from its own resources or with existing an central grant. Central government will always have a role in ensuring equity across the state through grants to devolved and local authorities. It is thereby impossible to avoid the need for a central authority empowered to ensure equalisation. Less prosperous areas will not have the same tax base to provide resources for greater public services that will exist in the prosperous area. Being born in a less prosperous area should not put any citizen at a disadvantage. The state's role in providing equity requires interventions and correctives in such situations.

We would want to ensure that there are minimum levels of welfare throughout the state. But does this mean that the same levels of welfare must apply everywhere? Public opinion opposes what is referred to as the 'postcode lottery' in public services – ie that the level of service provided is affected by where the citizen lives. But the public also want decisions made more locally. These are incompatible positions. There can never be the same level of all services across the UK or within Scotland. Not only do different citizens and communities have different needs but geographical, demographic and other factors come into play. Providing the same level of health service in remote parts of Scotland as in highly urbanised areas is all but impossible. It is not only the cost involved in ensuring that someone in the remotest part of Scotland has local access to all health procedures as someone living next door to a major hospital in a city. The inevitable lack of highly specialist health care professionals means that providing such medical expertise within easy reach everywhere is just not possible. Proportionality then becomes an important consideration. Expertise in health, as in other public services and life in general, grows with experience. It is far better to travel a distance to an experienced team of medical specialists for treatment than be treated by a local team with little opportunity to develop experience and expertise. This does not mean that people living in remote parts of Scotland should not have access to the best medical care only that they would not always have it on their doorstep. But they should expect excellent transport infrastructure to allow them easy access to the best medical care. Poor transport between Scotland's islands and the mainland provides a poor health service as well as damages local economies, highlighting once more the inter-connectedness of public services in delivering best outcomes for citizens. Anyone who has moved general practice or met different general practitioners will be aware of the simple fact that because human beings vary, uniform services can never be guaranteed.

There is a difference between these services and direct payments. Direct payments to individuals, such as pensions and welfare benefits, can be applied uniformly. The state pension does not vary from place to place. Payments made directly by public authorities to citizens provide immediate and direct benefits. They cut out the transaction costs involved in other policies and reduce the likelihood of bureaucratic and implementation failures. They also give recipients agency to choose how to spend the payments. Targeted direct payments nonetheless come with costs and challenges, though universalism comes at greater cost. There has been a tendency to adopt lazy thinking and a lack of honesty in policy making in this area. Scotland needs a serious, mature debate on policies, practices and procedures. Vacuous sloganising has led to unfair policies and failed to address inequalities as evidenced with the council tax freeze and inconsistent Scottish Government positions on winter heating payments.

US Supreme Court Justice Louis Brandeis coined the phrase 'laboratories of democracy' to describe situations in which a 'single courageous state [within the US] may, if its citizens choose, serve as a laboratory; and try novel social and economic experiments without risk to the rest of the country'. There has been some evidence of this in Scotland over the last 25 years but less than might have been expected, as noted by a previous Permanent Secretary referred to in chapter three. Intergovernmental relations are all too often seen as institutions for resolving disputes but should also have a role in policy learning and policy transfer. A decade ago, the late David Donnison, who played a significant role in social policy from the 1960s, reflected that the

> most important policy innovations of the past – the building of the first district general hospitals and subsidised housing, the creation of comprehensive schools, the invention of foster care for children previously consigned to institutions of various kinds – all began in local government, usually in the teeth of opposition from central authorities.

The opportunity to experiment and learn through devolved laboratories of democracy offers great potential, reminiscent of those Donnison referred to from an earlier age.

One view is that the gradual accumulation of devolved competences involves a process towards the end point of independence with any and all additional responsibilities sought. An alternative would be to adopt the principles of subsidiarity and proportionality in relation to more powers, and much could be learned in this respect from the EU. The EU's Open Method of Coordination, defined in the 2000 Lisbon Treaty, involves policy making through sharing best practice, benchmarking and evaluation over time but without legislation. This 'soft law' approach has much to commend it in relations between UK and devolved governments. Subsidiarity is the principle that the central authorities should have a subsidiary function and given only those responsibilities that cannot be performed better at a more local level. Proportionality is the principle that decisions on appropriate levels of decision-making should take account of costs and practicalities. One of the problems we have long known is that subsidiarity and proportionality are highly subjective and interpreted variously. In the 1990s, Margaret Thatcher invoked subsidiarity to defend UK autonomy in decision-making against the EU at the same time that Jacques Delors, then President of the European Commission, embraced subsidiarity when calling for more European decision-making and simultaneously more regional and local decision-making within member states. Around the same time, the Scottish Constitutional Convention linked subsidiarity to the case for a Scottish Parliament and Scottish local authorities insisted the principle meant more power for local government. Translating principles into workable practice requires negotiation and compromise after evidence is provided and reasoned debate occurs. These principles should apply across the system of government and not simply to what should be decided in London and Edinburgh. The logic adopted in the early extension of devolution to include railways, referred to in chapter two, was rooted in subsidiarity and proportionality. There was ample evidence that it made good sense. To move beyond subsidiarity as a slogan requires evidence and explanation.

But this still leaves the bigger question raised by Gordon Brown unresolved. Should power to redistribute wealth be centralised? While it is tempting to argue that such matters should be devolved, allowing more generous levels of welfare in different parts of the state, it means that many people living in other parts of the state will be left behind. This might be a price worth paying if, for example, areas with more generous support act as exemplars and catalysts for change elsewhere. The Scottish Child Payment discussed in the previous chapter is a policy innovation introduced in Scotland that could be extended and adopted in the rest of the UK.

The example of how the movement for the adoption of a living wage has developed exemplifies how local initiatives can become rolled out through example and learning. But there is also the danger of a 'race to the bottom' with competing governments within a state lowering levels of taxation – with consequences for funding public services. Recognising that there are often no easy answers is a good starting point in any such deliberations.

Scotland at the centre

The late Norwegian scholar Stein Rokkan, arguably the leading European authority on territorial politics and government over the latter half of the 20th century, described the centre as 'privileged locations within a territory'. It is their privileged position rather than geographic location that matters. There are many dimensions to this privilege. It may be political, economic and/or cultural. It may be where the central institutions of government, commerce and industry, finance and media are located. Or there may be different or many locations for each or some of these dimensions. Germany is the classic multi-nodal state. Berlin may be the country's capital but Frankfurt is the German financial centre and Munich has a similar status as Berlin in financial affairs. Eight German cities perform better than the European average but London is the only UK city to do so. What makes London stand out is its status as the capital and privileged location across a variety of dimensions. It accounts for around a quarter of UK Gross Value Added compared with Berlin's 4 per cent of Germany's GVA. This is reflected in the media with regional national newspapers. Newspapers with a base outside London capable of offering reports and analysis of events across the state and beyond is a healthy sign in any liberal democracy. Greater cognisance of the diversity of the UK is needed across all public institutions – not only in Government and Parliament but also within broadcasting and wider media, the Bank of England and regulatory bodies. Regional government is no guarantee that this will happen.

The UK is an executive-dominated polity. Reforms that ignore the executive branch of UK Government will have very limited effect. The form the Scottish voice takes in the executive in London needs attention. Some believe that having an embassy of an independent state in London will be sufficient though that would leave it in a similar position to the UK in relation to the EU as a rule taker rather than a rule maker. So long as Scotland remains part of the UK, an indisputable case exists that it should have a voice inside, not on the sidelines of UK central policy making and not the chance appointment of Scottish MPs to Cabinet. The Scotland Office cannot always perform the function of being Scotland's voice for the same reason that the Scottish Office could not – its Ministers are appointed on the basis of a UK-wide mandate and appointed by the Prime Minister regardless of support in Scotland. The office of Secretary of State for Scotland is much diminished post-devolution. Little attention had been paid to this and attention is now required. This need not mean a more powerful Scotland Office but better means of feeding Scottish opinion into Whitehall. The choice needs to be broader than having a Scottish Embassy in London lobbying on behalf of an independent Scotland or a Scottish voice inside the heart of government appointed by a Prime Minister who has little support in Scotland. But such means need to be based on tackling specific issues. Regularity is less important than relevance.

Scotland will continue to be directly affected by decisions made in London regardless of Scotland's constitutional status just as the UK is learning that decisions made in the EU continue to affect the UK. In 1969, Pierre Trudeau famously compared Canadian–US relations as like sleeping with an elephant, 'No matter how friendly and even-tempered is the beast, if I can call it that, one is affected by every twitch and grunt'. Scotland finds itself in a similar situation. That might be taken as an argument for or against independence but it is evidence that Scotland cannot be insulated from decisions made in London. Constitutional independence is not economic independence. One of the problems with the current constitutional arrangements is that Scotland lacks consistent political clout at the centre. As noted in a previous chapter, debate on devolution tended to focus on giving democratic voice in Scotland to Scots but neglected how the Scottish voice would be heard in London after devolution.

Defenders of the status quo may point to the House of Commons and the 650 MPs from geographical constituencies as evidence that territory is well represented. The argument might be put that Scottish MPs could work with MPs from other parts of the UK where a common interest exists. These arguments would be more convincing if the UK did not have an executive-dominated system of government and a strong whipping system in the Commons whereby the governing party's interests almost always trump geography. One of the weaknesses of the Commons' electoral system is that large tracts of the country may periodically be shut out of decision-making or be taken for granted. A winning party can devise a successful electoral strategy by focusing on where most seats are concentrated and ignoring or at least de-prioritising the rest. The case for electoral reform for the Commons has been well rehearsed but less often considered in terms of the geographic dimension. A good system should be one that encourages parties seeking to form or be part of a government to be competitive in every part of the country. A range of options exist but if electoral reform becomes a serious proposition again then this dimension merits attention.

One consequence of devolution was the reduction in the number of Scottish MPs in the Commons – down from 72 pre-devolution to 57 now (compared with 543 in England; 32 in Wales; and 18 in Northern Ireland) as the quota of electors for each constituency became the same in Scotland as in England. All constituencies have an electorate within 5 per cent of a quota (with the exception of Orkney and Shetland, Na h-Eileanan an Iar, Ynes Mon and two seats allocated to the Isle of Wight). Unless Scotland's relative population share improves then the number of Scottish MPs will continue to decline. It is difficult to argue against this but without other reforms this puts the idea of the UK as a Union of Nations in danger. As the Commons has become the chamber representing population, there is now a need for a chamber representing territories.

Little thought had been given to how Scottish business should be addressed in the Commons post-devolution beyond a reduction in the number of Scottish MPs. The Calman Commission report in 2012 recommended closer working relations not only between governments in Edinburgh and London but also between the Scottish Parliament and Westminster, with 'mutual respect' as the guiding principle. It recommended the establishment of a standing joint liaison committee of the UK and Scottish Parliaments to oversee relations and to consider the establishment of subject-specific ad hoc joint committees. An obvious example of a joint committee would be on Scotland's shameful record of drug deaths. But a joint committee in itself will not be enough. At best it might facilitate serious engagement and policy development. Institutions are not in themselves policy solutions or responses, only tools or facilitators when used constructively and focused on the subject that needs to be addressed. If they descend into blame games they will serve no constructive purpose. The tragedy of drug deaths afflicting many communities and families must then be considered jointly and taken out of the blame-game politics of recent years. Too often devolved and central governments have pointed the finger at each other. Joint committees have the potential to improve Parliamentary scrutiny and accountability in areas of shared responsibilities. The McKay Commission, set up by the UK Government to report on the consequences of devolution for the Commons, reported in 2013 and argued for a Devolution Committee in the Commons. The claim that this would mean other committees would be less inclined to scrutinise intergovernmental issues is odd given the lack of engagement other Select Committees have had with serious scrutiny of shared responsibilities. Calman's recommendation has more merit, especially in addressing the accountability gap discussed earlier.

Quasi-federalism and entrenchment

Different variations of federal-type options exist, opening up possibilities that require further debate. The Scottish Liberal Democrats produced a report in March 2014 following up on an earlier report in October 2012. The earlier report noted that the 'biggest hurdle in moving to a federal solution for the UK is the position of England and the lack of appetite, until recently, to discuss and decide how matters of purely English concern should be dealt with' but that 'proposals for home rule all round and federalism do not have to be achieved in one leap'. A set of proposals for Scottish Home Rule, in the liberal tradition, was set out in a book by Ben Thomson, who had spent a career in financial services, with a foreword by former Liberal Democrat leader Menzies Campbell. Thomson advocated a system based on subsidiarity, full fiscal autonomy and mutual respect between different levels of government operating within a written constitution. Full fiscal autonomy would be a step too far as it would leave poorer regions without the ability to provide adequate public services but otherwise these ideas reflect potential cross-party consensus and the book should be read as a useful contribution to debate.

There have also been stirrings on the right. In 2009, David Melding, former Conservative member of the Welsh National Assembly/Senate, produced a book in which he argued that if the UK is to survive to 2020 then the 'Home Nations' needed to be acknowledged in a system of shared 'sovereignty'. The UK has, of course, survived but this work is also worth attention. Britishness, he asserted, needs to 'accommodate the explicit character of Wales, Scotland, Northern Ireland and perhaps sooner than we think, England'. He called for a new settlement that would be federal in nature to replace the 'tacit consent'. His was undoubtedly a minority view in his party but it showed greater awareness of what was needed than found in a succession of Conservative Cabinets in London.

Debate in Wales on the idea of a federation has been more advanced than elsewhere in the UK, explained by the absence of an entrenched binary division as in Scotland and weaker electoral support for Welsh independence. Proposals for 'radical federalism' were drawn up under an agreement between Welsh Labour and Plaid Cymru. In 2021, the then Welsh First Minister Mark Drakeford welcomed the proposals remarking that reform should not be a 'defence of the status quo. It cannot be a surrender to the simplicities of Unionism or Nationalism. It has, instead to be a radical redrawing of the United Kingdom'. Debate on Welsh devolution, including proposals for reforming the Welsh Senate, highlight the kind of thinking needed in Scotland.

A notable report written for Labour during Jeremy Corbyn's leadership by lawyer Sean Griffin, *Remaking the British State* set out a radical model of federalism. The 'progressive federalism' advocated in the report involved a new federal, codified and legally entrenched constitution. The House of Lords, with its hereditary and life peers and bishops would be abolished with a fully elected Senate of the Nations and Regions in its place. The Scottish Parliament, the Welsh Senedd, Northern Ireland Assembly and Greater London Authority would have permanent constitutional status. Combined Regional Authorities in England would also be given permanent constitutional status. A new Council of the Union would be established as the supreme executive body on federal–devolved relations. It would bring heads of each of the governments together, including of the UK Government, and would be accountable to the Senate of the Nations and Regions. Much of this drew on German experience. There was much more to the proposal including an Interparliamentary Committee, proposals allowing for judicial review of primary and secondary legislation passed by Westminster, judicial confirmation hearings by the Senate of the Nations and Regions, a Charter of Workers' Rights, reinvigorated local government and Citizens Assemblies. The report was bold and radical and while much was unlikely to command support even within the Labour Party, it was an important contribution to the debate with elements that could gain broad support.

Another notable contribution was the report of a Commission chaired by Gordon Brown. This report was not simply a constitutional exegesis but started with and was embedded within a political economy critique of the UK. John Prescott's work 40 years ago on the *Alternative Regional Strategy* can be seen as a prelude to this report, combining constitutional, institutional and political economy reforms that recognised the need to tackle regional inequalities. Most of the commentary on and criticism of the Brown report focused on some or other recommendation with little appreciation of the central critique contained in the first section. This omission in critiques was astonishing given that the political economy element was crucial to the second part containing reform recommendations. The cause of a geography of discontent was an 'outdated neo-liberal economic dogma' combined with an 'unreformed, over-centralised' system of government. Covid had cruelly exposed weaknesses. The 'starting point' for any reform, the Brown report insisted, was a 'modern system of decision-making that does not start from the top – but starts from the people and is grounded in new ways of consulting, participating, and deciding'. This thinking exemplifies what John Smith had referred to back in 1992, discussed in chapter one, regarding the 'significant sociological shift' from subjects to citizens. The Brown report recognised that devolution on its own was not enough. And it recognised that many failings were to be found at the centre.

The Brown report asserted that the UK constitution was not 'neutral'. The UK was imbalanced, with many people feeling left behind, ignored and marginalised. It noted that the sense of alienation from London Government that had led to support for Scottish or Welsh independence/more powers was little different from the legitimate grievances expressed by many people in parts of England – the manifestation of this may differ but the source was the same. Drawing heavily on the work of regional economists, it set out the nature of imbalances. Half of the UK's population lives in areas no better off than poorer parts of the former East Germany. Half the population lives in areas where people are poorer than the poorest states in the USA. Gross imbalances were evident in a range of statistics set out in the report: 72 per cent of new research and development hubs were concentrated in London and the South East of England where 45 per cent of all private investment was concentrated. Double the average UK infrastructure per capita was spent there. It also had damaging consequences for London and the South East, creating congestion and house price inflation. This had not come about by accident but had been encouraged by public policy that stifled potential in other parts of the UK and contributed to legitimate grievances. The report argued for something bolder than 'Levelling Up'.

Entrenching the constitutional status of devolved bodies, providing a permanent voice in an Assembly of Nations and Regions as a reformed second chamber and a range of proposals for other institutions to allow for meetings to consult, coordinate, learn and take joint action were included in the report. The idea of a second chamber at Westminster that would represent a 'distinctive regional dimension' had been referred to in a speech by Robin Cook back in 2002. As Cook then noted, the form this took differed across the world: from Australia, where direct elections occurred; to systems in which elections are conducted by the regional parliaments, as in the Netherlands, Austria and India; or the German Bundesrat, consisting of representatives appointed by German Länder. The Brown proposals were for direct elections and would facilitate the prospect of devolved bodies operating as 'laboratories of democracy' which, as we have argued, has not been fully realised. Brown made a series of recommendations involving the empowerment of towns, cities and regions. His focus was largely on England but the same principles apply equally to governance within Scotland. It was altogether an attempt to marry political economy analysis, constitutional and everyday public policy concerns.

The idea of a reformed second chamber representing the nations and regions of the UK has been raised occasionally over the years. Supporters of federalism have pointed to the need for a chamber representing the component parts of the UK. The idea has had less appeal amongst devolutionists than might be expected largely because of difficulties inherent in the asymmetrical nature of devolved government. There were tentative moves in the direction of creating elected regional government across England but this was halted when the North East of England, then thought the most likely English region to support devolution, overwhelmingly rejected the idea in a referendum in 2004. When that happened it was felt that there was little point pursuing the policy elsewhere. Rolling devolution came to a juddering halt in the referendum in which an Assembly was presented as a great White Elephant and there was a demand that money for the proposed Assembly should be used instead for the National Health Service, a campaign in which Dominic Cummings developed skills and arguments later deployed in the Brexit referendum. This failure was at least partly due to an attempt to impose an Assembly without adequate prior public consultation. Had devolution been rolled out across England then the next step might have been reform of the second chamber. There was little appetite for a comprehensive revision of the constitution that would have linked the various parts. Creating an Assembly or Senate of Nations and Regions to replace the Lords might have required reform of government in England.

Much has changed since then. The experience of 14 years of Conservative Government has had a similar impact on many parts of England as 18 years of Conservative Government from 1979 had on Scotland and Wales. Wales had voted by four to one against devolution in 1979 but recorded a narrow Yes vote in 1997. The North East voted by almost the same margin against devolution in 2004. There may now be scope to further develop existing arrangements to give voice to the North East and across English regions. Two decades on and there is greater appreciation that a symmetrical model has little appeal but also that there is a growing awareness of the need for English voices both in the regions and at the heart of government. Whereas Scottish devolution was opposed in the past by many who represented English regions fearing that a Scottish Assembly or Parliament would give Scotland an advantage, there is now greater awareness of common territorial interests. In June 2023, Greater Manchester Metro-Mayor Andy Burnham spoke of his frustrations with Westminster saying he could understand Scottish sentiments as 'we all have our frustrations about the way Westminster treats the rest of the UK, the regions in England but also Scotland, Wales and Northern Ireland'. The form of regional governance that has emerged is very different from the devolution that had been advocated in the past. It is undeniably messy and very asymmetrical but it is the basis on which any newly emerging system of territorial government across the UK might be based. It makes sense that such reforms are not rushed and that publics in each part of England are fully engaged. It is possible that agreeing that the component nations and regions are represented at the centre, especially in a reformed second chamber of Parliament, may prove easier – though this is not to suggest that this will be without major challenges – than the form regional governance will take in England. But linking debates on combined authorities with such debates opens up possibilities and would be in the interests of Scotland and Wales as much as English regions.

The relationship between the Commons and a reformed second chamber will prove challenging. A more democratic second chamber would have authority currently lacking in a chamber of appointees (leave aside any hereditary element). This creates unease and opposition, in fear that it would make the reformed second chamber more assertive in its relations with the Commons. There would, therefore, need to be formal acceptance that the Commons remained, for most purposes, the primary chamber able to overrule the Chamber of Nations and Regions, except in areas affecting the powers and competences of devolved institutions.

The Scotland Act 2016 stated that devolution would be a 'permanent part of the United Kingdom's constitutional arrangements' and that the Scottish Parliament and Scottish Government would 'not be abolished except on the basis of a decision of the people of Scotland voting in a referendum'. This was an odd provision in a number of ways. First, it asserted permanence then explained how permanence might be removed suggesting an odd understanding of 'permanence'. Second, the assertion of permanence in statute could be superseded by later legislation passed at Westminster however unlikely. Third, leaving aside the legal status of devolved government, the prospect of the Scottish Parliament and Government being abolished without a referendum is politically highly unlikely. Vernon Bogdanor, in his book on devolution published shortly before the 1979 referendum, argued that it was only under 'pathological circumstances' that power could be recovered once devolved to the proposed Scottish Assembly. The supremacy of Parliament at Westminster would 'bear a different and a more attenuated meaning after the setting up of the Assembly'. But this would not prevent the gradual erosion of devolution. This reflects political realities. Any attempt to abolish the Scottish Parliament and Government against the wishes of Scottish majority opinion would create a political crisis. It is difficult to envisage a scenario more likely to lead to Scottish independence. This provision in the 2016 Act was a symbolic but otherwise superfluous gesture. However, the gradual erosion of devolved competences is not only conceivable but has happened with the unanticipated implementation of Brexit. The 2016 Act was unable to stop this erosion.

Brown proposed a solution that drew on UK constitutional history, updated for an era in which an Assembly of Nations and Regions existed. The new second chamber would be empowered to veto any attempt by the Commons to reverse or abolish devolved bodies anywhere in the UK. As the chamber would consist of representatives of the Nations and Regions, this guardianship role would prove more meaningful than the declaratory clause in the Scotland Act 2016. This idea drew on a provision in the Parliament Act 1911 that removed the Lords' power to reject legislation and replaced it with a power to delay. But there was one important exception. The Lords could reject legislation from the Commons that sought to extend the term of a Parliament, in effect providing a veto on a government keeping itself in office by postponing a general election. The Lords might, as happened during the Second World War, allow an extension. As the Brown report noted, 'Paradoxically enough, therefore, the unelected House of Lords acts as a safeguard for democracy in the United Kingdom'. Brown proposed that the new Assembly of Nations and Regions retain this power and is extended to have a veto over other constitutional statutes, which would include efforts to alter devolution. This neat proposal succeeds in being rooted in UK constitutional history and would provide an effective form of entrenchment.

The Sewel Convention currently means that the UK Parliament will normally only legislate on devolved matters with the consent of devolved bodies passing a 'Legislative Consent Motion'. This has been used about 200 times over the last 25 years, including about 100 times by the Scottish Parliament when the SNP has been in government. Holyrood has refused consent on 15 occasions, almost all since 2019 and primarily due to disagreements over Brexit's impact on devolution. Brown proposed that this provision should take statutory form that would be legally binding, making it a legal obligation rather than a convention of the constitution and apply always, removing the 'normally' provision which gave greater scope for Westminster intervention. In addition, the Commons alone would be unable to amend such a legal change or the powers of devolved institutions without also having the support of a reformed second chamber, the Assembly of Nations and Regions.

Conclusion

Machiavelli recommended a *riduzione verso il principio*, a return to first principles, when facing a crisis. Scotland is not facing a crisis, not even close to it but complacency can allow a constitutional crisis to creep up on us. We have witnessed dramatic challenges to democratic institutions even in formerly stable states. The pressure for Scottish independence may have receded but that is no reason to ignore the need for reform. In 1970, Donald Dewar warned, 'With the tide perhaps turning against the SNP there is a temptation to suppress discussion about reform in case this is seen as weakness'. The best time to reform institutions is during a period of relative quiet. The UK should be acknowledged officially as a Union of Nations and Regions and reforms accordingly built on principles, while accepting that reforms must be realistic. There is no blank sheet but there can be a sense of direction informed by principles.

The Brown report referred to the UK as a 'Union of Nations' and that this should be 'laid out in a new constitutional statute'. A statute of this kind cannot change much on its own. It would be expressive rather than justiciable; in other words it would send out a political signal rather than be enforceable through the courts. But that does not make it entirely pointless. A political signal is appropriate given the UK's 'political constitution' but more important will be changed behaviour. It was clear even in the early days of devolution that the establishment of the Scottish Parliament was seen across Whitehall as an event completed rather than an ongoing process requiring changed attitudes at the centre. Something akin to a 'federal culture' did not develop but its absence only became obvious later. As well as statute, emphasis on the importance of acknowledging the 'Union of Nations' would need to be spelled out clearly in the Cabinet Manual which sets out guidance, rules and procedures for the operation of government.

Efforts to impose, or be perceived to impose, symmetry in the UK will prove counter-productive and there is little reason to believe this will change in the foreseeable future. The language of debate has proved unhelpful. Federalism may come in a great variety of forms but tends to have negative connotations for many. In some respects, the term used to describe the UK is less important than the arrangements themselves but language is important in itself and the idea of a 'Union of Nations' lacks relevance in English regions. This speaks to the Balfour Commission's injunctions on the need to avoid 'thoughtlessness, lack of tact and disregard for sentiment'. The Brown report proposed a reformed second chamber as an 'Assembly of Nations and Regions' though any declaratory statute and embedding of language in official documentation might better refer to the 'Union of Nations and Regions'. The proposal to give the reformed second chamber a new function as guardian of the constitution, able to veto any effort to abolish or reduce devolved powers would provide such declarations with teeth. This leaves open the precise arrangements and prospect of the evolution of devolution in each and any part of the UK.

The responsibilities of the old Scottish Office were the starting point of devolved competences. The problem with this is that these competences had evolved piecemeal with little overarching rationale. The Scottish Office was part of UK central government and operated within that framework. There was no consideration of any major debates or understanding of which policy types would appropriately be devolved to a Scottish Parliament at each and every extension of administrative devolution. This cannot be reversed as there was no prospect, nor is there any prospect now, of constitution-making with a blank sheet. But greater balance needs to be struck between constitutional principles and constitutional ad hocery in future.

CHAPTER 5

Reforming Holyrood and Scottish Governance

The Scottish Parliament is quite distant from front line service delivery. That is a real issue... the next phase of devolution, whether or not we head for Independence, has to be getting the Parliament and the Scottish government closer to the realities of the pressures at the frontline, of service delivery and looking at some of these really tough issues about joining up health and social care.

Dr Robert Black, former Scottish Auditor General, 14 July 2014

Introduction

IN THIS CHAPTER we focus on reform of Holyrood and the wider governance of Scotland. Over the last decade, public debate has focused on Scotland's constitutional status. Parliamentary reform, relations with local government, the world of Non-Departmental Public Bodies (NDPBS), whole system approaches to governance, the role of publics and communities all require more consideration. Scotland now needs the same intense focus and debate on these matters as has been had on its constitutional status over the last decade. We need to consider Scotland's other constitution, its internal structures and operation within and beyond the Scottish Parliament and Government. Much was achieved by the establishment of the Scottish Parliament. But there is room for improvement. There are wider issues of governance that require our attention too. From the perspective of the citizen, as the late Robert Black's comment above made clear, it is at local level that decision-making is experienced. And to understand Scottish government requires engagement with questions of delivery.

As noted previously, changing an institution once established is difficult. Hannah White refers to the Commons as 'privileging tradition over innovation'. It might be thought that this should not be a problem in Holyrood given its relative youth but invented or inherited traditions can become embedded in a new institution within a short period of time. Time is not the issue so much as vested interests. Proposals for reform will come up against powers that benefit from limited oversight and scrutiny, from an executive branch that would be wary of a more assertive Parliament.

We start by considering Holyrood, which lies at the heart of Scottish politics. In one of the classic studies of comparative legislatures, Gary Copeland and Samuel Patterson identified three functions of any legislature: linkage; decision-making; and legitimacy. Hannah White in her study of the Commons noted its four functions: enabling government to pass laws; holding government to account; providing a forum for national debate; and representing the views and concerns of constituents. Together these observations on the functions of Parliament are a useful way of considering reforms for Holyrood. The Scottish Parliament differs from the House of Commons in ways discussed in chapter two but in practice it is a Westminster-style Parliament even if it does not have all the characteristics associated with Westminster. There is a concentration of power in the executive. But Holyrood is elected by a system that provides greater proportionality. While formal institutional differences exist, the practical effects have been more limited than many supporters anticipated.

Legislatures exist along a spectrum from 'arena' to 'transformative', to borrow terms used by American political scientist Nelson Polsby. The Chinese National People's Congress, with about 3,000 members, only meets for a couple of weeks each year to endorse whatever the Chinese leadership has decided and lies at the arena end of the spectrum. US Congress has long been viewed as lying at the other end as it has real power and has been very much involved in decision-making, capable of transforming proposals from the executive branch – though less so of late. The UK and Scottish Parliaments lie together on that spectrum, much further from the transformative end than the Scottish Constitutional Convention hoped though the 1997 white paper setting out the Labour Government's position stated that the 'relationship between the Scottish Executive and the Scottish Parliament will be similar to the relationship between the UK Government and the UK Parliament'. Moving the Scottish Parliament along that spectrum will require addressing its linkage and decision-making functions to rebalance the relationship with the Scottish Government. The Parliament will need to improve its capacity to hold the government to account. This is not to suggest that Holyrood can or should become like the US Congress where gridlock occurs when the legislature and executive are unable to agree.

Nor would we want pork-barrel politics that see members adding spending commitments for local electoral purposes that undermine effective policy making. There is plenty of scope for reforms that would move Holyrood along the spectrum without undermining effective government.

Linkage functions include providing the link between the public and the legislators and the link between the legislature and executive. The electoral system is key. Legislatures, as the name makes clear, legislate but Parliaments have wider decision-making functions. Decisions may be made that do not require primary legislation and resolutions may be passed which have little authority but may be expressive, offering a view on a matter that may be beyond the control of the Parliament. And finally, Parliaments provide democratic legitimacy to decision-making.

Reform of Scottish governance would be partial and imbalanced if it focused only on Parliament. Local governance, widely defined, has been neglected. In its reflections on 20 years of devolution, the reconstituted Consultative Steering Group (CSG) expressed disappointment that devolution had weakened local government. The CSG expectation that devolution would 'set us on a path towards a subsidiarity arrangement for local government' has not happened. Despite frequent references to multi-level governance, debate in Scotland has all too often been very narrowly focused. Local government and the extensive world of Non-Departmental Public Bodies (NDPBS) desperately need to be addressed. In *Making Laws that Work: How Laws Fail and How We Can Do Better*, Justice David Goddard of the New Zealand Court of Appeal and leading authority on drafting legislation, emphasised the importance of institutions that implement the law, 'applying it, interpreting it, enforcing it'. What matters, he pointed out, are the 'outcomes that users experience'. The 'user interfaces' of laws passed by Parliaments are the institutions through which implementation occurs and 'touch the lives of affected citizens', which are 'at least as important as the content of the legislation itself'. Passing a law cannot on its own make the world better. What he refers to as the 'Harry Potter' approach to law – 'wave a magic (legislative) wand and the problem is solved' appeals to some politicians. Pronouncements and grand speeches are all too easily delivered. Delivering improved outcomes is much more challenging.

The classic account of why implementation goes wrong was first published in 1973. Pressman and Wildavsky's study *Implementation* had a lengthy subtitle that summed up the theme of how well-intentioned policy can go wrong:

> How great expectations are dashed in Oakland [the focus of the study]; or, why it's amazing that Federal programs work at all, this being a saga of the Economic Development Administration as told by two sympathetic observers who seek to build morals on a foundation of ruined hopes.

The road to hell is paved with good intentions. The importance of thinking through the processes from announcing a policy to implementation is vital. Good policy making takes account of the importance of local government, the range of institutions in communities across Scotland and the central role of citizens. It requires the involvement, from the outset, of those involved at the 'coal face', who have expertise that is lacking or limited at the centre. Scotland has suffered from top-down pronouncements designed more to deliver headlines than improved outcomes. We have had too many 'Harry Potter' laws over the last decade.

Restored but fragile legitimacy

It is important to include the one function Hannah White omitted when we consider the Scottish Parliament's achievements. A system of government requires more than operating within the law to attain legitimacy. Its actions need to be justifiable, reasonable and have public consent. The pre-devolution system of government lacked legitimacy from this perspective. This was commonly referred to as a 'democratic deficit' though should more accurately have been described as a legitimacy deficit. There was nothing illegal in the system of government so much as a growing sense that decisions made by the Scottish Office lacked public consent and were often deemed by a majority of Scots to be unjustified. One of the unsung achievements of devolution was that it closed a legitimacy gap in Scottish politics. Sharp differences of opinion on Scotland's constitutional status and on most policies remain but few challenge the legitimacy of devolved institutions. We may not like, even strongly oppose, particular policies but there is little doubt that the system has legitimacy. Devolution broadly works well; it is particulars that are not working as envisaged or as they should.

While devolution appears secure there is reason to believe that challenges to its legitimacy might arise. Nothing should be taken for granted. In 2023, the Scottish Social Attitudes survey found a sharp decline in the proportion of people who trusted the Scottish Government to work in

Scotland's best interests, down from 61 per cent in 2019 to 47 per cent. There was also a decline from 56 per cent to 45 per cent in the proportion who thought the Scottish Parliament gave 'ordinary people more say in how Scotland is governed'. There should be no comfort in the much lower proportion of 21 per cent who said they trusted the UK Government to work in Scotland's best long-term interests, up from 15 per cent in 2019. The British Social Attitudes Survey, published in June 2024, recorded a record high 45 per cent of people who 'almost never' trusted any party and 79 per cent believed that the system of government could be improved quite a lot or a great deal. The CSG, re-assembled to offer reflections on 20 years of devolution, observed Holyrood debates were driven by 'party political tribalism' more than they had expected. This tribalism has done little to distinguish Holyrood from the Commons or to win support amongst the Scottish public. If devolved government is to regain high levels of acceptance, then a period of reflection, discussion and reform is needed. There is no reason to assume that growing disenchantment and distrust will be reversed without remedial action. And it contributes to distrust and an environment which populists can exploit.

Linkage with the electorate

More women were elected in the first elections to the Scottish Parliament in 1999 than all women previously elected as Scottish MPs. The highest proportion of women (58 MSPs – 46 per cent of the total) were returned at the 2021 election, lower than the proportion elected to the London Assembly of 52 per cent but higher than the 40 per cent of women MPs elected at the 2024 UK general election. Only six countries in the world today have achieved 50 per cent or more women in Parliament. Six current MSPs are of Asian heritage. One is a wheelchair user. A variety of languages were used when MSPs were sworn in: English, Gaelic, Punjabi, Zimbabwean Shona, Urdu and Sign Language. There has been commendable progress in making Holyrood more representative, a vast improvement on what had gone before.

But the process of choosing candidates by political parties remains fairly obscure, despite the fact that becoming a party's candidate is often tantamount to becoming an MSP. The selectorate and the processes used in the choice of candidates require far more attention than has been the case hitherto. Over 60 years ago, one of the great post-war American political scientists EE Schattschneider remarked that whoever 'has the power to make the nomination owns the party'. Given that nomination and selection processes have such an impact on who governs it is extraordinary that so little attention is paid to the processes of selecting MSPs or other elected representatives. In his book on *How Westminster Works...and Why It Doesn't*, Ian Dunt noted that the British press spends more time covering the Iowa caucus in the US than it does on any pre-election procedures in the UK. That may be changing, as evidenced by work on the selection of candidates for the 2024 general election by journalist Michael Crick. It would be beneficial if more attention was paid to this in Scotland especially given the opportunities to manipulate the List element. We know that selection processes can be rigged in favour of candidates who are more likely to toe the leadership's line; at the same time, they have the power to ensure that minorities are represented. Labour's adoption of twinning constituencies in the first elections to the Scottish Parliament ensured that exactly 50 per cent of Labour MSPs were women. As Professor Meryl Kenny has shown, even when formal rules are instituted to bring about fair representation, these can be undermined by informal practices. As she put it, 'masculinized practices of local patronage and the privileging of favourite sons' have 'detrimental effects on the representation of women and other under-represented groups'.

When Donald Dewar delivered the Brough annual lecture at Paisley University in November 1997 he welcomed one Scottish employer's decision to encourage employees to stand for the Scottish Parliament, 'I am keen to ensure that high quality candidates come forward from all parties.' But candidate selection processes did not encourage that to happen. Very small numbers of people are involved in candidate selection. There have been well-documented instances in recent years of MSPs who are out of favour with a party's leadership being effectively de-selected through rules that look on face value to be designed to achieve greater representativeness but are used in practice to remove independent-minded MSPs. Joan McAlpine, former newspaper editor and SNP List MSP, wrote about her experience as an MSP who occasionally disagreed with her leader on some issues and was 'forced out' of Parliament by an 'equalities mechanism'. Her party's leadership imposed new rules without the authority of the party's annual conference. In an article in the *Sunday Post* in April 2023, she explained that she had been subjected to additional vetting and despite still getting through the first stage in the process of seeking renomination, she lost out to a candidate with less support due to changes designed to empower the leadership's favoured candidates. Her party's leadership had been given advice that its approach might be illegal. McAlpine declined to challenge the process through the courts, as she might have done. This might be one of the most egregious examples but by no means the only case and it is not restricted to any one political party. It would be wrong to insist that all parties adopt the same process of selection. Each party may place greater weight on different criteria for selection but all parties ought to adopt greater transparency and fairness in their processes of candidate selection. Term limits have been suggested and are worth considering though they would come at the cost of losing MSPs who have gained experience and are themselves repositories of institutional memory. The counter to that is that an influx of fresh blood might bring fresh thinking with Members not tied to old practices.

This also applies to councillors, though one of the greatest challenges is often getting people to stand for election to local government. The most recent survey of Scottish local councillors, released by the Scottish Local Authorities Remuneration Committee (SLARC) in February 2024, addressed barriers to elected office. It showed that councillors were unrepresentative with regard to women, younger people and people with a disability: 36 per cent of councillors are women (cf 52 per cent of the population); 56 per cent are over 55 years old (cf 39 per cent of the Scottish population); 17 per cent are disabled (cf 20 per cent of the population); though the ethnic make-up of councillors broadly reflected the population as a whole. COSLA's Barriers to Elected Office Special Group concluded that there were many reasons for this disproportional representation. Remuneration, childcare and the reputation of politics puts many people off. The aforementioned tribalism and aggressive form of party politics also discourages candidates. Personal safety, especially online abuse, was highlighted. The demands of being a councillor do not sit well with family or caring responsibilities, issues that are an impediment to standing in the first place and consequently a reason many councillors have stood down after only one term. Career considerations have proved an obstacle, especially amongst young people. Financial barriers were key problems encountered by a number of disabled councillors. Gaining employment alongside being a disabled councillor has proved an impediment to taking on or remaining a councillor. It is no surprise that such a high proportion of councillors are older, often retired, with more time available. Remuneration is poor given the time and commitment involved.

While the parties often provide support and training for prospective candidates, there is a perceived need to tackle the bullying and misogyny, along with other examples of poor behaviour, which act as deterrents. The nature of being a councillor, MSP or MP requires extensive engagement with the community. Elected representatives are expected to be available. Some councillors quoted in the SLARC report expressed a concern that they might be pilloried for making legitimate expense claims for taxis on dark, wet evenings for example. Not only has the rise of social media changed the nature of work but cuts in local spending and the tendency of Scottish central government to pile more responsibilities and demands on local authorities without compensating resources, has made being a councillor more challenging and less rewarding. The creation of new bodies post-devolution, such as the Integration Joint Boards covering health and social care, added complexity and new demands. Legislation requiring participatory budgeting and community asset transfers have been widely welcomed but again have arrived with inadequate attention to the impact on the role of councillors. The introduction of STV elections, discussed in chapter two, has also had implications. This has led in some instances to members of the public contacting more than one ward councillor resulting in duplication of effort, though it has helped with representativeness (by party though not necessarily other criteria). But unrepresentativeness has not been restricted to elected representatives. As research in the early 1990s had shown, only 18 per cent of appointees to Quangos were female. More monitoring of this has taken place since devolution. Legislation passed in 2018 set a target of 50 per cent of women on public boards in non-executive positions in Scotland. By the end of 2022, 130 listed public bodies (68 per cent) had achieved the target. While this gender scrutiny is welcome there needs to be much broader scrutiny of the appointment process given the range of responsibilities, powers and funding of Quangos.

MSPs have developed innovative ways of engaging with the public over the last quarter century. The Citizens Participation and Public Petitions Committee has been at the centre of this activity in Holyrood but the committee is not the sole means through which MSPs engage with the public. Each committee makes an effort, where appropriate, to engage with the public and MSPs cannot fail to have some public engagement, whether through constituency work, attending meetings or the usual gamut of community activities in areas they represent. The extent to which some of this work should be channelled elsewhere, notably to local councillors, is debatable but the visibility of Holyrood means that MSPs will often be the first port of call for aggrieved citizens. Sensible practices were developed in the early years of the Parliament regarding how constituency and list MSPs should cooperate but relations with local councillors vary considerably. In a system of multi-level democracy, there needs to be mutual respect between elected representatives at all levels, not least as this contributes towards public respect and legitimacy.

The electoral system is important in this linkage function, as we have noted. This had been thoroughly debated within the Constitutional Convention and developed by a Commission established by the Convention. Agreement was initially reached on the need for an alternative to first-past-the-post (FPTP). This had been a major step forward for the Labour Party given that FPTP had long given Labour a great advantage. The next step was to identify key principles. These principles were set out in the Convention document *Towards Scotland's Parliament* in 1990:

- that it produces results in which the number of seats for various parties is broadly related to the number of votes cast for them;
- that it ensures, or at least takes effective positive action to bring about, equal representation of men and women, and encourages fair representation of ethnic and minority groups;
- that it preserves a real link between the member and his/her constituency;
- that it is as simple as possible to understand;
- that it ensures adequate representation of less populous areas; and
- that the system be designed to place the greatest power in the hands of the electorate.

No electoral system could meet all of these laudable criteria; the next stage required prioritisation and trade-offs. The mixed Additional Member System (AMS) was adopted as a workable compromise. It was more proportional, retained constituencies and was reasonably simple to understand. Equal representation was more a matter for the parties and the selectorate, as noted above, than the electoral system. Less populous areas were no less well represented than had been the case under Westminster. Giving voters a constituency and list vote gave them more choice but fell short of giving them the choice that other systems offered. An enquiry into different constituency boundaries for the Commons and the Scottish Parliament reported in 2008 proposing that the List system should be open, that is that voters would be able not only to choose from a list of candidates but also choose between individual candidates. It also recommended consideration of introducing Single Transferable Vote (STV) for the Scottish Parliament. STV encourages competition not only between parties but within parties. Its primary function is not, as commonly asserted, to create greater party proportionality, though that can happen, but to offer voters more choice. A voter with a strong affiliation to a party may not be enamoured by the selected candidate but under STV would have the opportunity – as it will often be possible, depending on the number of seats in any constituency – to choose between candidates for the same party or indeed for voters to express preferences that need not all be from the same party.

According to Ian Dunt, in his aforementioned book on Westminster, FPTP has four consequences: it reduces scrutiny; increases tribalism; corrupts policy making; and allows the two main parties to 'amass complete executive power on the basis of a minority of the popular vote'. The Westminster system, he argues, aims 'remorselessly to crush and eradicate independent judgement'. AMS in Holyrood has done little, if anything, to address these four weaknesses. If anything, the hierarchies of the parties have more control of elected members given their control of the rules governing the Lists. There is a case for further reform, though with realistic expectations. An electoral system cannot be expected to eradicate all weaknesses. The criteria set out by the Constitutional Convention provided a reasonable set of principles, even if they cannot all be found in any electoral system. There is also a case for initiating debate on whether and what alternative reforms might be suitable, incorporating informed public opinion through means of a deliberative assembly or similar arrangement. We now have had the experience of STV in local elections since 2007, AMS since 1999 and FPTP from much earlier to help inform any debate. More radical ideas might be considered. In 2009, the English Conservatives experimented with open primaries in a small number of constituencies, allowing voters to choose candidates from a short list chosen by the party hierarchy. Dr Sarah Wollaston, a local general practitioner, was chosen and won Totnes the following year. However, her defection to the Liberal Democrats in 2019 would likely make all parties see open primaries as a step too far.

As well as considering alternative voting systems, there is a need to think about how to encourage MSPs to be more independent and more constructive. In his reflections on experience as an MSP, left-wing Labour Neil Findlay recounts how he, Jackson Carlaw of the Tories and Alex Neil of the SNP worked constructively together on the issue of mesh implants. It was, he stated, 'an indictment of the way the parliament works that we are treated as such a novelty for this'. This collaboration may have been possible because each was confident in their core beliefs and none feared accusations of 'selling out'. Margo MacDonald and Dennis Canavan were significant independent voices in Holyrood. Margo's independence cost her a high place on the SNP's List in 2003 but her public profile and popularity meant she was able to be elected as a List MSP in 2003, 2007 and 2011. Dennis managed to win his constituency seat as an Independent from 1999 until he retired at the 2007 election. While a Parliament of Margos and Dennis's might be difficult to manage, Holyrood benefits from having such independent voices.

One of the most significant examples of members from a range of parties working well together came in reaction to the ill-thought-out policy on gender recognition. The failure of the Sturgeon Government to pay heed to legitimate concerns and warnings from women MSPs across Holyrood and campaigners outside resurrected cross-party campaigning that had not been seen since the successful advocacy to ensure women were better represented in the devolved Parliament than had historically been the case in Scottish politics. This cross-party cooperation was a better reflection of the kind of politics the founders had hoped for rather than the top-down antithesis that has commonly marked Scottish devolved politics.

Governing would become very difficult if this was taken too far with too many independent MSPs but there is ample scope for more independent-minded MSPs without endangering good government. More independent-minded MSPs can help improve government by raising questions, issues and concerns that would otherwise not be raised, and act as early warning systems of poor policy development. Members are representative of their parties but also their constituencies and regions. We have recently seen some MSPs of the governing SNP assert themselves in exasperation having been ignored or traduced by the leadership. It has not helped that parties are accused of being 'split' whenever there are internal differences, often by the same people who demand that MSPs show greater independence. More openness and honesty about differences within parties would help. The tendency to pathologise internal party differences undermines good government. The common assertion that political parties are 'broad churches' is less often evident in how they operate in Holyrood. The late Margo MacDonald, former SNP and later Independent MSP, brought a plant sprayer into the chamber and would ostentatiously bring it out and mockingly pretend to use it whenever she detected a planted question from a backbencher intended to help a front bench party colleague. A more relaxed attitude is unlikely to be adopted by whips or front benches though MSPs may become more assertive if a career path, other than achieving Ministerial office, was available along with more open candidate selection processes.

Participants in Holyrood debates are often decided by party whips. Lists of approved MSPs are submitted and allocations made to each party depending on the number of seats held by each party. The Presiding Officer simply names the speakers from the order on lists supplied. This means that dissident backbenchers, often with more interesting contributions, struggle to be called as the lists tend to fill the allocated time for debate. This makes life much easier for the Presiding Officer but it also adds to the staged nature of debate and undermines the role of MSPs as individuals with minds of their own. There may be lessons from other Westminster-type Parliaments. In Canada, for example, a previous Speaker challenged the Government whips by telling elected Members that they should not feel constrained by party whips when it came to making statements or asking Questions. The Government Whip hit back stating that the Speaker was a 'referee' and it was the prerogative of the parties to 'coach' or decide which 'player to play at any given time'. Presiding Officers (POs) can stamp their authority on Parliament, within limits, and Holyrood would benefit from more assertive POs. The limited amount of time available for Members to make a speech in the chamber allows more MSPs to contribute but prevents the development of arguments. Quantity of speakers over quality of speeches has resulted. Change is required to improve debate.

Linkage with the Scottish Government and its agencies

As a Westminster-style Parliament, the executive is chosen from within the membership of Holyrood. Bernard Crick and David Millar, in their previously mentioned proposals before devolution, recommended that not more than ten members should at any one time be Scottish Government Ministers. There were initially nine members of the first Scottish Cabinet (the Lord Advocate and Chief Whip also attended) plus ten junior Ministers, excluding the law officers. The numbers crept up until 2007 when Alex

Salmond appointed six Cabinet members. John Swinney's Cabinet in 2024 consists of 11 members (plus the Lord Advocate and the Minister for Parliamentary Business) with 14 junior Ministers, down from 18 under Nicola Sturgeon. The growth in devolved responsibilities over the last quarter century might be expected to lead to an increase in the number of Ministers but the number is nonetheless large. There is no Holyrood equivalent to the legal maximum of paid Ministers under the Ministerial and Other Salaries Act, 1975 at Westminster, which includes a limit on the number of Ministers sitting in the Commons. There are also Parliamentary Liaison Officers (PLOs) in Holyrood, who replaced Ministerial Aides in 2007, whose function, defined in the Scottish Ministerial Code, is to 'support the Cabinet Secretary in the discharge of their Parliamentary duties' who are expected to be loyal supporters of the Government. PLOs were able to serve on Parliamentary committees until a change of rules in 2016. As with Parliamentary Private Secretaries at Westminster, PLOs are seen as part of the 'payroll vote' on whom the Government can always rely for support. Appointments, requiring First Ministerial approval, are seen as the first rung on the Ministerial ladder. Taken together, Ministers and PLOs plus the leadership's control of committee appointees, especially with aggressively assertive leaders, reduces the number of backbenchers able to operate with autonomy.

The dual functions of the Lord Advocate – as head of the independent prosecution services and principal legal adviser to the Scottish Government – is an anomaly that has persisted as it had not been seen as a problem until recently. In recent years there have been calls for the two roles to be separated. The Venice Commission of the Council of Europe recommends ensuring that state prosecution systems act independently of Parliament and Government. Justice not only must be done but must be seen to be done and separating the roles removes any suggestion of impropriety. While nobody has questioned the professionalism of successive Lord Advocates, it is important that there should be no prospect or even the appearance of a conflict of interest in these two functions. This would require legislation at Westminster to permit the Scottish Parliament to make the change. A Bill to this effect was presented in the Commons in January 2024 by former SNP MP Joanna Cherry KC but did not progress. There now needs to be progress on this matter.

The number of Special Advisers (SPADs) has grown in British politics. SPADs play an important role in adding a 'political dimension to the advice and assistance available to Ministers', according to the Scottish Government's 'Code of Conduct for Special Advisers' but there is little transparency in appointments, their qualifications and how they operate. There are now too few SPADs with policy expertise. Too many owe their position to loyalty to the leader and/or their communication skills. A policy specialist can be expected to offer quite different advice from someone focused on presentation. As decisions made are the responsibility of Ministers, who will take account of party political, including electoral and communication concerns, the role of the policy adviser is best seen as operating independently of such considerations. One area that requires attention is accountability. At present, the Code of Conduct states that SPADs are 'accountable to Scottish Ministers, who in turn are accountable to the Scottish Parliament'. It is, however, no secret that SPADs often act as gatekeepers on matters such as Freedom of Information requests and have considerable influence inside Government, with some having greater access to the First Minister and senior Cabinet Ministers than junior Ministers, not to mention backbench MSPs. This is not to suggest that SPADs should be banned, only that they should be brought out of the shadows. Crick and Millar's proposal, referred to previously, had included a Public Appointments Committee. If that was to be considered for NDPB appointments, as they suggested, then it would make sense to extend this to SPADs. At present, SPADs have power with little responsibility or accountability, an unacceptable situation in a liberal democracy.

The range of interactions in the budgetary process that a legislature has with the executive branch provides great insight into the legislature/executive relationships. Parliamentary roles include setting tax and spending priorities as well as scrutiny. It is widely accepted that Westminster has weak budgetary influence compared with other advanced liberal democracies. David Heald, a leading authority on budgetary processes in the UK, explained how the executive branch dominated the budgetary process in evidence to a Commons Select Committee enquiry in 2016. The Government had a 'vast advantage'. There were well established practices of leaking and planting before budgetary statements. The Treasury Committee was overstretched resulting in an inability to function continuously and effectively as a spending and tax committee. The Scottish Parliament is even weaker despite good intentions at the outset of devolution as discussed below. Insufficient changes have occurred to take account of Holyrood's increased fiscal powers. One suggestion made by tax experts Charlotte Barbour and Moira Kelly was that Holyrood should introduce a tax committee allowing MSPs to develop specialist expertise and ensure sufficient time is made available to scrutinise taxation.

There are a number of dimensions to fiscal scrutiny and accountability. Joachim Wehner, a leading scholar of Parliamentary budget processes, identified a number of factors that affect the institutional powers and capacity of legislatures in this crucial area. These include the extent to which a legislature can amend budgets; whether a legislature can hold up a budget; whether the executive can make changes within budget with or without limited approval of the legislature; and the time available to scrutinise budgets and prepare a response (three months is regarded as international good practice); and the access a legislature has to budgetary information. Westminster-style systems lie towards the bottom end of international leagues of liberal democratic legislatures for their capacity in this area and this is certainly true of Holyrood. In part this is a result of decisions made in London that arrive late with insufficient time for the Scottish Government to produce its budget, thereby limiting Holyrood's scrutiny capacity. This is an area in which reforms are required both at Westminster and Holyrood. The implications of the sharp turnaround in timing not only affect Holyrood's ability to engage with the budgetary process but also leaves little time for local authorities and others to determine budgets.

In 1998, the UK Government established the Financial Issues Advisory Group (FIAG) to inform the operation of the Scottish Parliament which set out a series of budgetary objectives:

- providing opportunities for the Parliament to comment on expenditure priorities and to influence the Governments' preparation of budgets;
- providing the opportunity for the public to have the opportunity to put their views to subject committees, as well as individual MSPs at an early stage in the process;
- providing sufficient time for the Parliament to consider and debate proposals fully;
- providing balance between the requirement for parliamentary scrutiny and the needs of the Executive;
- providing some degree of certainty so that ongoing activities can continue without prolonged uncertainty;
- providing an efficient mechanism to deliver motions to be debated

by the Parliament;

- providing a meaningful role for subject committees and the Finance Committee;
- delivering timeous decisions on tax-varying powers and the budget (as well as the interim spending approval and budget amendments);
- engaging all MSPs;
- facilitating the Executive's formulation of proposals; and
- providing for the right of amendment.

These principles remain important and together offer a guide for reform.

In 2017, the Budget Process Review Group (BPRG), established jointly by the Scottish Parliament and Government, concluded that scrutiny required a broader understanding of decision-making. The BPRG felt that there was little consideration of long-term impacts and little on outcomes of budget decisions or prevention from the Government. It argued for a more strategic approach, with scrutiny taking place all year round rather than squeezed into a few weeks. The interaction of components of budgets required more attention – revenues, spending, borrowing and reserves should not be seen in isolation. Budgets' impact on economic performance should be taken into consideration to a greater extent. Increased responsibilities and increased complexity ought to be accompanied by comparable increased resourcing and time for scrutiny. Various efforts have been made to lay down principles which should govern budgetary processes. Evidence from the Chartered Institute for Public Finance and Accountancy (CIPFA) to the 2017 review of budgetary processes recommended a budgetary process that allowed for long-term financial planning, linking financial decisions to improving outcomes through Programmes for Government, ongoing year-on-year monitoring of budgets and meaningful public engagement. There needs to be more progress on all of the above. The main innovation following the Group's work was the Medium-Term Financial Strategy (MTFS). The first MTFS was first published in 2018 and set out a medium-term outlook on the sustainability of Scottish public finances. A range of data was required to enhance the Parliament's scrutiny of public finances: the Scottish Government's broad plans over the next five years; forecasts of taxes and spending, including demand-led spending; the impact of different economic scenarios on budgetary affairs; and policies explaining how fiscal powers would be used and managed.

Scrutiny and policy making

One of the most frequently quoted comments on legislatures was made by Woodrow Wilson, 28th President of the USA, in his days as an academic. In his 1885 book *Congressional Government*, Wilson asserted that 'Congress in session is Congress on public exhibition whilst Congress in its committee-rooms is Congress at work'. Committees in many legislatures, including the House of Commons and the Scottish Parliament, are seen as where the real work is done. This was what had been anticipated by the founders of the Scottish Parliament. But Holyrood's committees have proved less effective than hoped for. In his John P Mackintosh Memorial lecture in November 1999, Donald Dewar warned that the committees' agendas should avoid being 'dominated by the morning headlines and their potential for spawning press releases'. His belief was that an effective committee system was the best way of examining legislation and testing government action. Presiding Officer David Steel publicly disagreed with the then First Minister and argued that the Scottish Parliament's legislative system was superior to Westminster's. Experience over time has shown that Dewar was right to be concerned about the weakness of the committee system.

The problem lies with the system as much as with individual MSPs or staff. The all-purpose committees had been established in the expectation that there would be less legislation requiring committee deliberation and therefore more time for policy development and scrutiny of government and its agencies. It had been hoped that combining legislative and scrutiny committees would help develop expertise amongst committee members. But there were unforeseen problems. The committees are unable to devote as much time as initially anticipated to enquiries and agenda setting due to the unexpected volume of legislation passed by Holyrood. A strong case can be made for having separate legislative committees but this would add to MSPs' workload. Separating the functions of committees is probably only feasible by increasing the number of MSPs. There is certain to be public opposition to having 'more politicians' but the choice is clear. Either we accept that Parliament has a limited role in policy making and scrutinising Government or Holyrood is significantly reformed with more MSPs. An argument can be made to that we should simply accept outright that Parliament has very limited scrutiny and policy making capacity but that would undermine the main *raison d'être* of devolution. Two options are worth considering: increasing the number of MSPs or including a small second chamber solely focused on revising legislation. Increasing the number of MSPs might be addressed through cross-party agreement or by an independent Commission. The experience of the last 25 years combined with the growth in responsibilities leaves no obvious alternative. It should be noted that there has been a (small) reduction in the number of Scottish MPs at Westminster without any increase in the number of MSPs. This has been raised for consideration by Murdo Fraser MSP in a thoughtful paper published by Reform Scotland in 2024. There is potential cross-party consensus which could go some way to ensuring Holyrood moves closer to the ideals it originally set itself.

A second elected chamber, smaller than the main chamber, perhaps by Single Transferable Vote, focused on revising legislation is also worth consideration. Political scientists Alan Convery and David Parker have suggested that Scotland might consider a bicameral legislature with regional members populating one Chamber and constituency members the other. Bicameralism is not unusual in sub-state legislatures. All US states but Nebraska are bicameral. In Germany on the other hand, all 16 Land Parliaments are unicameral after Bavaria abandoned its senate in the same year that the Scottish Parliament was formed. Canada has had experience of bicameralism. Four provinces were bicameral but are all now unicameral. The last to abandon bicameralism was New Brunswick in 1992. Graham White, a leading authority on Canadian provincial government remarked that these unelected second chambers in Provincial legislatures proved 'at best benignly useless, at worst obstructionist' to the elected lower House and lacked regional representation. Most were soon abolished. One lesson from this is that the basis of the composition of the second chamber should differ from the first. A case can be made that Scotland's elected local authorities might be represented to ensure that the much-neglected local dimension is given a central place.

There are a variety of arguments in favour of bicameralism. An argument for efficiency is that a second chamber allows the quality of legislation to be improved. A further argument is that bicameralism distributes and balances power, avoiding concentrating power in one chamber or a chamber controlled by the executive branch. A third reason is that a second chamber allows for more variety of representation. A bold idea that has been raised is that a second chamber could be selected by sortition. Sortition involves selection by lot, in a similar way as juries are chosen. Its justification lies in addressing weaknesses in representative democracy which it is claimed offers a mechanism for political accountability but, according to political philosopher Arash Abizadeh, sortition offers a mechanism that provides equality, impartiality and enhances responsiveness. This is likely to be a step too far for Scotland's political parties and would require careful work on implementation but the critique of representative democracy inherent in the case for sortition should be taken into account in any discussion of a second chamber.

There has been no equivalent in Holyrood to the Committee on Reform of the House of Commons, chaired by Tony Wright MP, that was established in 2009. And there has been no equivalent to the reforms seen at Westminster over the last 25 years. There is much to learn from developments in the Commons. Commons Select Committees introduced reforms that are now widely acknowledged to have succeeded in rebalancing the relationship between Parliament and Government. A House of Commons Backbench Business Committee was established, consisting of elected backbenchers responsible for allocating time for debate in the Commons and Westminster Hall. Chairs of Commons Select Committees were elected by secret ballot rather than chosen by party whips for the first time in 2010. Members of Select Committees are also elected. Evidence shows that Committee chairs are now more expert in the relevant policy area and some chairs have been innovative in how they operate. A study by Hannah White of the *Institute for Government* concluded that some chairs had higher profiles than some Cabinet Ministers and that the chair of a select committee determines the committee's impact more than any other factor. Major enquiries were held that helped inform the public on issues such as phone hacking, multinational corporations' tax affairs and standards in banking. It has led to greater demands on staff which requires more resourcing of committees. There is an argument for excluding Ministers and Parliamentary Liaison Officers (PLOs) from voting for Holyrood Committee convenors, as it would seem odd to allow those who are to be scrutinised to have a say in who should scrutinise them. But the case for elected conveners is now difficult to challenge other than by those who benefit from a lack of scrutiny.

The procedure in the Commons for electing Select Committee chairs is instructive. The first stage involves the allocation of committee chairs to parties reflecting the number of seats in the Commons. A ballot then occurs. Nominations to chairs require the support of fifteen or 10 per cent of MPs from the allocated party, whichever is lower, though up to five MPs from other parties can accompany these. An election is held if more than one candidate is nominated. Otherwise the nominated MP becomes chair. MPs vote by ranking as many candidates as they want in order of preference. The count takes place using the Alternative Vote system. Candidates win with over 50 per cent of first preferences, or if no candidate gets 50 per cent then the candidate with least first preferences drops out with second preferences re-allocated. This process continues until a candidate wins more than half the votes cast. There is a term limit of two full Parliaments or eight years, whichever is greater, for any chair. The Commons awards Committee Chairs additional remuneration in recognition of workload and status. This also means that there is an alternative Parliamentary 'career' path other than becoming a Minister. Ian Dunt, in his aforementioned book, maintains that power has shifted back to the Commons over the last half century in 'small but important ways' through the emergence of Select Committees, the Wright Reforms and the changes introduced by Speaker John Bercow through his more activist role and allowing the Commons to amend business motions to change the order and timing of business and vote on emergency debates. Holyrood needs similar reforms to achieve the same objective.

Ken Macintosh, Presiding Officer 2016–2021, established a Commission on Parliamentary Reform, chaired by former BBC Scotland Controller John McCormick, which reported in 2017. It gathered evidence and made recommendations, all of which had been well articulated over many years but had not been implemented. The report offered a wide range of proposed reforms from elected committee convenors, a review of the size and remit of committees, improved resourcing of committees, changes to Parliamentary Question time, a five-stage process to legislative scrutiny, a stronger role for the Presiding Officer, regular reviews of Standing Orders, greater scrutiny to achieve diversity amongst other recommendations. Little that was proposed was new but bringing it together in this way was useful. While the report was widely welcomed across Parliament in a debate in June 2017, little progress has been made to act on the recommendations.

Parliamentary privilege is another area that needs reform, again drawing on Westminster experience. Parliamentary privilege gives MPs rights and protections greater than other individuals or organisations. MPs have freedom of speech in debate and cannot be prosecuted for what they say in Parliament. But MSPs have no such privilege. This is an odd omission and after a quarter of a century MSPs have earned the right to be able to speak freely without fear of prosecution. There has been the perverse example of the Member of Parliament for a Yorkshire constituency using Parliamentary privilege in the Commons to make reference to a matter concerning the conduct of the Scottish Government in its handling of complaints against a former First Minister. This anomaly should be fixed.

Of course, not everything should be copied from Westminster. First Minister's Questions (FMQs) were introduced at the outset of the new Parliament based on Prime Minister's Questions, the most characteristic feature of the Commons. FMQs are a poor form of scrutiny. First Ministers and staff spend considerable time preparing for these weekly jousts. It is, however, difficult to imagine this being abandoned, even though they exaggerate adversarial politics, contribute little to policy scrutiny and involve the First Minister and staff spending considerable time and effort in preparation. More care needs to be taken to avoid reforms that would further emphasise these exaggerated adversarial politics that create more heat than light.

The Scottish Government

The Scottish Government has attempted to operate more collegiately though such efforts go back a long way before devolution. There is no easy fix and silos tend to reassert themselves even when reforms are instituted to address the problem. This does not mean that efforts should not be made but that any sense that this can be fixed with a one-off reform is naïve. One of the reasons for a more comprehensive approach to decision-making is to assist with prioritising. An idea that has been proposed by economist and former policy Special Adviser John McLaren is that a new Treasury department should be created at the heart of the Scottish Government. This makes sense not only to help improve decisions on priorities of spending to focus on growth and value for money but would reflect the important fiscal competences that are now devolved. It is, of course, more than likely that such a department would be unwelcome across much of the Scottish Government. Maynard Keynes compared Treasury control to conventional morality, 'There is a great deal of it rather tiresome and absurd once you begin to look into it, yet nevertheless it is an essential bulwark against overwhelming wickedness'. His essential point was that there needs to be an institution in central government that scrutinises spending decisions. This is especially important given Holyrood's weakness in this area. A case can certainly be made to separate tax and spending in one part of

Scottish central government from an Economics Ministry but there is little doubt that there is a need for more emphasis on these two areas under the current devolved arrangements. Efforts to create a counterweight to the dominance of the Treasury in Whitehall have not been successful over the years. Whether it might work to create a Treasury responsible for fiscal policy, plus a separate Department for Sustainable Growth and Productivity, is well worth considering.

Debates on reforming the inner core of government in London are also worth considering. In a report on government at the centre, the *Institute for Government* (IoG) has proposed an executive Cabinet Committee, essentially an inner core of key Ministers, to ensure a programme set out at the start of each new Parliament is implemented, a senior Minister given responsibility for delivery and for the civil service, and a reformed performance management system. Though the IoG's proposal of an inner Cabinet is not directly relevant, the case for a reduction in the number of Ministers and a smaller Scottish Cabinet makes sense. Professor Patrick Dunleavy has countered this with a proposal drawing on Australian experience that would involve the creation of a new Department of Finance, Procurement and Productivity as a counterweight to the Treasury. The Dunleavy proposals seem more relevant from the perspective of Scottish Government. What is clear is that we need to pay far more attention to such matters in Scotland and draw on relevant debates. While there are disagreements on what is required in Whitehall there has at least been serious debate.

Governance beyond the centre

Another area that Scottish central government ought to give far more consideration to is the delivery of public services. The disconnect between decisions made at the centre and implementation has been a major weakness of devolved government, as Bob Black made clear in the epigraph to this chapter. New Labour established a Delivery Unit in Downing Street and over time reflected on and reformed how it operated. Lessons from this period ought to be learned and though the model then adopted may not be exactly what is required in Scotland, the idea of a unit responsible for ensuring that ideas are implemented and 'Harry Potter' laws and policies are avoided is needed. Its role as an Outcomes Unit would include ensuring that robust thinking about delivery was built into the policy process from the outset of a policy's germination. Such a unit should be directly accountable to the First Minister. Its focus on outcomes would be welcome – and it would make sense to call it the Outcomes Unit - and it would not need anyone communications skills to be attached to it. It could take charge of rigorous examination of existing spending commitments to consider the extent to which sufficient progress is being made to achieve improved outcomes or whether there is a need to alter spending patterns. A second focus would be on prevention. There has not been the shift to prevention hoped for by the Christie Commission. Lessons can be learned from the experimentation in Victoria, Australia as has been discussed by Professor Ken Gibb of Glasgow University.

There is a need to ensure that laws and policy making more broadly takes proper account of how an idea or objective will be delivered. This will require much closer collaboration with local authorities and those involved at the 'coal face'. Related to this is a need to find means to turn the rhetoric on public service reform (PSR) into reality and focus on outcomes. Indeed, PSR has become a hackneyed and over-used term that provokes cynicism even when articulated by advocates of genuine reform. A shift to more focused thinking, approach and language is required. What we need is a focus on outcomes. Once more the challenge is to create an arrangement whereby reform is given greater priority inside the Scottish Government but is not isolated from but integrated into the work of the whole government. Unlike a Treasury, such arrangements for delivery and public sector reform lack the power of the purse that make a body such as a Treasury impossible to ignore. Such a unit would be strengthened if it reported directly to the First Minister. An Outcomes Unit would need to draw heavily on outside expertise.

One of the striking features of Scottish governance is how extremely centralised Scotland has become. This has happened gradually over many decades. Devolution has failed to reverse this long-term trend. Many Scots like to think that the system of government is 'European' but Scotland, in common with the rest of the UK, is an outlier with an extremely centralised system of governance and with a diminished range of local responsibilities. Reform is required that links with the above discussion of delivery.

As discussed in chapter two, a Commission chaired by Sir Neil McIntosh had been established after the 1997 devolution referendum to consider relations between local government and the prospective Scottish Parliament. The report's recommendations remain relevant. It described the two essential features of local government: serving the people with an unparalleled range of services and having a democratic mandate to represent communities. Local government has a direct relationship with central government. There is, as the report noted, an 'inescapable tension in this relationship, but it can be creative if it is managed positively'. McIntosh described local government's representational function as 'fundamental' yet unrealised. Local government ought to be in a position to 'take the lead in drawing together the plans and activities of the whole range of public bodies, as well as the business community and the voluntary sector within their areas' to address community needs. This remains relevant. It is clear that devolution has been deeply disappointing in this respect though there have been some positive initiatives. The development of Community Planning Partnerships (CPPs) as a way of bringing a range of public, private, and voluntary institutions together with communities was well-intentioned but has not made the progress anticipated. Over the last quarter century, new organisations and structures have added to complexity and made coordination more difficult. There is now a need to revisit the McIntosh report, consolidate the institutional arrangements and empower local communities. Community empowerment requires resourcing otherwise it local communities become a dumping ground for difficult decisions.

The McIntosh Report called for mutual respect and parity of esteem between devolved and local government. This should be enshrined in law by adopting the European Charter on Local Self-Government. Nobody should be under any illusions that while this would be an important development it would not in itself be enough to change relations but we need to find means of ensuring such laudable objectives become embedded nonetheless. The first decade of devolution witnessed growth in spending including local government spending. But even then there was a tendency for Scottish central government to impose demands upon local government. The 2007 Concordat between Scottish central and local government, discussed in chapter three, reflected a partially positive change though at considerable cost with a council tax freeze. It was negotiated from a position of weakness by local government and when many of the controls were lifted the council tax freeze weakened local authorities considerably. Over time other controls were imposed while the freeze continued. Fundamental change is now needed. Relations with central government, especially financial relations, need to be reformed.

The changes required are unlikely to happen overnight but a process of change needs to begin with a clear set of long-term objectives. A road map towards a more representative and responsible system of local governance is needed. This is as much about improving outcomes as it is about democratic accountability. Top-down paternalism has not served Scotland well. Mistakes will be made but local mistakes that are locally accountable are less costly than the mistakes made by a centralised authority. And just as there is a need, discussed in chapter four, for devolution across the UK to become 'laboratories of democracy' so too do we need local government to operate as laboratories of democracy. Holyrood has, as had been warned by Jean McFadden (see chapter three), sucked up power. There has been a tendency for MSPs to march into territory that belongs to local government and for Ministers to interfere in such matters. This has contributed to the continuing process of centralisation. It is, nonetheless, inevitable and not necessarily bad that MSPs should want to raise local issues at national level. But the relationship has become imbalanced and needs more consideration. Many problems encountered by citizens do not easily fit into neat devolved vs local categories. But in the absence of clarity of responsibility, which is indeed often impossible to achieve in policy terms as discussed previously, there have to be guidelines on how matters are dealt with. The aim is to provide local authorities with the capacity, not just legal competence, to act so that Scottish Government Ministers can legitimately hand responsibility for decisions made locally to locally elected representatives.

Governments are understandably nervous when it comes to big changes in tax policy. The two boldest examples of tax change in modern times proved disastrous – the introduction of the poll tax over 30 years ago and the Truss Government's mini-budget in 2022. The fear of a taxpayers revolt contributes to conservatism. But as Ken Gibb and Chris Leishman note in their recent report on a sustainable housing policy, it is possible for an informed public through a citizens' panel to engage with the complexities of housing taxation and reach reasonable and progressive conclusions. While a citizens' panel might be criticised as an artificial construct and there is no doubt that engaging with the wider public in a highly adversarial, not to mention populist, environment would be challenging, there is evidence that serious deliberation can have constructive results.

The rebalancing of relations with local government will take time and monitoring progress will be essential. Scottish local authorities need far more financial autonomy. This does not mean they ought to raise all or even close to all of the money that they spend. But the overall proportion of grants to own resources needs to change, while authorities in less prosperous areas will continue to need considerable central grants. Governments should always be careful, even hesitant, when it comes to changes in tax policy. The first stage is to end council tax freezes once and for all. This must be part of a new settlement, acknowledging that setting the council tax, or whatever local taxes exist in future, should be locally determined. Another immediate change would be to address the wholly dated valuations on which council taxes are based. Revaluation of properties is long overdue. The valuations still being used are over 30 years out of date and that evaluation was done on the cheap and has been questioned for its accuracy. The problem is what has happened in the intervening period rather than the time since the last valuation. Property values have increased much more in wealthier parts of Scotland than in poorer areas, leaving probably at least half of Scottish properties now in the wrong band on which council tax is determined. There has been frequent and broad support across at least some of the parties in Holyrood for change. But while a consensus might exist in theory, this breaks down when opposition parties see an opportunity to take advantage of middle-class resentment at prospective increased bills. The Welsh Government has shown that change is possible, even when met with criticism. In 2005, changes were introduced that resulted in about 40 per cent of Welsh domestic properties changing bands. Scotland needs to learn from Wales in this area. There will be important consequences of revaluation that will need to be taken into account. Resource equalisation principles will require attention to reflect local needs as a consequence of revaluation. Policy interventions, however well-meaning and necessary, often have unintended consequences that must be acknowledged and thought given to how to proceed. We might well also look at Northern Ireland as an example. Northern Ireland introduced the Burt proposals (see chapter 2) for a tax on current capital values. While rates have been capped, this was evidence that a bold tax change is possible.

Council tax revaluation is only one immediate step that needs to be taken. Other changes allowing local authorities to raise revenue using alternative sources were proposed during a Local Governance Review that started before the pandemic. While this was a welcome step, tourist taxes raise limited sums and are of value only where there is a thriving tourist trade. There have been a number of reviews and proposals for reform over the years. There is less need for another review than the political will to act on reviews and research already conducted, though future work on details will be needed too. Some degree of consensus is required across Holyrood. A Commission on Local Tax Reform, co-chaired by an SNP Minister and Labour President of COSLA, reported in late 2015. The title of its report *Just Change: A New Approach to Local Taxation*, could be interpreted to mean a change that was socially just but also 'let's do this'. It recommended 'multiple forms of tax' to 'allow local taxation as a whole to be fairer'. Transitional arrangements would be needed to ease in reform. The Commission concluded that a 'system of land value tax is promising' but would require more detailed consideration over the next Parliamentary term. That work has not been done. To make progress on a 'locally variable income tax presents substantial administrative challenges', including dialogue with the UK Government. Its concluding comment was, 'This is an opportunity that must not be missed.' But missed it was.

A considerable amount of money allocated by the Scottish Government to local authorities is ring fenced, that is allocated for specified purposes with penalties applied if the money is not spent according to Scottish Government demands. Autonomy requires choices to be made by local authorities to allow room for different local needs and preferences. Well-intentioned decisions made at the centre on what a local authority can spend its money on fail to appreciate alternative ways of spending public money that would have more impact. An example is teacher numbers. There is no doubt that additional teachers can make a difference but a blanket policy applied in every school makes little sense. Improving educational outcomes depends on a wide range of factors. There are schools in which a more generous supply of teachers is needed, greater than that set by the Scottish Government, while elsewhere resources would be better spent on other support. There are, of course, problems with budget lines that make viring, ie transferring funds to other services difficult but this is where a more flexible and relaxed approach is needed. The one-size-fits-all attitude prevails and is the antithesis of effective policy making and indeed devolution.

As discussed in chapter two, the role of what were then referred to as Quasi-Autonomous Non-Governmental Organisations (QUANGOs), and now as Non-Departmental Public Bodies (NDPBs), had been criticised pre-devolution for the lack of oversight and dubious appointments. There was an effort to streamline the number and effectiveness of these bodies in the early years of devolution and there have been far more opportunities to call board members to account before Parliamentary committees.

There are 115 public bodies, of which 92 are regulated, with members appointed by Ministers. Coordinating the activities of different public bodies is challenging especially when dealing with some of the most intractable problems. On paper this looks simple as well as sensible but each organisation has different lines of accountability, different funding streams and different foci despite the existence of national objectives set out in a National Performance Framework (NPF). When everyone is accountable it can mean that nobody is accountable, as John Sewel noted in discussions of accountability in areas of shared UK and devolved governments. What might seem straightforward is complex. Cooperation needs to be simplified, reducing this complexity and increasing accountability. One way forward, though not without problems, would be to consider whether and which responsibilities currently under NDPBs might be better brought under local authority control. Local Government is, as noted above, already responsible for an unparalleled range of responsibilities compared with other public bodies, facilitating the possibility of coherent government. The range of local authority responsibilities today is much reduced compared to the past. Over a long period of time, local authorities have lost responsibilities to central government or its agencies. We have come to take current arrangements for granted. An example is health which tends to be associated in the public mind with the National Health Service. But as the former Chief Medical Officer Harry Burns frequently noted, the NHS is really a National Ill-Health Service, designed to deal with illness and health problems. We forget that local authorities once had Directors of Public Health and ignore the important public health responsibilities already held by local government, including responsibilities for leisure and recreation, which impact on both physical and mental well-being. This is not to suggest that major hospitals should come under local government but there is a need to consider whether and which health services should be accountable locally and allow for greater emphasis on prevention. An experiment on partially elected Health Boards was abandoned but that would have done nothing to help coordination. Health should not be looked at in isolation but along with other related policy areas, drawing on historical and comparative experiences.

The Scottish islands have long been recognised as requiring different structures of government. The case for different versions of a Single Public Authority has long been canvassed by the islands' councils. Though these models have varied not only between authorities but over time, there has also been a tendency for the Scottish Government to pay lip service to support for the idea, with little progress. There is a strong case for allowing innovation, in the spirit of laboratories of democracy, but this will take far more application than has been the case. This might be an area in which the above discussed Outcome Unit within the Scottish central government might take a lead.

One of the great losses to governance in Scotland was the abolition of Scotland's regional councils in 1996. The possibility of combining local authorities to work cooperatively with increased powers at a regional level needs to be considered. Tentative efforts have been made in different parts of Scotland. These differ across Scotland's regions, avoiding the one-size-fits-all approach. Many challenges faced by government require larger units than most of the current 32 local authorities. Transport, major infrastructure, economic development and skills development are examples of matters that would be candidates for greater regional cooperation. This does not negate the case for decentralisation and community empowerment within existing local authorities. Lessons should be learned from the development of Combined Authorities in England, whether or not this includes elected mayors. What is clear is that a rigid system imposed from the centre is not the best way to organise local democratic accountability and deliver public services.

Conclusion

The Scottish Parliament is now an accepted part of the furniture of Scottish politics. Government decisions are now scrutinised to an extent never possible before devolution. The Parliament is more representative of Scotland than what had gone before. Laws and policies flow from legitimate decision-making at a pace that has surprised many who had long advocated a Scottish Parliament. It has been a success. But there is always room for improvement and threats to democratic politics are now evident across the globe so there should be no room for complacency. Holyrood remains more like Westminster than had been intended. The legislature is dominated by the executive. In the early years, the Scottish Parliament had a justified claim to be a more modern and effective institution than the Commons but that is no longer the case. There is much about the Commons that Holyrood should avoid but there are also lessons to be learned.

UK politics suffers from an overconcentration of power in London. The

Westminster bubble syndrome damages the country as a whole. Scotland has its equivalent Holyrood bubble. Too little attention has been paid to governance and policies in Scotland, the institutions and structures beyond the centre. Subsidiarity needs to be extended to local government and into Scottish communities. Local governance arrangements have developed piecemeal over a long time. There has been a tendency to patch up problems where they have arisen and add new institutions and arrangements as and when deemed necessary. Form should follow function in reforms but will take time to be introduced and implemented. The next generation must address these needs with the same dedication and focus as the founders of the Scottish Parliament a quarter of a century and more ago.

CHAPTER 6

The Challenges and Opportunities Ahead

...first, there are no simple solutions to the tough problems of public policy. And second, there are nearly always trade-offs and choices to be made.
Paul Johnson, former director of the Institute for Fiscal Studies, *Follow the Money: How much does Britain cost?* 2023

Introduction

IN THIS CHAPTER we offer ideas that we hope will provoke debate on policy options and encourage others to make contributions. We cannot offer a comprehensive policy agenda for the next quarter century. Too much is unknown and the breadth of devolved competences is wide. There are some obvious issues, challenges and opportunities that are not going to disappear. We assume that Holyrood may well see some changes in its competences – perhaps Scotland will become independent – but our starting point has to be what can be achieved with the current powers, not least as there is much that *can* be achieved within these powers.

The main policy motivation, or at least mobilising factor, behind the successful campaign for a Scottish Parliament had largely been negative. Supporters of devolution knew what they opposed in public policy terms. The prospect of another poll tax or something similar fuelled demands for a separate Scottish Parliament. Given the need for a broad coalition in the 1997 devolution referendum, it was hardly surprising that it was easier to build support around what devolution would prevent happening rather than a set of new policies. The powers and responsibilities of the Scottish Parliament were inherited from the Scottish Office. They were not the fruits of detailed deliberation or informed by ideas of fiscal federalism or any set of principles. This is not a criticism but recognition of the pragmatism and desire to get a Parliament established as soon as possible. It made sense to start in this way. But the experience of devolution showed that other responsibilities needed to be devolved. There can be no definitive answer as to what should be devolved and what should be retained. This remains a matter that will continue to be argued over and evolve over time. But supporters of independence, as well as devolutionists, acknowledge that there will continue to be a need for cooperation and sharing of responsibilities. This is vital to Scotland's future.

This leaves us with big questions, not only about what kind of polity we have but whether the policies we have are appropriate as we look ahead to the next quarter century. This is not simply a constitutional or institutional question. On one hand, constitutions are important. They say something about who we are, who belongs, how our institutions operate and where institutional power lies or should lie. But institutions and constitutions only frame debate. Previous chapters discussed these institutional arrangements. It is what happens within these structures, the policies advocated in pursuit of some vision or goal that are crucial to the future of devolution.

Back in 2002, US Defence Secretary Donald Rumsfeld responded to a question about the lack of evidence on weapons of mass destruction in Iraq with what became known as the Rumsfeld matrix. He said,

> we know, there are known knowns; there are things we know we know. We also know there are known unknowns; that is to say we know there are some things we do not know. But there are also unknown unknowns – the ones we don't know we don't know.

Leaving aside Rumsfeld's politics, these categories can be helpful in looking to the future in any polity. But public policy needs to be more than reactive, responding to current concerns and crises. Future needs and challenges and taking advantage of opportunities which might have short-term costs but long-term gains are essential and need to be considered. The problem, as frequently noted, is that politics operates in electoral cycles; policies are devised taking account of public opinion in the here and now. Pollsters are unable to ask future generations for their views on issues in a decade or even the current generation other than through hyper-hypothetical questions. There needs to be more vision, a sense of direction towards a better Scotland. But visions without a clear pathway or that make heroic assumptions are at best dreams and at worst deceits. Too often in recent times, visions of a better Scotland have been painted without serious effort to explain how they are to be achieved. Paul Johnson's observation quoted in the epigraph to this chapter should not be ignored. There are no simple solutions to tough problems. There are always trade-offs and often hard choices to be made. We need to abandon the pretence that a speech committing to some goal delivers anything without a clear pathway to that end.

Known knowns, of course, are fairly straightforward though that does not mean we know how to respond. Known unknowns refer to things we know that we do not know. We may have a good idea that a problem or issue exists but the parameters, detail and full implications are often unknown. Governments need to make decisions with incomplete knowledge. Most problems confronting governments have an element of uncertainty about them. John Kay and Mervyn King's *Radical Uncertainty* offers an incisive and useful account, as well as advice that Scottish policy makers would be wise to heed. It may make decision-makers uncomfortable but discomfort should lie at the heart of many challenges we face. Though time may reveal the extent and nature of the problem, decisions often have to be made before much is revealed. Judgement is called upon. It is often only with hindsight that we look back and think that a problem ought to have been addressed earlier or in some other way. There is a common tendency to be critical after more facts are known and to judge government action unfairly.

Mistakes will be made, understandable mistakes that can be justified when account is taken of available evidence when a decision is made. We need to take care not to expect perfection – or fall into the 'nirvana fallacy' of comparing reality with unrealistic, idealised alternatives. That tendency leads to risk aversion or a habit of covering up mistakes. Public policy has much to learn from sectors that openly acknowledge and learn from mistakes as that is the surest way to learn and avoid the same mistakes in the future. The *Library of Mistakes* is a free-to-use library in Edinburgh dedicated to financial history that has existed since 2014. It would help if something similar existed, a safe space, in which lessons could be learned from public policy mistakes. We learn most from our mistakes. A repository of lessons learned would be useful. But politics does not lend itself well to this kind of activity, especially adversarial politics.

There is almost always an alternative voice questioning whether a problem really exists or is as bad as some suggest. The tendency to prevaricate, especially when action may be costly – financially or politically – is common, using imperfect or limited evidence as an excuse. A generation ago, climate change was not taken seriously across a wide spectrum of opinion. That perspective has increasingly been marginalised as evidence has mounted but even now it has not yet resulted in concerted efforts to address the manifold problems and introduce necessary responses to climate change. Governments across the globe have been slow to acknowledge the growing evidence of problems. We know that across the parties in Holyrood there is often agreement that offers a basis for consensual policy development. That opportunity has not been realised with effective policy making. Given the scale of challenges ahead, and recognition that the 'other side' does not consist of liars and charlatans, we could realise the ambition of a better way of policy making.

It is right to set targets but setting a long-term target is easy. What is needed is evidence, so far as possible, of how that target will be met – a theory of change. Targets, milestones, gateways and effective monitoring are needed, otherwise long-term goals can become little more than vague aspirations. We have seen this in housing policy and other policy areas. Despite much-praised policy on homelessness, Scotland now suffers from a classic implementation failure in housing policy, with over half of Scotland's population living in local authorities that have declared a housing crisis. Homelessness in Glasgow and Edinburgh has reached chronic levels. Scotland lacks affordable, good quality social housing.

Given its importance and the near certainty that all the main parties represented in Holyrood will at some point have governed in Edinburgh and/or London, then the case for broad agreement to avoid major disruptions to long-term policy development is essential to improve outcomes. For that to happen, a shift from short-term campaign mindsets to long-term concerns for the sake of future generations is urgently required.

Demographic change and Scotland's welfare state

One of the known challenges is the growing pressure on welfare programmes. Demographic change is in this category, even if the precise figures and trends may be uncertain. In common with much of the world, Scotland is experiencing very challenging demographic change. In one respect, this is a cause for celebration. People are living longer. The older population is not a burden but a major societal asset, as anyone familiar with the voluntary sector cannot fail to appreciate. The contribution retired people – especially women – play in community life, not to mention in family support, is immense and difficult to quantify. It is no exaggeration to say that much of what we take for granted in our communities would grind to a halt without these contributions. While we celebrate this development, we cannot ignore deeper trends. The proportion of those growing older has not improved in all sections of society. In 2008, a Commission on the Social Determinants of Health and the Health Divide for the World Health Organisation, chaired by epidemiologist Sir Michael Marmot, found that the 'health of the worst off in high-income countries is, in a few dramatic cases, worse than average health in some lower-income countries'. The example given was of a boy in the deprived area of Calton in Glasgow city centre who would likely have an average life expectancy of 54 years, compared with a boy growing up 12 kilometres away in affluent Lenzie who could then expect to live to 82. The boy from Calton had a lower life expectancy than the average life-expectancy in India. In January 2023, the Health Foundation reported on health inequalities in Scotland. It found a 24-year gap in the time spent in good health between people living in the most and least deprived 10 per cent of local areas in Scotland. Avoidable mortality amongst women in the most deprived parts of Scotland had increased by 8 per cent since 2010, despite reducing for others. Social class remains important and the divide in life expectancy has grown. It is easy to forget about those who do not live long enough to come close to needing help in old age. A large part of the Scottish population dies before reaching pensionable age. Many such people will have required considerable support from the state throughout their lives. Indeed, those who live to a ripe old age are almost by definition people who have generally enjoyed a healthy life.

The devolution of welfare payments under the Scotland Act 2016 created opportunities to develop a more distinct Scottish welfare system. One of the most effective ways of tackling these issues is through direct payments to citizens who need support. This provides money but also gives people agency, avoids paternalism and resources being channelled towards those least in need. One consideration is whether the cost of administering an alternative system would make targeting worthwhile and cost-effective. Care must be taken not to remove monies for services designed to help the less well-off.

We know that the Scottish Child Payment (SCP) has made a significant difference. The first payments were made in February 2021 with low-income families receiving £10 a week for each child. This was later increased to £25 and extended to under- 16-year-olds of qualifying families. Over 100,000 payments were initially paid and over three times that number of payments made later. The impact of the payment is direct. It has been a means of reducing dependence on food banks. While investment in education can improve opportunities, it can take a generation for the impact to be felt, whereas direct payments, such as the SCP, have an immediate impact. Both types of public spending are needed. Proposals to 'triple lock' the SCP, in similar ways to state pensions – in line with inflation, earnings or 2.5 per cent whichever is highest – have been proposed and would ensure that it was not devalued over time. There is a need to increase the SCP significantly. This should be a priority if we are serious about reducing inequality.

A serious debate is also needed on selective and universal benefits. Do all 60-year-olds and over really need a free bus pass? Is the cost of baby boxes the best use of limited resources? The impact of these policies requires more evidence. This does not mean that the oldest and youngest should all experience a withdrawal of support but that there may be better, more direct ways of providing that support. The current array of welfare support across the range of public services under devolution is an assortment of universal and selective benefits that arose with little reference to principles and was much more informed by political and electoral considerations – the problem of campaigning drowning out good government. In a perfect world, the need to consider whether services should be selective or universal would not exist. Everyone would get every service, allowance or benefit. But resources are finite and too often generosity has followed politically powerful interests or in pursuit of performative headlines. Scotland's much-trumpeted progressive politics has been tested over the last quarter century and has been found wanting. This needs to be confronted and, we hope, progressive choices will emerge even if it will be politically difficult and unpalatable for many.

The dependency ratio

The National Records of Scotland show that Scottish birth rates have been low and are expected to remain so over the coming decades. The proportion of people over 65 is anticipated to grow from 22 per cent to 31 per cent of the total population over the next half century, while those aged between 16 and 64 will fall. In 2023, the Scottish Fiscal Commission projected demographic change over the next half century. It calculated that the rapidly growing older population and decreasing number of children would result in Scotland having 74 dependent people for every 100 people aged between 16 to 64 by 2073–73. While such projections involve a considerable margin of error as much might happen to make this less, or indeed more, of a problem, it would be foolhardy not to prepare for the challenge involved. We referred earlier in this book to Thomas Jefferson's concern about decisions made in one generation that have an impact on later generations. This concern for inter-generational justice applies in the case of the dependency ratio – the ratio of those dependent on state support to the working-age population – and is a double-edged problem. The latest census shows that Scotland has the lowest rate of population growth of any component nation of the United Kingdom. The total Scottish population would have fallen without people moving to Scotland from elsewhere. Demographic change creates numerous public policy challenges. Pensions and other welfare payments, public health, transport, and housing are amongst the areas affected. Every generation had seen higher real terms wages from those preceding it since 1945. But that has stalled, with young people who entered the workforce since the first five years of this century experiencing the same wages as the previous generation. There were shocks to the system that partly account for this but indications of problems had already been evident before austerity.

The existing devolved tax powers came with an inevitable decrease in grant from London and greater economic responsibility. This needs to be acknowledged and addressed urgently. Not only are many taxes now devolved but so too are many welfare benefits. Laudable objectives of creating a fairer, more dignified and more respectful welfare system will not be achieved by words alone. The growth in the elderly population will place growing pressure on public services while the relative decline of the population in work and paying taxes contributing to the public finances will create a major challenge. The failure to address this problem now will leave future generations with an almighty set of problems. We cannot put off the need to increase public funding for social care for ever. The longer we take to do this, the more difficult it becomes. There are options on how the funding should be provided – call it a tax, contribution or whatever – but this cannot be avoided. The Scottish Parliament will have to work with Westminster to deliver what is needed.

One of the possible means of addressing the lack of working-age citizens is through immigration. Scotland's largest in-migration comes from the rest of the UK. That needs to be encouraged, not least as it is the likeliest source of skilled people. This could also relieve pressure in congested parts of England. There is also scope through negotiations with London to allow for more direct immigration into Scotland from outside the UK. Scotland would not be alone as a part of a state that has a more relaxed immigration policy than the rest of the state. The *Fresh Talent – Working in Scotland* initiative, discussed in chapter two, was a modest experiment that demonstrated that it was possible to have a different policy north and south of the border. There are technical means of ensuring that immigrants could only work in Scotland if the UK Government was to resist the same policy on migration.

Brexit

It was clear from the outset that Brexit would have a negative economic impact across a wide range of public services. It removed opportunities certainly, but the precise impact was, and indeed remains, unclear. Much depended on the outcome of negotiations between UK Government and the EU but even then much remained unclear. It was obvious that there would be problems following the end of free movement of people and that this would affect public services and economic activity that rely on EU citizens. Brexit has had an impact from the construction industry to seasonal berry picking work to the care sector and health. Trade has been adversely affected with more 'friction' at borders. The UK continues to have relations with the EU and these relations will continue to evolve. How they evolve will depend on decision-makers across the UK. Scottish Government can play a constructive part in that development or seek to play politics from the sidelines.

The best option by far would be for the whole of the UK to rejoin the EU, whether or not Scotland was independent. There would be obvious costs and difficulties for Scotland as a member of the EU if the rest of the UK remained outside. It is understandable that the SNP sought political advantage from the fact that 62 per cent of Scots voted Remain but it should acknowledge that the best course would be for the whole of the UK to rejoin together. Scotland cannot afford to exchange one set of economic dislocations for an even more damaging set. We need close relations with the EU but also close relations with the rest of the UK. It would be far better for Scottish politicians to contribute to encouraging greater cooperation along with the rest of the UK, than to make political capital and exaggerate differences between Scotland and the rest of the UK on this issue. The

Scottish Government can seek to exploit the problems resulting from Brexit and keep demanding immediate return to membership. Or it can engage in constructive dialogue.

Constructive engagement is required by both devolved and UK Governments. While Brexit necessitated agreement on a UK internal market, which would be required regardless of Scotland's constitutional status, the imposition of rules and regulations by London ran contrary to the spirit of devolution. The return of decision-making to the UK affected a vast array of policy areas. The UK Government identified 129 policy areas affected. Tensions were inevitable when it came to debating the issues involved in the United Kingdom Internal Market Act 2020 (UKIM) but these became caught up in and exacerbated by the UK Government's refusal to engage constructively. Decisions on the UKIM could have been made through negotiations conducted in the spirit of mutual respect and parity of esteem, as discussed in chapter five, or through imposition by London. The European market had allowed for a degree of leeway with public interest taking account of a range of considerations. But the UKIM was more restrictive with the application being described by Welsh Ministers as having a 'chilling effect' on devolved decision-making.

Various reforms have been proposed including legislative and procedural changes but more radical changes are required to ensure not only that this particular issue is resolved and there is no repeat of similar problems, especially if the UK, or indeed devolved, Government was keener on having a public fight for party political campaign purposes rather than resolving differences in the public interest. The proposals outlined in chapter 4, drawing on the report of the Brown Commission, *A New Britain: Renewing Our Democracy and Rebuilding Our Economy*, to create a new second chamber in Westminster empowered to veto attempts by the Commons to reverse the powers of or abolish devolved bodies is needed. At the end of the day the fundamental need is for much more constructive and cooperative efforts and less cheap political point scoring to secure closer relations and ultimately rejoin the EU.

Scotland's economic performance

The United Kingdom suffers from serious economic imbalances as discussed in chapter four. This has long been widely recognised across politics. In his maiden speech in the House of Lords back in 1992, Lord Norman

MacFarlane, one of Glasgow's leading business leaders, criticised the 'concentrated and congested area of economic activity in the South East' and suggested that a

> recast regional and urban policy must look beyond the excitement of the East Thames corridor and London Docklands and aim at the economic revival of the United Kingdom's proud provincial cities. A national programme is needed for the revival of the provincial cities which can be the economic powerhouses of the 1990s...

MacFarlane was a Tory but worked cooperatively with Glasgow's elected representatives on regeneration. His critique is not so different from that found in many reports and comments made by other unionists on the right and left. His comments were also remarkably similar to critiques of the UK economy found over many decades in SNP publications and speeches. In the same year as Lord MacFarlane's speech in the Lords, Nigel Smith, one of the great advocates of a Scottish Parliament in the business community remarked,

> To this day, the UK remains highly centralised on the south-east. It continues to see £20bn spent squeezing more people into the South-East as better than spending half the sum on an effective regional policy. The South-East takes the predominant share of the decision-making units in planning, design, and development in both business and government. No country which so inadequately understands its own regions can properly represent them in other forums.

He saw devolution as offering part of a solution but recognised that devolved government would have to work cooperatively with UK central government.

Constitutional reform cannot change everything but Scotland can play a part along with elsewhere in the UK in rebalancing the economy. Scotland cannot walk away from these imbalances. They will persist to our disadvantage regardless of Scotland's constitutional status. The creation of a very different form of devolution in parts of England should not be dismissed as irrelevant to Scotland. It would create allies to make the case for change in economic policy. This opportunity needs to be grabbed. One of the costs of devolution has been a weakening of Scotland's voice in UK central government. There is little prospect of a significantly strengthened Scotland Office at the heart of Whitehall and even if that was possible it would still run up against the problem of lacking the authoritative ability of a Scottish Government, drawn from a Parliament in Edinburgh directly elected by the Scottish people to speak for Scotland. Opportunities need to be recognised and exploited and so far this has not happened. The potential here, as in central–local relations, is to appreciate that benefits for all are greater through cooperation. Greater investment in infrastructure, including transport, across the whole of the UK will benefit all. There will be resistance to rebalancing the economy from many, though by no means everyone, in London and the South East. Any transition to creating a more balanced economy will involve more than regional rebalancing but also requires sectoral rebalancing. The UK's financial services contribute much to the economy. The challenge is to avoid damaging this sector while strengthening other sectors.

New technologies and moving to a Green economy offer opportunities not only to address geographical but also related sectoral imbalances. Nobel Economics Laureate Robert Solow's comment on information technology – the Solow paradox or productivity paradox – is apposite. 'You can see the computer age everywhere but in the productivity statistics'. Information Technology, big data and now Artificial Intelligence have the potential to transform public policy in positive ways and such technological advances need to be harnessed but nobody should be under any illusion that tech will be a panacea. Expectations of easy solutions all too often crash into harsh realities. That being said, Scotland, as elsewhere, is awash with data that we have yet to harness either in growing a sustainable economy or delivering public policies. Once more, the message is that much more thought needs to go into delivery to improve outcomes and not just provide more innovative inputs.

There is much that can be done by the Scottish Government. There have been many ideas, debates, strategy documents and plans issued over the last quarter century. It is easy to criticise what some see as the mountain of documents on the economy surrounding a vacuum of substantive policy ideas. Many problems are deep-rooted and existed long before devolution. The economic challenges may now be much more pressing given the new fiscal arrangements of devolution but they have long existed. Shocks that had not or could not have been anticipated have had a negative economic impact in recent years. Brexit and COVID-19 have made matters much more difficult.

But even before these shocks, devolved government had not had the economic impact hoped for by many founders. There is a fair degree of consensus on the nature of the problem, which is a good starting point. Scotland suffers from low levels of business start-ups and low business growth; research and development spending does not match what is required; and there are skills gaps (and in many cases skills mismatches with many people overqualified for jobs they are doing, while many are underqualified for work required). All of this creates the problem of low productivity.

A tension is often identified between investing in existing winners, investing in potential winners and dealing with weak parts or 'lame ducks' in the economy. As with whether to invest in prevention or tackling acute problems, the answer is finding a balance. Scotland possesses many great assets relevant to a thriving economy and society. These include a highly skilled workforce, albeit with significant skills shortages and mismatches, world-leading higher education institutions, and many key areas in which Scotland already has a comparative advantage. The need for a transition from oil and gas to renewable sources of energy is both challenging but also offers a major opportunity. The speed of the transition is debated but essential, and investment is required. The most successful way of achieving this is if it is done cooperatively with the UK Government and local bodies. It will take time and any pretence that this can be done speedily is misleading and will be harmful. While Scotland has a skilled workforce, more attention needs to be paid to skills gaps and this is where Scotland's Colleges, which have been neglected in recent years, have a major role to play.

Scotland's institutions of higher education offer great potential but also need to address weaknesses. The Scottish higher education funding model has proved to be flawed. Basing significant investment on the unstable income strand of overseas graduate student applications was short-sighted and made worse by a failure across the sector to prepare contingency plans for what has occurred. Added to this has been the policy of inadequate replacement government funding for tuition fees. The Scottish Government portrays its policy of no tuition fees for Scottish students as evidence of its progressive policies when in reality it has left universities needing to compensate by cross subsidising from other income streams. It has long been clear that the current financial arrangements were unsustainable, even if the sector's leadership and Scottish Government has only recently wakened up to the crisis. But academics engaged in teaching and research have contributed to important initiatives and created great opportunities for economic development and social wellbeing. Amongst these has been the work in brain science which contributes to addressing challenges associated with the aforementioned growing elderly population. This work has been acknowledged by the Davis Alzheimer Collaborative and the US based Global Alzheimer's Platform amongst others. A series of brain health summits have been and continue to be held. Progress in this area will require investment to build further capacity and innovation.

The Scottish economy cannot be understood in isolation. Scotland is a trading nation and its economic and trade relations are important. Scotland has long had a good record in attracting inward investment from the days of the big manufacturing industries well before devolution. This inward investment brought significant employment opportunities over a number of generations but also a this involved what was referred to as a 'branch factory syndrome' in which senior positions as well as research and development investment tended to occur elsewhere. The loss of many of these branch factories in the latter decades of the 20th century along with the decline of other traditional industries left scars across much of Scotland. The discovery of North Sea oil and gas went some way to compensating for these losses but was regionally focused. Oil and gas are now following a similar trajectory to Scotland's old heavy industries of coal, steel and shipbuilding. There is a real danger that the North East will suffer as so many parts of central Scotland did when traditional industries declined without alternatives in their place.

There is a further reason for greater focus on the economy, as already noted. The Scottish Parliament was largely a spending institution in its early years but has since gained fiscal powers. This change has led to greater complexity and fiscal and economic autonomy which has resulted in more uncertainty. The performance of the Scottish economy will impact on how much or little demand there is for welfare spending and how much or little money there is to address social problems that accompany poor economic performance. Scotland's relative economic performance will directly influence the amount of money available to the Scottish Government for spending and investment, as well as driving the level of spending on areas like social security. As Caroline Gardner, Auditor General 2012–2020, noted,

> It's hard to overstate the importance of these new powers. They give the Scottish Government incentives to grow Scotland's economy and more scope to raise money to pursue its own policies.

As she observed, growing the economy and creating a fairer Scotland are not mutually exclusive. Indeed they are mutually reinforcing. John McLaren, a former Treasury economist with expertise on the Scottish economy, has warned against the fixation on 'negative economic growth and externalities' – on issues such as unemployment, inequality and pollution – rather than on how to improve productivity and raise Scotland's growth rate. His prescription is more positive, more forward thinking and should be embraced. Far from suggesting that Scotland should ignore its social problems, he proposed a focus on sustainable economic growth to address social and economic problems. That shift in thinking is now unavoidable unless we are to abandon a fairer Scotland. The most successful way to achieve a healthier, socially just society is to create the virtuous cycle of sustainable growth with well-paid, secure and satisfying employment.

The reorganisation of local government in the 1990s saw the demise of Scotland's regional councils. This has deprived Scotland of institutions operating at that scale to assist with public service development and delivery as well as much needed economic growth. A wholescale reorganisation of local government is not anticipated, at least not in the immediate future, but the case for creating conditions for and incentivising more collaboration across existing local authorities including placing functions, responsibilities and budgets currently held by some unelected public bodies under regional collaboratives is needed. Whether this requires elected mayors is open to debate and could be a decision left to people living within putative regional authorities. There is variable interest in such developments across Scotland but that should not hold back reforms when and where desired. Policy ideas and prescriptions cannot – should not – be provided by central government without consideration of regional and local impact. The release of intellectual energy, drawing on a range of local institutions including further and higher educational institutions, is essential.

Subsidiarity revisited

We have also known that increased centralisation and underfunding of local authorities by the Scottish Government undermines the delivery of public services. There is a need to reverse this process. The starting point is not to outline a series of detailed policy reforms for local government but to recognise that the relationship between central and local government has become dysfunctional. It is undermining the common goal of providing public services. Scottish central government needs to recognise that a mutually respectful relationship is in its interests, that it does not have the necessary expertise or experience on its own to deliver public services and that centralisation and uniform approaches to policy making involves turning its back on those who have much to contribute to improving outcomes. Ministers deliver speeches but little else. The conveyor belt assumption of the policy process – that a policy is announced and then moves seamlessly along a conveyor belt to improved outcomes – is an affliction that leads to poor outcomes.

In a lecture in 2013, Dr Bob Black, the late former Auditor General quoted earlier in this book, remarked that,

> Bringing services close to Scotland, a better level of debate, fits with a civic society. That is probably a good thing but I had not grasped that the Scottish Parliament does not deliver anything. It takes money from Westminster, approves a budget, passes laws and speaks for the people of Scotland, but it does not deliver anything. It is quite remote in systemic terms from frontline service delivery. That is a real issue.

It was honest of Dr Black to acknowledge this in public and would be beneficial if this was further acknowledged and acted upon by Parliamentarians and Scottish Government Ministers and officials. Both central and local governments benefit from cooperation. This needs to become embedded in our system of government and that should be the basis on which further, including detailed, policy formulation occurs. There can be no doubt that a fundamental change in this direction is essential. Sharing power was identified as one of the key principles set out by the Consultative Steering Group a quarter of a century ago for very good reason. These local voices should be heeded as they act as early warning systems, identifying potential problems and opportunities and are essential for delivery. They are also sources of good policy ideas.

Local government finance lies at the heart of much that is wrong with the current governance arrangements in Scotland. There has been no shortage of analyses, enquiries, reports and recommendations over the years and there is remarkable consistency in identifying what is wrong and broadly in what should be done. Minor changes have occurred but the unfairness and weaknesses of the local finance system gets worse as time goes by. It has been a case of a small step forward and many steps back. The current arrangements are indefensible other than by those who want to protect the better off. So why is it so difficult to reform? And what reforms might be considered?

There are a number of inter-related reasons why reform has proved so difficult. First, tax reform is generally difficult and reforms will have unintended consequences. This is why decision-makers are often wary of tax reform and any reform is best introduced incrementally. Radical change may be needed but it will take time through a step-by-step incremental process of change. It has been suggested that tribal politics has paralysed Holyrood in this area. This is certainly true but what lies behind this tribalism is important. The fear of being attacked by opponents inhibits progressive change, not least boldness. Local tax reform will result in losers as well as winners and it is the losers the parties fear. The beneficiaries of the current system are those with the highest propensity to vote. They have most to lose from reform. This makes reform very difficult for any single party unless it is riding on the crest of a major electoral wave. There have only been two moments in the last 25 years when that might have been possible. The first was after the SNP won an overall majority in Holyrood but instead it pursued its constitutional agenda and the opportunity for radical policy change in other areas was lost. The second was in the immediate aftermath of the independence referendum when the goodwill towards the SNP was at its height, even amongst many of those working in public services who had voted against independence. But that moment has long since passed.

It is difficult to expect all-party agreement on reform. The Conservatives would doubtless see any effort to reform as an opportunity to regain their long-lost place as Scotland's party of the middle classes. Agreement between Labour and the SNP on this issue ought to be possible and with a chance that the Liberal Democrats and Greens would also lend support. The biggest challenge would be party political rather than public policy. Agreement on reform is easier to envisage than to deliver. The prospect of gaining sufficient cross-party trust is slight. But while the risk may be great, the reward would be greater with a much-improved system.

But what might the shape of reform look like? Adam Smith outlined the classic four canons of taxation in *The Wealth of Nations*:

i) The subjects of every state ought to contribute towards the support of the government, as nearly as possible, in proportion to their respective abilities.

ii) The tax which the individual is bound to pay ought to be certain and not arbitrary.
iii) Every tax ought to be levied at the time, or in the manner, in which it is most likely to be convenient for the contributor to pay it.
iv) Every tax ought to be so contrived as to take out of the pockets as little as possible, over and above that which it brings into the public treasury of the state.

These canons involve trade-offs – a general theme of this book – when it comes to choosing taxes. The costs of administering and effective implementation of a tax must be taken into account. The impact of taxation on welfare and the economy cannot be ignored. Transparency is also seen as important though transparency has its cost. The poll tax was designed with transparency of a sort in mind and fuelled a major revolt, though it was a tax that failed Adam Smith's test on grounds of fairness and was hopelessly inconvenient administratively given the nearly insurmountable implementation challenges. It is notable that when it was replaced by the council tax, money was found to pay for the fiasco by raising another tax – Value Added Tax (VAT) – and this hardly raised an eyebrow. VAT is the third largest tax in the UK, behind income tax and national insurance contributions, and is largely invisible as it is a sales tax that is hidden in the price of the goods and services on which it is levied. VAT illustrates another important point about taxation and indeed much public policy. There are always likely to be anomalies or idiosyncrasies. VAT is not imposed on food but it is on pets. Rabbits are thereby exempt as they are edible. Perfection in public policy, as in life, is the enemy of progress. This is all too true when it comes to taxation.

The council tax is dysfunctional but not because it is a tax on property. Property taxes existed before income tax and are attractive as property is immobile and it is relatively easy to identify who should pay (though there has been debate on whether and what proportions might be paid by owners and those renting property). The immobility of property makes it particularly attractive for financing local government. Complexity arises when it comes to *how* property should be taxed. Proposals have been made over the years to replace the property tax with a local incomes tax (LIT). George Younger, as Scottish Secretary under Margaret Thatcher, was the only Cabinet member to support a LIT when a replacement for domestic rates, the previous property tax, was debated in Cabinet back in 1981.

The SNP fought the 2007 election with a commitment to do the same but lack of an overall majority meant the SNP dodged what would have been a very challenging task and subsequently quietly dropped the policy. The Local Tax Commission, jointly chaired by the COSLA President and a Scottish Government Minister, reported in December 2015 suggesting that 'if it could be proved feasible then a LIT should be considered'. This would require cooperation with the UK Treasury. COSLA's submission to the Commission on Local Taxation, which was accepted, argued for 'multiple forms of tax' and could see no reason why other taxes should not be considered including environmental, resource, sales or tourist taxes. A move towards giving local authorities access to a wider range of sources of income does not mean that the total tax take would increase. As the Commission noted, 'There is no intrinsic link between the numbers of taxes operated and how much is collected in total'. But reforms in local taxation would have implications for other aspects of fiscal policy that would require careful consideration and modelling. While this makes policy sense, it would be naïve to ignore the political difficulties and the near certainty that opposition would be whipped up equating more sources with paying more in tax. Cross-party consensus will need to be present for this reform.

A land value tax was described by the Local Taxation Commission as 'promising' though acknowledged that much more detailed investigation would be needed, which it suggested should be completed during the next (2016–21) Parliament. A report commissioned by the Scottish Land Commission noted the administrative challenges in introducing and maintaining such a tax. The prospect of a 'big bang' approach of introducing a land value tax to replace the council tax is unrealistic in the short or even medium term. But it is conceivable, if the will is there, to start a process of laying the foundations for the introduction of a land value tax. Broadening the taxable base, leaving aside the amounts generated, would provide more security and less instability with less dependence on mobile and more elastic taxes.

Taxation has functions other than revenue raising. Changes in taxation have an economic impact. We would be wise to keep the council tax but need to acknowledge its weaknesses according to the above canons and criteria. One obvious reform is to revalue all properties and legislate for annual revaluations. Annual revaluations are now possible in a way they previously were not – or at least previously proved prohibitively expensive and thus breached Smith's canon that a tax should not require to be raised at high levels simply due to the administrative costs involved. Decisions on when and whether revaluations occur should be taken out of the hands of government. Primary legislation is required so that any effort to prevaricate would at least make it more difficult to avoid regular revaluations. Revaluation has not occurred since 1991 as discussed in the previous chapter and for reasons explained there. But much more is needed. Of the various options that might command sufficient cross-party support to win acceptance, the most likely are those that involve more bands, something the Scottish Government started but this needs to go further.

The Land Building Transactions Tax (LBTT), which replaced Stamp Duty in Scotland in 2015, is applied when properties are exchanged. Taxes on property sales create barriers to sales and limit labour and housing mobility with adverse impact on productivity and opportunities. The late Sir James Mirrlees, Nobel Economics laureate and member of the SNP's Council of Economic Advisers, made this clear in his review of taxation for the Institute of Fiscal Studies. While referring to Stamp Duty, the equivalent of the LBTT, Mirrlees noted that transaction taxes were inefficient, discouraged 'mutually beneficial transactions' and ensured that 'properties are not held by the people who value them most'. There was 'no sound case for maintaining' such a tax. This highlights the unintended consequence of a tax that may generate income for Government but has otherwise damaging properties. Getting rid of the LBTT would make sense but would require an alternative source to replace lost revenue. The LBTT was reviewed by the Scottish Government resulting in a surcharge on land and building transaction tax on purchases of second and rental homes. The amounts raised through LBTT vary depending on how many properties are sold and growth in property values, each in turn relate to the state of the economy. Transactions may be reduced resulting in making mobility, including workforce mobility, expensive. It inevitably distorts housing markets and as the LBTT is a 'lost value' it is not something lenders are keen to cover. Overall, this once more raises the tricky question of trade-offs – it may raise money but can have a negative economic impact. Reforming the system of annual land and property tax has been raised in various reviews and will need to be considered. Unless and until an alternative source of revenue is found we are stuck with this tax.

Wicked problems

The distinction between 'tame' and 'wicked' problems was first made over half a century ago. Tame problems are those that are relatively straightforward, even if costly to address, and can be 'solved'. There is a linear quality at least in abstract to such problems – a problem would be defined, diagnosed, options considered and a solution found, though few policies conform to such straightforward linearity. Even when a solution is found, there is a constant need to monitor, review and where necessary revise a policy. Wicked problems are more complex. The nature and causes of wicked problems are unclear and contested, not least because they have a multiplicity of causes, can be very disruptive in unpredictable ways and do not lend themselves to 'solutions'. An array of bodies – public, voluntary, private – need to work together even though each might have a different understanding of the nature of the problem and the response required. An analogy can be drawn between a painful but straightforward broken limb of a child as a tame though serious problem – usually easily diagnosed, treated and ultimately sorted satisfactorily with little or no evidence of the problem persisting into adulthood. A wicked problem would be tantamount to an elderly patient with multiple morbidities and chronic conditions. These might be less easily diagnosed, a response to one condition might aggravate another and ultimately there is little prospect of 'solving' the problems, though alleviation and reducing the onset or extent of problems may be possible. Major issues occur when medical professionals fail to engage with one another in such cases. Similarly, lack of cooperation and coordination in tackling wicked problems creates more problems.

Complex case management is essential for complex conditions. And just as each individual's chronic condition will be unique, wicked problems demand more attention, greater resources and consistent application because each wicked problem will be unique. Broad agreement on long-term responses is needed and that will require mature consensual politics. Consensus does not mean seeking a position lying halfway between two alternatives. Consensus in response to wicked problems is difficult to achieve as it requires serious engagement with issues, a willingness to be open-minded and build agreement on responses that can be pursued long-term. Empathy is essential both for affected citizens but also with other professionals in what ought to be a team effort. Such responses will not be easily found, not least as multiple agencies are involved, and responses

– not solutions in the sense of a point when those involved can say 'job done' – are costly. And necessarily iterative. They require mature politics.

Wicked problems are abundant and Scotland has its fair share. Paul t'Hart, a leading scholar on public leadership, offered a list of wicked problems faced today across many countries: urban stress, cyber crime, climate change, refugee flows, obesity epidemics, religious fanaticism, alcohol and drug abuse, problem gambling, child trafficking, genetic engineering, resource depletion, poverty. Scotland is not unique and anyone familiar with Scottish public policy will recognise most of these problems. Behind each of these lie fundamental problems that require attention to prevent, or at least limit, the scale of these issues. As the same scholar noted,

> These are complex problems because they involve a large number and diverse range of stakeholders, values and interests. They entail irreducible uncertainties or conflicts about the nature and scope of the problem as well as the likely impacts of alternative ways of tackling it.

There are many causes and very different reasons for these challenges but one that stands out, to Scotland's great shame given claims that Scotland is a progressive nation, is the record on drug deaths. As Annemarie Ward, a leading campaigner on the issue, powerfully expressed it, 'The rich get rehab, and the poor get methadone'. Scotland has been trying to manage the problem, perhaps because the cost of really tackling it is too high or perhaps politicians and society do not care enough and all too easily take their eye of the ball while more electorally appealing issues demand their attention. Scotland needs to hold a mirror up to itself and address the gap between the rhetoric of caring for the most vulnerable and taking appropriate action. It would be more honest, though depressingly defeatist, to acknowledge that responses required are so costly as to be politically unacceptable. This is a challenge not only to our politicians and decision-makers but Scottish society. One of the CSG principles that has been neglected was the sharing of power between the people of Scotland, the legislators and the Scottish Executive. Meaningful sharing of power requires the public to be informed and share responsibility for policies or the lack of policies. The tendency to engage in limited forms of 'community empowerment' is evasive and performative. The public should be more than recipients of messages and providers of votes. The public need to be engaged with honesty, requiring them to share in the collective decisions involved in trade-offs and painful decisions. There is evidence from a range of democratic innovations that the public engage constructively with big policy problems given the chance.

We also now refer to 'super wicked problems'. Such problems are defined as having four features in addition to those characterising wicked problems: time is running out to avert catastrophe; those who cause the problem need to be part of the response though may be reluctant to accept responsibility and would lose out by assisting; there is a tendency to push the problem further into the future with, for example, unrealistic long-term goals; and government and others lack the authority to act. The most obvious examples of super wicked problems are found in international environmental challenges. The European Union made great strides in this area and continues to offer an important framework for common policies to address climate change. This does not preclude devolved government playing its part not least in articulating demands for action and following EU initiatives where possible. Even UK central government will be limited in what it can achieve but has greater access to international bodies in which demands for action can be voiced. We should not pretend that such problems can be resolved solely by the actions of Scottish Government, but need cooperation with others especially, though not exclusively, the rest of the UK. Climate change is creating myriad problems and challenges.

For one, pests, diseases and invasive non-native plant species are likely to thrive. We do not know the precise implications for health due to changes in the weather and resulting patterns of diseases. Well over a quarter of a million Scottish homes and premises are at risk of flooding, a figure that is expected to grow. Institutionally, Scotland is reasonably well placed to address some of this with a Scottish Fire and Rescue Service capable of moving resources to areas of need at short notice. Much more is needed. Super wicked problems require greater international cooperation to confront those creating the problems. Rejoining the European Union is unlikely to happen any time soon but we should re-engage with the rest of the EU when the opportunity arises on issues such as this.

As we can see, wicked problems cannot be solved in known, affordable and easily managed response modes. We can and should learn from elsewhere. In seeking to learn from elsewhere we need to avoid thinking we can simply 'copy and paste' responses. Care needs to be taken to ensure that appropriate lessons are learned. And lesson learning needs to be driven by public policy thinking, not in pursuit of some effort to frame responses for party political purposes. Scandinavian experience is rich and extremely varied – indeed referring to a Scandinavian model in policy terms raises the question of which Scandinavian model. The tendency to assume either that a 'Scandinavian policy' would be suitable or to frame initiatives as 'Scandinavian' has no place in serious policy development. And we should not ignore lessons from elsewhere in the UK. This is not to suggest that we should only look south of the border for ideas but that experiences elsewhere in the UK are likely to be relevant. It makes sense to look to our nearest and most similar neighbour at least as a first port of call.

Much debate over the last 25 years has focused on the extent to which Scotland has diverged in policy terms from the rest of the UK. The primary concern ought to be to find policies that ensure Scotland diverges from current poor performances and poor outcomes for its citizens. If that means policy convergence with England or the rest of the UK then that should trump any desire to be different. It would also be a sign of political maturity. The question as to where ideas come from, whether Scotland diverges or converges in public policy terms with the rest of the UK, should be irrelevant. There are many lessons from the rest of the UK in what not to do but there are equally lessons in what might be appropriate, for example the remarkable achievements in addressing educational attainment gaps in London a couple of decades ago, or lessons in Combined Authorities across England. In 1986, the respected journalist Neal Ascherson delivered a lecture at the SNP's annual conference in which he quoted Tomas Masaryk, the first president of an independent Czechoslovakia. Masaryk's advice to the new state was 'Don't be afraid – and don't steal', meaning that citizens should be bold and honest. That advice applies equally in Scotland today, though with one important caveat. Scotland needs to be bold in addressing public policy challenges, while at the same time politicians need to take the public with them. Honesty is required but they should have no hesitation in 'stealing' ideas from elsewhere. If there is one form of theft that is acceptable, even welcome, then it is the theft of policy ideas. There is much to be learned from outside Scotland but there are lessons in policy transfer that need to be heeded in so doing. Policy transfer requires appropriateness and involves adaptation, not simply lift and paste.

The transfer of powers over welfare proved much more complex than Scottish Government Ministers anticipated and had to be delayed as a result. It is a common assumption that policies are easily implemented but much can go wrong at the implementation stage. Policy making and implementation should not be seen as separate processes. It is easy to assert that a policy is fairer but much more difficult to ensure that what is delivered is fairer. The ultimate test is always how citizens are affected. Fine language and laudable aims slip easily off the tongue. As we have seen with the transfer of welfare responsibilities, the difficult part is the establishment of necessary institutions to implement improvements in outcomes. There is a need to reduce demand on services through preventative action. The old adage that prevention is better than cure applies to public policy. The problem is that shifting resources to preventative measures comes at the cost of existing commitments unless operating in a period of considerable economic growth. The focus on early years has been welcome but the tendency to view policy making as a tick box exercise undermines much good work. There is ample evidence that early years, and indeed preconception, are crucial in life chances but we also know that improved life chances through positive early years interventions are reversed over the following years unless followed through with later interventions. Early intervention requires follow through and that has all too often been missing. Early interventions followed by later interventions are often needed.

Known unknowns

Rumsfeld's three categories of knowledge ignores one vital category. We note that a fourth type, identified by the philosopher Slavoj Žižek, is highly relevant to Scotland: *unknown knowns*. These are the matters we know about but to which we have turned a blind eye. Facing up to big challenges is difficult and has often been politically easier to ignore. Scotland cannot afford to hide behind progressive rhetoric, constantly measuring ourselves in highly subjective and often dubious ways against what happens in the rest of the UK. This is perhaps the biggest challenge we face in Scotland. Pre-devolution it was politically easy and appealing to blame London for all Scotland's woes. Devolution ought to have at least limited this. Blame games continue and difficult times encourage that tendency. There are, of course, many cases when blame can justifiably be placed at UK Central Government's door. London remains all too conveniently available. This temptation will always exist and due to economic ties, regardless of constitutional status, will always be possible. But the challenge of devolution over the next quarter century must be to be more confrontational not with London, or with political opponents in Scotland but with our challenges and problems.

An early achievement after devolution was the establishment of the Violence Reduction Unit in Strathclyde Police at the instigation of John Carnochan and Karyn McCluskey. In his book *Conviction: violence, culture and a shared public service*, John Carnochan tells the story of 'David' and walks us briefly through his life. The story is one of lives ruined, lost potential and escalating cost to the taxpayer as the range of additional services 'David' required grew and grew. This anonymised story exemplifies the importance of early intervention and follow-through. There is a massive cost involved in failure demand, that is demand for public services caused by a failure to address a problem or issue. One of the greatest challenges is to shift resources, especially when money is tight, from acute services to prevention. David's story is not simply, nor most importantly, one of escalating costs. It is a story of lost potential, of our failure to provide opportunities for all.

As has been noted earlier in this book, prevention has become a buzzword, with prevention hubs and other paraphernalia of a public service reform industry. Too much that is now presented as prevention is at best downstream prevention, aimed at softening the impact of ongoing harm. Policy needs to have a greater focus upstream, indeed what has long been referred to as 'primordial' prevention in the medical literature. Primordial prevention had been introduced half a century ago by those working on cardiovascular disease to refer to reducing social and environmental risk factors targeted at the whole population. To put this at its simplest, we need to tackle poverty head-on. Tackling poverty is the primordial response to a vast array of social and economic problems. Much follows positively when poverty is tackled seriously. We know this but we do not act accordingly.

One of the most obvious examples of unknown knowns is found in our over-crowded prisons. The Scottish Prisons Commission, chaired by one of the authors of this book, issued its report in 2008. It had been set up by Kenny MacAskill, then Justice Secretary, who had asked

> Why does Scotland imprison so many more of its people than its neighbours in Europe, and what does it say about a system of justice that so efficiently collects those in our society who are the least well-off, and with the most complex health and well being issues?

He was wont to argue, in characteristic pithy style, that we should lock up the bad ones and not the sad ones. At that time Scotland imprisoned more people than most of Europe with the prison population having increased each year of the new century and projected to reach 8,700 by 2016. Prisons were being used to lock up and hide away social problems. They have failed in recidivism terms. The report included 23 recommendations aimed at realising the vision set out by its chair in which there were fewer people in prisons which would hold the most serious offenders presenting the greatest threat; Scottish prisons would be recognised internationally as models of safety and security with Scotland hosting visitors seeking to learn from success; staff would provide effective programmes to produce change and accountability; greater use of community-based sentences; communities should create hope and pride. A theme running throughout the report was the need for a shift to prevention with greater investment in communities but also for sentencing purposes. Community supervision sentences were advocated which should become the default position for dealing with less serious offenders. There should be fewer sentences of six months or under and judges should be required to provide reasons for short sentences. A concern raised by the Commission was that judges who then might have imposed sentences of less than six months might 'simply impose longer sentences to make sure offenders still got to prison'. The Commission included a target of an average 5,000 prisoners daily. A key driver of the increased prison population was the increasing number of women who were given prison sentences. The Commission found that 90 per cent of women in prison had drug and alcohol problems and 75 per cent had a history of abuse and major health problems and not dissimilar figures existed for young offenders and men. A staggering 37 per cent of women prisoners had attempted to commit suicide.

Many recommendations were accepted and implemented over succeeding years. A review of progress ten years later, conducted by leading criminologists, found that the prison population had fallen but was still high at over 7,500 but had been declining over the previous five years. There had been a fall in the number of short sentences of three months or less but a rise in sentences over six months to two years. An exceptional number of prisoners released on licences, remaining under supervision in the community within strict requirements, had been returned to prison due to failures in meeting these requirements though not reoffending. Community Payback Orders were successfully implemented along with supporting institutional infrastructure. Ten years on the number of women in prison had fallen but only slightly. A further enquiry focused on women in prison, chaired by former Lord Advocate Elish Angiolini, reported in 2012. It had been established with the backdrop of a doubling of female imprisonment over the previous decade and serious problems of over-crowding in Cornton Vale Prison which had become unfit for purpose. The Commission offered a wide range of recommendations under a series of headings: service redesign; alternatives to prosecution; alternatives to remand; sentencing; prisons; community reintegration; leadership, structures and delivery. Women in prison are amongst the most vulnerable people in society. There was a proposal to build a new women's prison in Inverclyde but this decision was reversed and instead a smaller prison on the Cornton Vale site was chosen with a capacity for 80 prisoners as opposed to 300 in the old prison. The problem of recidivism looms large and is exacerbated when so many who leave prison lack skills, leaving aside a criminal record. But Canadian experience suggests that smaller, better facilities do not always work as intended. As ever when trying to tackle complex wicked problems, there are no easy options and even when progress has been made there is a need for constant monitoring, careful consideration of evidence and recognising the limitations of any policy as well as a willingness to be bold when necessary. There has been significant progress but more work will always need to be done.

The World Prison Brief, produced at Birkbeck, University of London, shows that Scotland's incarceration rate, taking account of population size, is almost three times that of Finland. The Finnish prison population has been reduced over the last half century in part due to a decline in crime but also policies pursued by a succession of governments. Recidivism amongst those who had committed low-level offences was tackled and there has been greater emphasis on restorative justice measures. A high proportion of people in Scottish prisons have drug and alcohol problems as well as physical and mental health problems. Many people in prisons are there for fairly petty crimes associated with poverty. In this respect, Scotland is very British, and this is one case where Scotland should diverge from England's approach to achieve better outcomes. Having a high prison population is extremely costly and counterproductive, as testified by recidivism rates. The evidence on the failure of imprisonment for many crimes is well known yet we continue to lock up a much higher proportion of our population. Two questions are immediately raised. Why does this policy of high levels of imprisonment persist against massive evidence of policy failure? And what should be done to address the underlying source of the problem?

The answer to the first is straightforward. Populist politics all too often trump serious policy analysis and prescription. It would be easy to blame sections of the media, though there is no doubt that sections of the media do contribute to the problem. But the political parties play populist games even when their leaders know full well that this is illogical in policy terms. If one party advocates a bold progressive measure, then other parties all too often struggle to resist the temptation to play a populist card in opposition. The duty of the opposition may be to oppose but should also be to engage critically and constructively with policy development. We are failing to do so. At root, of course, is the question of the fundamental causes of problems, so often leading us back to levels of poverty, lack of opportunities and a lack of voice for those most in need in Scottish society.

The late Professor Steve Raynor referred to 'uncomfortable knowledge' and the 'social construction of ignorance' in policy debates. He maintained that institutions use four strategies to avoid uncomfortable knowledge: denial, dismissal, diversion and displacement. These strategies have become all too common in recent times. As with wicked problems, particular means are required to address this uncomfortable knowledge. 'Clumsy solutions' was a term first used by Michael Shapiro, which are necessarily pluralistic and inclusive. Facing up to the challenges with honest appraisal and openness will be required. The next 25 years needs to see more emphasis, time, resources and reward for governing pluralistically and less on spin, communication and campaigning.

Conclusion

Much public policy is necessarily reactive. Crises come along unexpectedly. Even when a crisis is anticipated, it cannot be assumed that the form it will take will be as expected. A global pandemic had long been anticipated but the precise nature of COVID-19 could not have been predicted. This applies to less challenging crises. But the need to respond speedily, more often with limited information on how the crisis might unfold, applies regardless of the scale and nature of the crisis. Anticipatory policy making can never be perfect but we have to learn from past experience without allowing ourselves to 'prepare for the last war', ie expect a future crisis will be the same as the last one. Flexibility needs to be built into anticipatory policy making. We are likely to experience more complex and fast-developing crises in the future and will require institutional mechanisms and as much preparatory work as feasible in anticipation. Technological change is happening at breakneck speed in our globalised world. Policy making will need to be smarter, fleeter and more interconnected than in the past. Scotland's size combined with greater decentralisation should put us in a good position in this respect. Political, economic and technological turbulence and unpredictability look set to be features we will have to live with into the foreseeable future. Once more, this requires cooperation and learning from elsewhere. Scotland needs to be open for business but also open to ideas.

We need to start with a better way of approaching policy making that avoids populist measures, blame games and evading difficult questions. Recognising explicitly that policy making involves difficult choices and that there are nearly always trade-offs would be a good start. It is understandable that political parties should compete fiercely at election times but we need to create more space to build consensus for long-term policy making. Scotland has been drifting along on a wave of progressive rhetoric while failing to get to grips with deep underlying problems. There has been progress over the last quarter century but much more needs to be done.

Climate change, economic challenges and demographic change are not separate challenges to be put into different policy making silos. A policy response to one problem might exacerbate or help address another problem. It would be easier to pursue economic growth by ignoring climate change but that would be irresponsible. Growth based on polluting the environment which enriches a few was not what those who campaigned to see the creation of a Scottish Parliament envisaged nor mainstream opinion today wants. It would be foolish to ignore what is referred to as the wellbeing economy, though this needs to become more than a slogan to be included in speeches. Neither can we ignore the need for a growing tax base to pay for the growing pressures from demographic change by green purism. As Paul Johnson, quoted in this chapter's epigraph, stated, 'there are no simple solutions to the tough problems' and there are 'nearly always trade-offs and choices to be made'. This will require mature and reasoned debate. There will always be a need in any Parliamentary system for voices keeping up pressure on government decision-makers. Strong environmental voices need to be accompanied by strong voices for economic growth, with trade-offs unavoidable where synergies are not possible. It is the job of government to weigh up arguments, make responsible decisions with consideration of the long-term costs and implications.

As HL Mencken famously remarked, 'there is always a well-known solution to every human problem – neat, plausible, and wrong'. What might appear at first sight to be a sensible policy may have unintended negative (or indeed positive) consequences. There have been examples of blundering into decisions that might have been thought to be attractive but have had to be reversed because well-informed voices were ignored. Gender recognition reform may have been well-intentioned but genuine concerns were dismissed and the handling of this issue by Scottish Ministers contributed to ugly scenes, intolerance and deeply flawed policy making with appalling outcomes. A more nuanced and thoroughly prepared approach could have avoided at least much of the heat generated in this sensitive area. The Deposit Return Scheme and Highly Protected Marine Areas (HPMAs) were other examples of what were presented as environmentally necessary innovations that had simply lacked serious considered analysis. The desperate need to address adult social care has been delayed by allowing rhetoric to run ahead of serious policy making, resulting in performative drafting of legislation that subsequently had to be scrapped. The late Bernard Crick in his classic work, *In Defence of Politics*, referred to this type of politics as 'student politics', though that does a disservice to students but captures the kind of policy making divorced from serious consideration of implementation challenges. There is also no value setting targets that claim to be 'world leading' which are unrealistic, just designed to grab a headline. This only leads to cynicism and evades real progress. The immense nature of these interconnected challenges should be acknowledged. Progress will only be made through honest appraisal, serious engagement with the issues and collaborative efforts.

CHAPTER 7

Conclusion

What do the people want of the place?
They want it to be filled with thinking
persons as open and adventurous as its architecture.
A nest of fearties is what they do not want.
A symposium of procrastinators is what they do not want.
A phalanx of forelock-tuggers is what they do not want.
And perhaps above all the droopy mantra of 'it wizny me' is what they do not want.

Edwin Morgan, 'Open the Doors!', poem dedicated to the opening of the Holyrood Parliament, 9 October 2004.

JOHN SMITH'S COMMENT that devolution was 'unfinished business' is frequently quoted in debates on devolution. His comment was made after the failure of devolution back in the 1970s. It was a reference and commitment to deliver devolution when Labour came back to power. He did not live to see that happening but that commitment was fulfilled. Contrary to much commentary, Smith had not always been a supporter of devolution. As late as 1974, only two years before he was made Minister responsible for devolution, he had expressed concerns that it meant a diminution of Scotland's voice at the heart of government in London. He changed his mind and became an ardent supporter of devolution but our experience shows that he had been right to express a concern regarding the impact of devolution on Scotland's voice at the centre. We now need to take this criticism, and others made by opponents as well as supporters of devolution, into account as we look to the future.

In this book we interpret unfinished business in a wider sense. Another well-used phrase associated with devolution, coined by then Welsh Labour leader Ron Davies, was that devolution was a process, not an event. Davies' hope and expectation was that Wales would gain more powers, including primary legislative powers. But there was also an awareness that devolution could never be truly settled. This has been well understood in the academic community's study of institutions. Institutions do not survive by standing still. They become ossified when the changing political, social and economic environments around them are ignored. The notion that devolution was the 'settled will of the Scottish people' was yet another of those well-worn phrases, again associated with John Smith from a speech he delivered at Scottish Labour's conference in 1994. But what Smith was referring to at the time was that there was a settled will in favour of a Scottish devolution as against the then status quo. He could not say what might happen after its establishment. Constitutional and institutional arrangements, especially when new, need to be reviewed and, where necessary, revised through experience. It is in this sense that we approached writing this book. We cannot, nor should we attempt to, create arrangements that will last in perpetuity.

Devolution was always going to be unfinished business in another sense. Creating devolution could only be the start. How devolved bodies operated, the relations that would develop and the policies made would evolve. The ideas and policies debated and scrutinised would be never ending. As Donald Dewar stated, devolution was a 'new stage on a journey begun long ago and which has no end'. It was, 'Not an end: a means to greater ends'.

Circumstances and contexts change thereby raising questions as to the suitability of any institutional arrangement or policy. But it is not just the constitutional status of Scotland that will be affected. Priorities, new challenges and opportunities arise that require new thinking on public policies. Too often constitutional change has been the response to enduring problems in Scottish society, economy and environment. Constitutional politics offer an important framework in which policies are developed but it is the policies themselves that matter. Policies will not succeed without appropriate institutional and constitutional arrangements. The institutional arrangements should facilitate good policy making but demanding more fiscal and welfare policies is not enough on its own. Even worse is to use soaring rhetoric in making demands for more powers. To fail to take tough choices seriously is either naïve or cynical. We accept that demanding more powers as an end in itself is a legitimate political position for some but it should never be seen as a substitute for policies.

We also acknowledge that the business of government is always unfinished. Whether it is constitutional relationships or any area of public policy, no institution or policy should be held in aspic. We have made reference throughout this book to Jefferson's argument that the 'earth belongs to the living, not to the dead' and 'one generation is to another as one independent nation to another'. New challenges, opportunities and learning mean that what is fit for one generation may no longer be relevant to the next. This is not to cast aside principles and values which should endure. Social justice is timeless. But go back a couple of generations and we would find that climate change was on very few people's political radars. It is one of the most pressing issues today and ought to have been pressing much earlier. It hardly merited attention in the deliberations of the Constitutional Convention meeting almost 40 years ago. Over 150 countries today include environmental provisions in their constitution. The UN Human Rights Council recognises that a clean, healthy and sustainable environment is a human right. That places responsibilities on institutions at the most local through to the global levels. Other challenges will emerge, currently unknown or barely visible, over the next quarter century. We need to be far more alert to such emerging challenges and opportunities than we have been with climate change.

Vindictive negativism

Fifty years ago, John P Mackintosh noted the 'vindictive negativism' of some in his own Labour Party regarding the rise of the SNP. The same applied and applies to the SNP's attitude towards Labour. There are decent people and good ideas in both, indeed all, parties represented in Holyrood. No party has a monopoly of wisdom though party politics operates as if this is the case. There is considerable – in some cases more – diversity within any of the parties than between the parties. Many MSPs privately acknowledge this. Only a few feel the need to announce that they have no friends in one or other mainstream political party. This speaks of a deeply hyper-adversarial mindset, an extreme version of the campaign mindset and/or a pettiness that undermines good government.

Electoral campaigning is an inevitable and positive part of democratic politics but space must be found for governing. In chapter three, we referred to different campaign and governing mindsets that Gutmann and Thompson identified a decade ago. Such cognitive and dispositional attitudes view politics in very different ways and lead to distinct types of politics. Politics is framed adversarially and simplistically in campaigning while governing requires a very different mindset to be effective. The tension cannot be avoided but greater effort is required to separate the two. Distrust, mutual antipathy that can verge on mutual loathing, or at least come across that way, and exclusivity might excite and mobilise supporters in a campaign but can be destructive when it comes to governing. It can make for good copy for journalists and those focused on the latest opinion poll. When opponents become enemies, disagreements become entrenche and, energies and thinking are channelled into unproductive disagreements. Political trench warfare follows and society and the economy suffer. The nature of modern politics, especially the advent of the 24-hour media cycle combined with the rise of social media, has contributed to invasive campaign styles into governing.

The Scottish Government has developed an unhealthy top-down approach that treats consultation as a tick box exercise. Consultation needs to be more than simply being in a position to claim a large number of individuals and groups have sent comments on proposals. Relations with local authorities is a stark example of a failure to engage, share, listen and hear respectfully. Awareness that there is expertise and experience at local level that does not exist in Scottish central government is essential.

One of the challenges over the next quarter century that should lead to better policy making and thereby better outcomes is to create more space for collaborative efforts. The changes required are less institutional than behavioural. Self-interest should lead to this conclusion but runs up against short-term campaigning pressures. There is ample scope for such a change but leadership is required, a greater willingness to acknowledge publicly, and not just privately, that political opponents might just have a point worth considering. And by leadership we refer not simply to formal leaders – though they have a key role in this – but to all elected politicians who are leaders in their own communities. Building collaboration from below may prove the most fruitful approach.

Part of this is to recognise that policy choices are rarely binary but operate along a spectrum, indeed a range of intersecting spectrums, as most policies involve a range of different choices. It is also important to recognise that many decisions are made with limited information at the disposal of decision-makers. Learning on the basis of new information or greater experience is essential in improving policy outcomes. And openly learning from mistakes, more often made with good intentions and limited information, will be important.

Conclusion

We have consciously avoided engaging in debate on whether Scotland should be independent or whether more powers should be devolved. This is not that these are unimportant matters but that we believe there are other matters demanding our attention that are being neglected. We need the same focus that has gone into debating whether Scotland should be independent applied to these other concerns. There are many who will see constitutional and other matters as intimately intertwined. We do not suggest that these issues should be debated separately and respect those on both sides of the independence debate who see connections. But it is self-evident that there are many issues that can be taken out of the constitutional debate allowing for greater collaboration across the constitutional divide.

Countless people were involved in the long campaign for a Scottish Parliament. The focus has tended to be on the political parties and elected politicians for good reason. But there were many others, unaffiliated to a party but deeply committed who played their part. Most of these, given the decades-long duration, are now no longer with us. Each had a distinct motivation and singling out any individual is difficult. The late Nigel Smith, who chaired the *Scotland Forward* referendum campaign in 1997 admitted that the Scottish Parliament had been 'only a partial success, certainly less successful than campaigners hoped for'. It had failed 'too often on the bigger issues'. Perhaps the idealism that inspired campaigners created unrealistic expectations. Perhaps too little time was devoted to thinking about what the Parliament might do in the long years prior to its establishment as time was devoted to thinking about the institutions, avoiding policy differences amongst supporters and simply campaigning for its establishment. There was a consensus that Scottish politics should be different, better with more transparency, greater accountability, diversity and a focus on Scotland's long-term challenges. Much has been achieved – and much more than would have happened without a Scottish Parliament – but as we look to the 50th anniversary of the establishment of the Scottish Parliament we see areas for improvement, more focus. This book does not have all the answers and our main aim is to be provocative in the best sense, to provoke debate on how we can best ensure that the Scottish Parliament, whatever powers it has, accelerates as a means to greater ends.

Acknowledgements

WE ARE GRATEFUL to countless people with whom we have engaged over many decades and have shaped our thinking. It would be impossible to list everyone, not least as many who will have affected our thinking will have done so unwittingly and, from our perspective, often unconsciously. We also asked a range of people to offer comments on drafts – these include people involved across a range of political parties, as well as practitioners and academics. Euan Cram Mitchell read through the manuscript and identified parts that needed improvement. We are also grateful to Gavin MacDougall and his colleagues at Luath who have once more proved the value of an independent publisher.

Luath Press Limited

committed to publishing well written books worth reading

LUATH PRESS takes its name from Robert Burns, whose little collie Luath (*Gael.*, swift or nimble) tripped up Jean Armour at a wedding and gave him the chance to speak to the woman who was to be his wife and the abiding love of his life. Burns called one of the 'Twa Dogs' Luath after Cuchullin's hunting dog in Ossian's *Fingal*.
Luath Press was established in 1981 in the heart of Burns country, and is now based a few steps up the road from Burns' first lodgings on Edinburgh's Royal Mile. Luath offers you distinctive writing with a hint of unexpected pleasures.
Most bookshops in the UK, the US, Canada, Australia, New Zealand and parts of Europe, either carry our books in stock or can order them for you. To order direct from us, please send a £sterling cheque, postal order, international money order or your credit card details (number, address of cardholder and expiry date) to us at the address below. Please add post and packing as follows: UK – £1.00 per delivery address; overseas surface mail – £2.50 per delivery address; overseas airmail – £3.50 for the first book to each delivery address, plus £1.00 for each additional book by airmail to the same address. If your order is a gift, we will happily enclose your card or message at no extra charge.

ILLUSTRATION: IAN KELLAS

Luath Press Limited
543/2 Castlehill
The Royal Mile
Edinburgh EH1 2ND
Scotland
Telephone: 0131 225 4326 (24 hours)
Email: sales@luath.co.uk
Website: www.luath.co.uk